Piranesi drawings

visions of antiquity

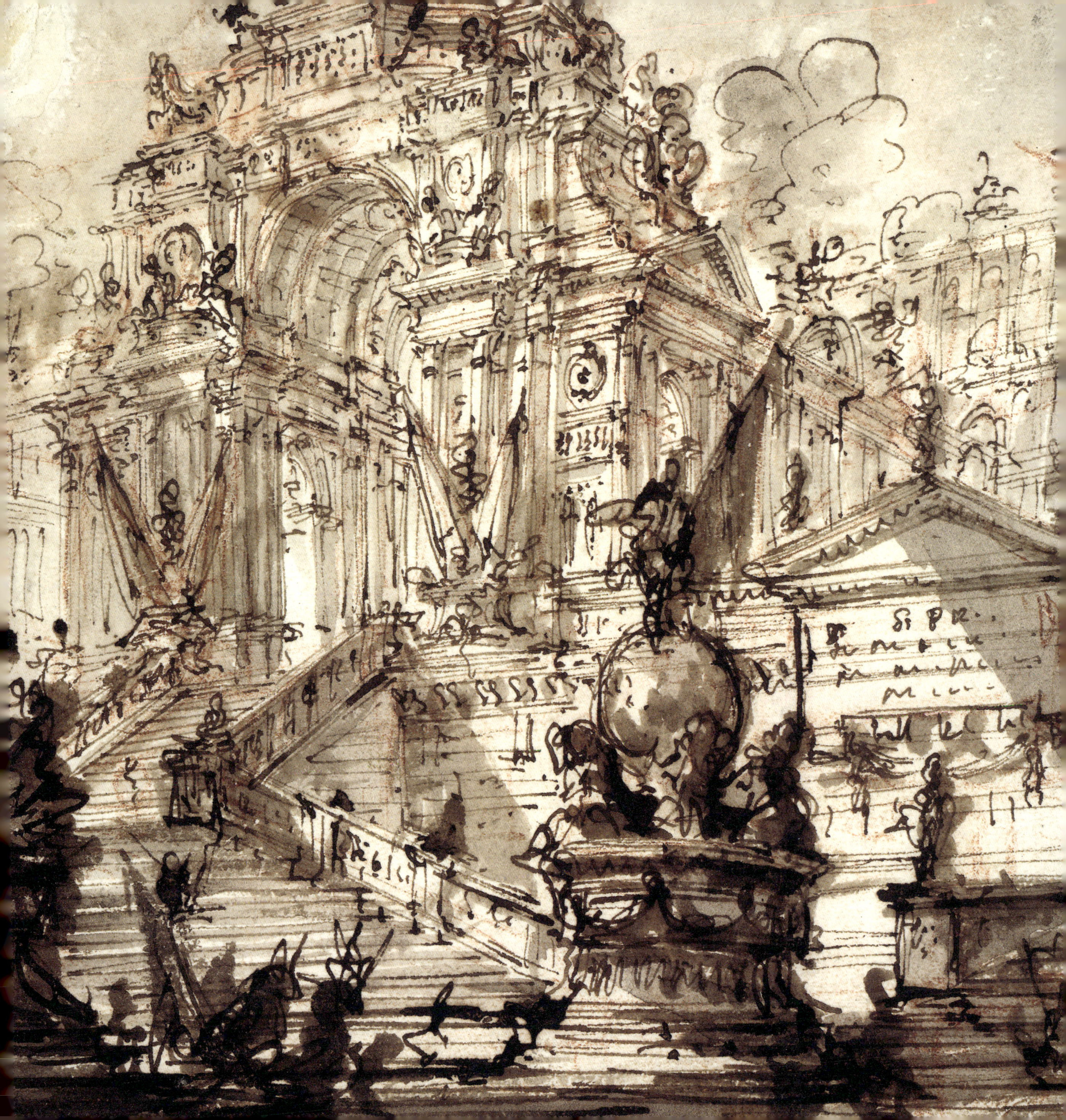

Piranesi drawings
visions of antiquity

Drawings from the British Museum

Sarah Vowles

Preface by Hugo Chapman

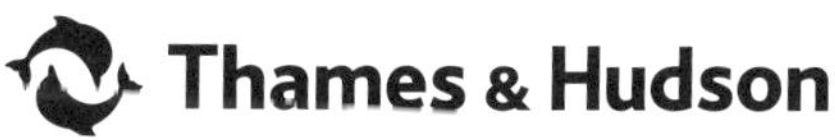 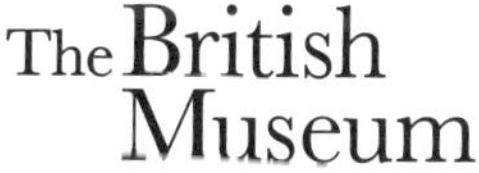

All works have been reproduced at actual size or smaller, except in instances where enlarging the work aids their study. All works are by Piranesi unless otherwise indicated in the caption.

p.2: *An ornate triumphal arch with a grand staircase* (detail), c. 1747–50 (cat. 26)

Published to accompany the exhibition *Piranesi drawings: visions of antiquity* at the British Museum from 20 February to 9 August 2020.

The exhibition is supported by the Tavolozza Foundation.

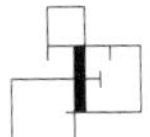

TAVOLOZZA
FOUNDATION

First published in the United Kingdom in 2020 by Thames & Hudson Ltd, in collaboration with the British Museum.

British Library Cataloguing-in-Publication Data
A catalogue record for this book is available from the British Library

ISBN 978-0-500-48061-8

Printed and bound in Italy by Printer Trento

Thames & Hudson Ltd, 181A High Holborn, London WC1V 7QX

To find out about all our publications, please visit **www.thamesandhudson.com**. There you can subscribe to our e-newsletter, browse or download our current catalogue, and buy any titles that are in print.

For more information about the Museum and its collection, please visit **britishmuseum.org.**

Contents

Piranesi at 300

HUGO CHAPMAN

To celebrate the 300th anniversary of the birth of the Venetian etcher and architect Giovanni Battista Piranesi, the British Museum is mounting its first ever show devoted to its collection of his drawings. Edward Croft-Murray included all that were available to him in 1968 in his expansive exploration of the roots and European-wide reach of the artist's graphic output, *Giovanni Battista Piranesi: his predecessors and his heritage*, but this show centred largely on prints. However, focusing on the drawings alone makes sense today for two reasons. The first is purely pragmatic: the institutional split in 1973 of the British Library from the British Museum means that Piranesi's work as a printmaker is far more comprehensively covered in the bound volumes of his etchings now at the Library than at the Museum. But secondly, there is great value in a focused examination of his drawings alone. This became apparent to me more than a decade ago from my struggles to make sense of their function in Piranesi's practice, not to mention their chronology, when as part of my curatorial duties I had to catalogue them for the Museum's online database.

Mercifully my successor as Italian curator, Sarah Vowles, readily took up the challenge, although both of us are aware that our conclusions on such matters will remain tentative until the foremost Piranesi scholar, Andrew Robison, publishes his long-awaited catalogue of the drawings. The need for such a comprehensive overview has been heightened by Georg Kabierske's discovery of a large cache of drawings by Piranesi and his studio in the Kunsthalle Karlsruhe (published in *Master Drawings* in 2015). Research on these, led by Christoph Frank among others, has revealed that many of the same assistants were responsible for studies now in the Morgan Library and Museum, New York, drawings which had hitherto always been regarded as solely by the master. The growing awareness of studio participation has undoubtedly now complicated the assessment of other works previously regarded as entirely autograph, such as the fifteen pen-and-wash studies from the 1770s of the Doric temples of Paestum, now held in the Soane Museum in London. Piranesi's drawing-centred

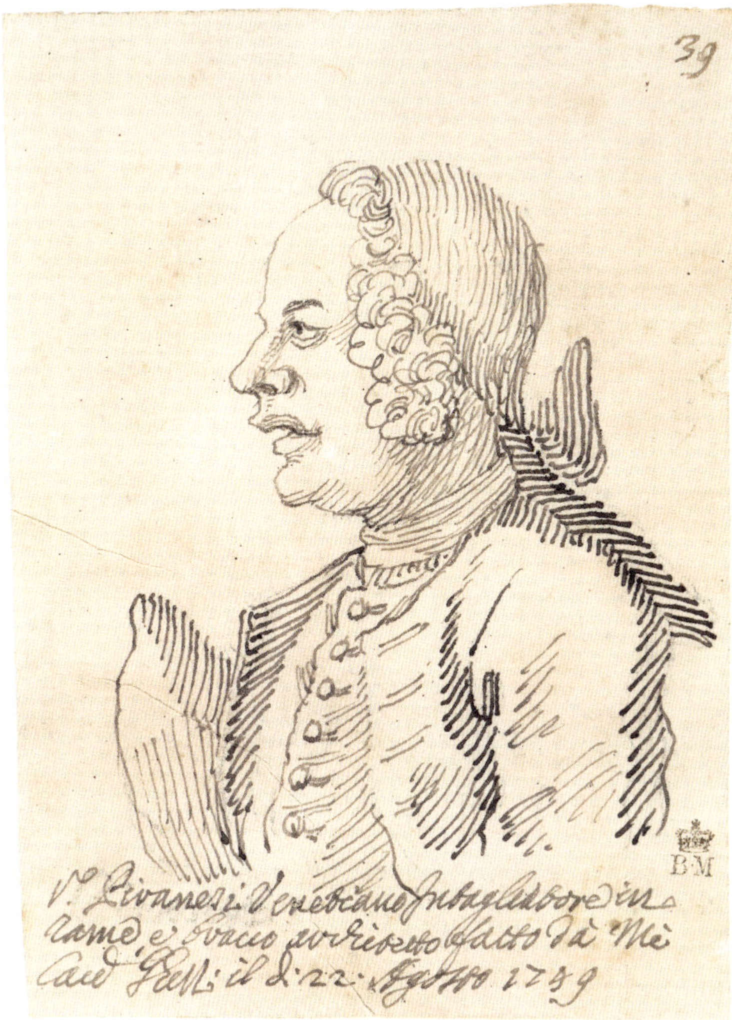

training of family members and associates to work in his style should on reflection come as no surprise, as it tallies with how most Italian artists operated from the Renaissance onwards, not least in Venice, where art was often a dynastic family business.

Questions of studio involvement are only relevant to a handful of the British Museum holdings. For wherever John Gott – or, as we can infer thanks to Sarah's new research, more likely his father, William – acquired the forty-six Piranesi drawings that the British Museum subsequently bought in 1908, it was from someone who had an extraordinary trove of autograph works (the only exception being two studies from Piranesi's circle, not included here). The chronological spread of the works documents the entirety of Piranesi's career from its beginnings in the early 1740s right through to the 1770s. Moreover, the Gott group provides a marvellously rounded picture of Piranesi's inventiveness and energies as a draughtsman, touching on almost every aspect of his diverse activities – as printmaker, architect, designer of imaginatively reconfigured classical fragments, and, most frequently, as a visionary interpreter and increasingly polemical standard-bearer for the eclecticism and grandeur of ancient Roman architecture.

What emerges from studying the British Museum holdings is how, for all the differences in style, Piranesi remained remarkably consistent in his approach to drawing. Perhaps surprisingly, in view of his prolific output as an etcher, he used the medium predominantly for exploratory rather than preparatory ends, and also as a means of sharpening and refining his powers of extemporary invention. That is not to say that he did not sometimes make drawings to rehearse his work on copper, which he presumably kept on hand when translating their compositions in reverse onto the plate (such as cats. 3, 29 and 42), but they are far removed from the carefully calibrated studies, with their contours incised for transfer and their design transposed in readiness for reversal, that artists tended to make in preparation for prints.

Occasionally the drawings provide a glimpse of Piranesi's ability to aggrandize and dramatize the architectural vistas that are in front of him, such as in the black chalk sketch of the Hospital of Santo Spirito (cat. 8) overworked in pen from the first half of the 1740s, in which the octagonal tower of the Corsia Sistina swells in size, or the pen studies of the interior of the Pantheon (cat. 46). The latter document his efforts to merge a wide-angle view of the space in a convincing way, while also showing the oculus at the centre of the domed ceiling, an irresolvable conundrum he neatly sidestepped in his boldly executed study in red chalk by adopting a vertical format, with the view framed by an opening (cat. 42). But such are his extemporizing skills that it is hard, and perhaps impossible, to be sure whether Piranesi is drawing in front of the motif or relying on his prodigious visual memory back in his studio to warp and transmute a real architectural scene. This ability is exemplified in a pen study from the late 1750s that moulds together a vast crossing space, much like that of St Peter's, with plunging diagonal vistas derived from the work of the Sicilian stage designer Filippo Juvarra (cat. 36). The drawing is one of many instances in which Piranesi's enduring debt to Juvarra and the theatrical designers of the Bibiena family, who shaped his sense of architectural space, shines through. Initially, this appears in a straightforwardly derivative manner, as in the studies relating to the *Prima Parte* from the early 1740s, but later develops into something much more dynamic and incisive, as seen in the slashing pen lines that define the circular space in *Interior of a circular building with arches and flights of steps* (cat. 37).

Piranesi's propensity to use drawing repeatedly to revisit closely related ideas and motifs over a long period of gestation can be seen in the group of drawings (such as cats. 12, 15, 17, 23 and 27) loosely associated with the two editions of the *Carceri* prints. This repetitive, circuitous way of working on paper has in the past arguably been underplayed and explains why establishing a chronology is so tricky. If this notion of his working habits is accepted, it can no longer be assumed, as was often the case in past scholarship, that a similarity to a print means that a drawing is necessarily preparatory for it (see for example cat. 33).

What is clearly articulated in mature drawings such as the *Carceri* group, but is nascent even in Piranesi's earliest works as a draughtsman, is a very Venetian sensitivity to how light and shade can be manipulated to lead the eye around and backwards into the fictive space. The white of the paper is a charged and active element in his thinking on paper, so that the play of solid and the void in architectural space becomes thrillingly apparent. The drawings demonstrate that he sometimes tested himself by successfully conjuring up monumental spaces on a miniature scale (as in cat. 26). Piranesi was so skilful in exaggerating scale that visitors to Rome who had first experienced the city through his etchings, most famously perhaps Goethe, felt slightly underwhelmed by what they actually saw.

For all Piranesi's undoubted greatness as an archaeological and topographical artist, arguably his most enduring legacy is his ability to evoke architectural space and vistas that hover between the real and the fantastic, and that simultaneously glorify man's ingenuity and grandeur of imagination while showing how such grandiose structures dwarf and make insignificant the figures that inhabit them. The dualistic tension in Piranesi's imagined world between time-worn magnificence and oppressiveness still resonates in the gloomy dystopian war-torn landscapes of computer games, and memories of his prints can be unexpectedly stirred by contemporary spaces with labyrinthine angles and gantries, such as the ticket hall and platforms built for the Jubilee line extension at Westminster Underground station. As cities and buildings have grown ever bigger and denser, Piranesi's dizzying fantastical architectural visions seem increasingly prescient; and it is through looking at his drawings that it is possible to gain an understanding of how he developed and honed that singular imagination, the power of which continues to haunt and inspire us to this day.

'Architetto Veneziano':
The Life of Giovanni Battista Piranesi

SARAH VOWLES

Giovanni Battista Piranesi would sign himself 'Architetto Veneziano' throughout his life, placing this claim to city and profession at the heart of his identity. He was born on 4 October 1720 in Mogliano Veneto, on the Venetian mainland, into comfortable circumstances. His father, Angelo, was a master mason who had married up in society, while his maternal uncle was Matteo Lucchesi, a practising architect with special responsibility for the vast stone defences of the Venetian water-walls out on the lagoon.[1] Alone among his siblings, Piranesi was granted the distinction of an aristocratic godfather, Giovanni Widman, a relation of the Rezzonico family and thus of Pope Clement XIII, whose papacy (1758–69) would coincide with Piranesi's maturity in Rome.[2] The young man was trained in the small world of the Venetian construction business, first studying draughtsmanship with Lucchesi and then, when their volatile personalities clashed, moving on to work with Giovanni Antonio Scalfarotto, another successful architect with connections to the Piranesi clan.[3]

At first glance, Piranesi's activities during these early years suggest a lack of focus. His early biographer Legrand speaks of time spent studying stage design and perspective with the celebrated Bibiena family in Bologna, followed by a period in the studio of the Valeriani, stage-painters and interior decorators who moved to St Petersburg to work for the Russian court in 1742.[4] It is possible that Piranesi also gained a rudimentary knowledge of engraving with the print publisher Carlo Zucchi.[5] He gained practical architectural experience from his work with Lucchesi and Scalfarotto, and probably accompanied the latter in 1735 when he went to restore the Triumphal Arch of Augustus in Rimini.[6] This must have excited Piranesi's existing fascination with ancient Rome, which had been nourished by the stories of his elder brother Luigi, a learned Carthusian monk, and probably further encouraged by conversations with the eccentric Lucchesi. His uncle passionately believed in the supremacy of Etruscan architecture, and had published a polemical tract in 1730 that foreshadowed the arguments adopted by Piranesi in his own later, much more celebrated, theoretical pursuits.[7]

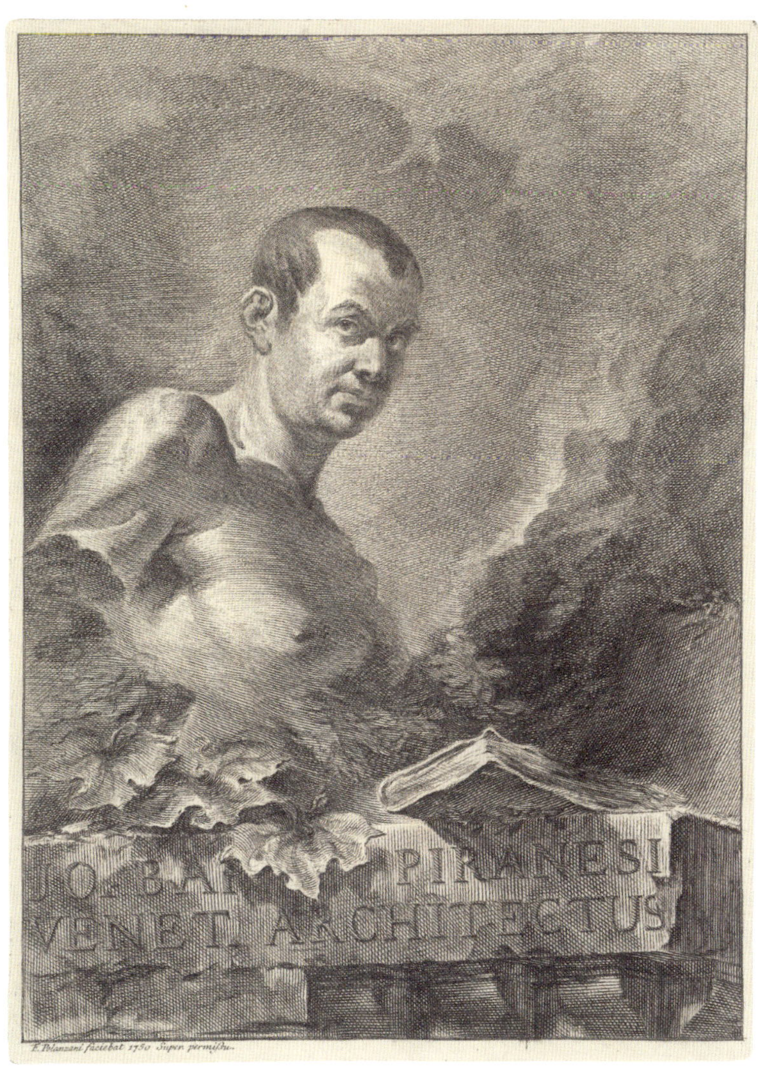

Fig. 2

Francesco Polanzani
(1700 – after 1778)
Portrait of Giovanni Battista
Piranesi in imitation of an
antique bust
From *Opere varie di Architettura*
1750
Engraving
270 × 133 mm (10¾ × 5¼ in.)
The Metropolitan Museum of
Art, New York

This variety of training does not suggest an inability to settle: on the contrary, Piranesi was wisely gaining experience in the many fields on which an architect had to be able to call, in order to maintain a viable career at times when commissions for buildings were few. He could design stage architecture; produce architectural views; survey, restore or publish on ancient monuments; and engage in lively printed debates about the classical world.

For all its opportunities, Venice offered limited openings for a young man of ambition like Piranesi, but in September 1740 he was given the chance to travel to Rome in the entourage of Francesco Venier, the Venetian ambassador to the new pope, Benedict XIV. Once established at the embassy, Palazzo Venezia, he threw himself with passion into his studies of Roman architecture (cat. 8), apparently making a single pot of rice last all week to save time on cooking.[8] He spent long hours reading in the library of Nicola Giobbe, a well-educated master mason who took

Piranesi under his wing. He also studied printmaking with the engraver Giuseppe Vasi:
Piranesi learned a great deal from Vasi very quickly, but their professional relationship
was tumultuous and short-lived.

Eventually, he found work making small engraved views of the major sights of Rome,
as part of a larger team that included several young French artists from the Académie
de France at Villa Medici, not far from Palazzo Venezia. These loose-leaf prints could
be bought by travellers and bound into their guidebooks, but were far from the ambitious
enterprises that Piranesi had dreamed of. He had prepared himself as far as possible
for the life of an architect, but his timing was simply wrong. He arrived in Rome at
the tail end of the Baroque building boom, which had given the city the churches of
Bernini and Borromini, but he may have hoped that the election of a Venetian pope
from the Rezzonico family would lead to a new climate of patronage weighted in
favour of Venetian architects. Unfortunately, there proved to be few openings for a
young man whose buildings still looked more at home in the theatre than in reality.

Piranesi focused instead on his first independent print series, the *Prima Parte di
Architetture, e Prospettive* (1743), which reflects the stage-set training of his youth. Its title
refers to an influential publication of theatrical architectural fantasies, *Architetture, e
Prospettive*, published in 1740 by Giuseppe Galli Bibiena.[9] The dedication, addressed to the
kindly Nicola Giobbe, laments the lack of visionary patrons who would commission such
extravagant buildings, condemning them to exist only on paper. But time was running
out for the young Piranesi: his father back in Venice was growing worried about his
prospects and was threatening to cut off his allowance. He made the most of the time he
had left, visiting Naples in 1742 or 1743 to admire the paintings of Luca Giordano and,
more significantly, to visit the excavations at Herculaneum.[10] He briefly went home to
Venice in the summer of 1744, perhaps to arrange accommodation for a longer visit, and
then, after spending the winter of that year in Rome, returned to Venice in early 1745.

Piranesi remained in Venice for the next two years, developing and expanding
his skills. He seems to have spent some time working with the Tiepolo family, whose
fluid draughtsmanship and fantastically Rococo subject-matter crept into the
impressionable young artist's work (cat. 11). By 1747, however, he had found a way
to return to Rome, by striking a bargain with the Venetian print publisher Joseph
Wagner, for whom he agreed to run a Roman outpost. Armed with a newly Venetian
outlook, Piranesi gathered his belongings and travelled south. His work for Wagner
gave him a certain level of financial independence, allowing him to create more
experimental and individual prints. His first offering, the series of peculiarly Venetian
Grotteschi (1747–49), does not seem to have been particularly successful – perhaps its
eerie strangeness failed to strike a chord among visitors to Rome. But he was already at
work on another series, the *Antichità Romane de' Tempi della Repubblica, e de' primi imperatori*
('Roman Antiquities of the Time of the Republic and the First Emperors', 1748),
which proved far more popular. Accompanied by methodical copies of the inscriptions
found on the bridges and arches represented in the prints, this publication announced
Piranesi as a scholarly printmaker of archaeological exactitude.

For the first ten years after his return to Rome, Piranesi worked tirelessly to establish himself. The *Antichità Romane de' Tempi della Repubblica* was swiftly followed by the first of the *Carceri* ('Prisons', 1749–50), a beguiling series inspired partly by Bibiena's stage sets and partly by Venetian *capricci* – compositions combining real and imaginary elements. These dark prisons, like those which frequently appeared in contemporary operas, tantalized the eye with labyrinthine staircases, arches, bridges and shadowy cranes hidden in dark corners. Alongside these fantastical visions, Piranesi continued to depict archaeological subjects: in 1750 he produced *Le camere sepocrali*, a series showing ancient Roman tombs; and in the same year, he publicized the entire range of his work to date by reissuing prints from all his extant series in the retrospective *Opere varie di architettura, prospettive, grotteschi, antichità*. The collection was accompanied by a frontispiece: a witty engraved portrait by Francesco Polanzani (Fig. 2), which emphasized Piranesi's passion for antiquity by showing him as an antique bust. Another archaeological study, *Trofei di Ottaviano Augusto*, followed in 1753.

As if to place the seal on his success, in 1752 Piranesi married Angelica Pasquini, whose generous dowry effectively alleviated his financial difficulties and made it possible for him to focus on the grand projects he had hoped to initiate ever since his first arrival in Rome.

The first of these more ambitious works was the *Antichità Romane* (not to be confused with Piranesi's earlier series), a four-volume set published in 1756. The enormous expense of producing such a work – from the copper for the plates to the paper for the printing – meant that Piranesi still needed patrons to underwrite his projects, and he had secured a promise of funding for the *Antichità* from the young Irish aristocrat Lord Charlemont. When payment failed to materialize, Piranesi displayed the first signs of his flair for public argument. He reworked the original copper plates and republished the dedicatory pages of the *Antichità* with Charlemont's name 'chiselled off' the laudatory tablets, in a dazzling act of *damnatio memoriae*. He explained his actions at great length in his *Lettere di giustificazione scritte à Milord Charlemont* (1757), which also publicized the correspondence over the promised patronage. Fortunately his work on the *Antichità Romane* was soon recognized in other ways, with his election as an Honorary Fellow of the Royal Society of Antiquaries in London in 1757 and as a member of the Accademia di S. Luca in Rome in 1761. In that year Piranesi published his next monumental project, *Della magnificenza ed architettura de' Romani*, a polemical treatise that sought to defend the creativity and innovation of Roman architecture in the face of growing scholarly appreciation for the Greek style.

This dispute, which dominated much of Piranesi's later career, was not a simple argument about the relative merits of two schools of architecture. It touched on much deeper and more sensitive matters, which explains the intensity of feelings that it provoked, in Piranesi especially. For centuries, Rome had been regarded as the intellectual and artistic centre of Western culture, as well as its spiritual heart: no artist's training was complete without a sojourn there. This admiration for the finishing gloss of Rome had been expressed most obviously by the foundation of the

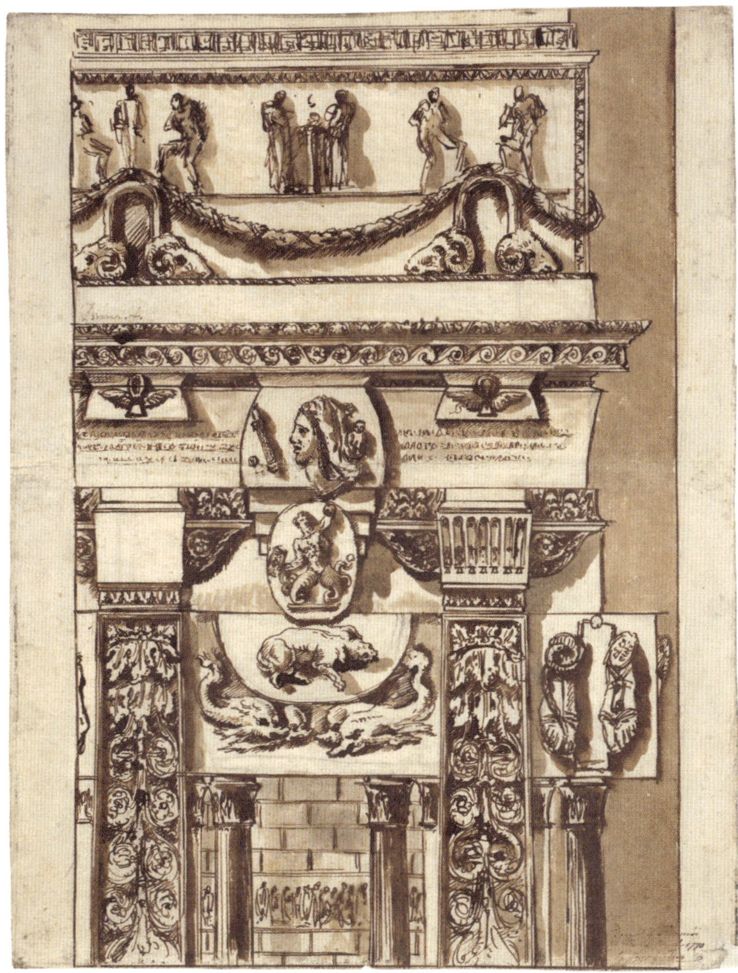

Académie de France, with whose students Piranesi had fraternized during his first days in the city. Times were changing, however. The increasing knowledge of Greek remains caused some thinkers, notably in France, to contest the assumed pre-eminence of Roman architecture – thereby challenging the very significance and primacy of Roman culture. Piranesi and his peers closed ranks to defend their city, whose celebrated monuments were suddenly dismissed as workmanlike shadows of the pure simplicity of Greek taste.[11] For Piranesi, the creative vivacity of Roman architecture, with its domes, curves and arches, rendered it far more sophisticated than its Greek counterpart, an argument that he made with witty effect in a drawing, dismissing these innovative techniques, tongue-in-cheek, as 'outrages' to the Greek style (cat. 28).

Piranesi's arguments in *Della magnificenza* predictably ruffled feathers in France, where they were dissected and challenged in articles in the *Gazette Littéraire de l'Europe*, a mouthpiece for Enlightenment philosophers. It seems that all the articles discussing Piranesi's ideas at this time were written by Pierre-Jean Mariette, who had previously admired his work, but found himself unable to accept Piranesi's spirited defence of

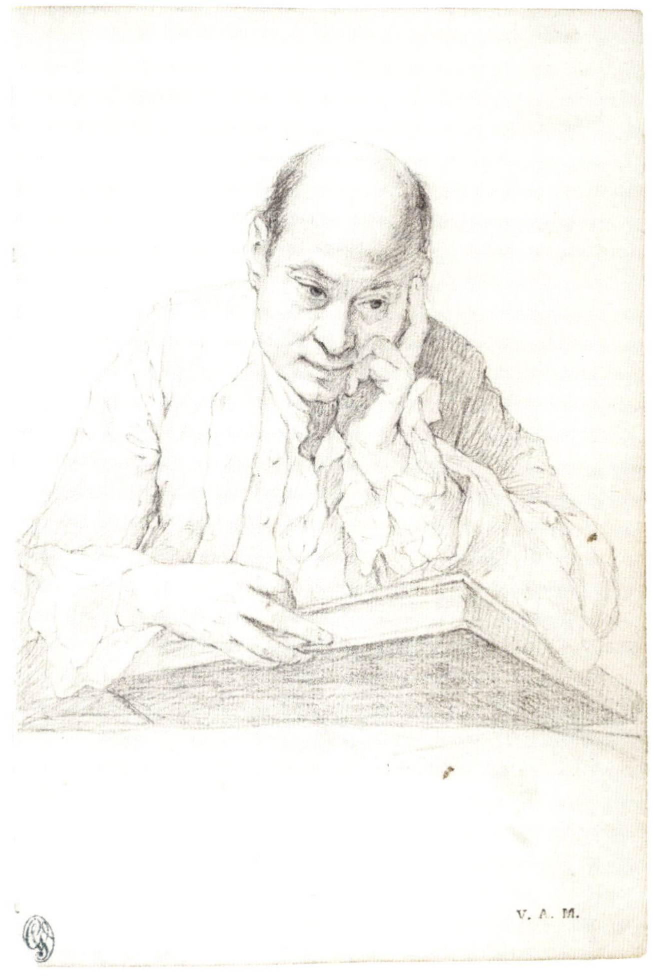

Roman architectural supremacy.[12] Most articles were anonymous, but in one, which was signed, Mariette's rebuttal of Piranesi's theories was so vehement that Piranesi felt compelled to reply.

The result was the *Osservazioni di Gio. Battista Piranesi sopra la Lettre de Monsieur Mariette aux Auteurs de la Gazette Littéraire de l'Europe* (1765), which explained in great detail how Mariette had misunderstood Piranesi's arguments, and argued that Greek architecture had actually developed from the Etruscan, so regaining the intellectual advantage for Italy. This publication also contained the *Parere sull'architettura*, an ambitious series of plates, which juxtaposed Egyptian, Etruscan and ancient Middle Eastern details alongside Roman motifs, in order to demonstrate the rich results of creative cross-fertilization. Four years later, Piranesi would explore these other ancient schools of architecture in further detail in his *Ragionamento Apologetico in difesa dell'Architettura Egizia e Toscana*, which served as the introduction to his series of ornamental designs, the *Diverse maniere d'adornare i cammini* (1769). Now, at around the age of fifty, he found himself championing the very Etruscan culture that his uncle Lucchesi had so admired,

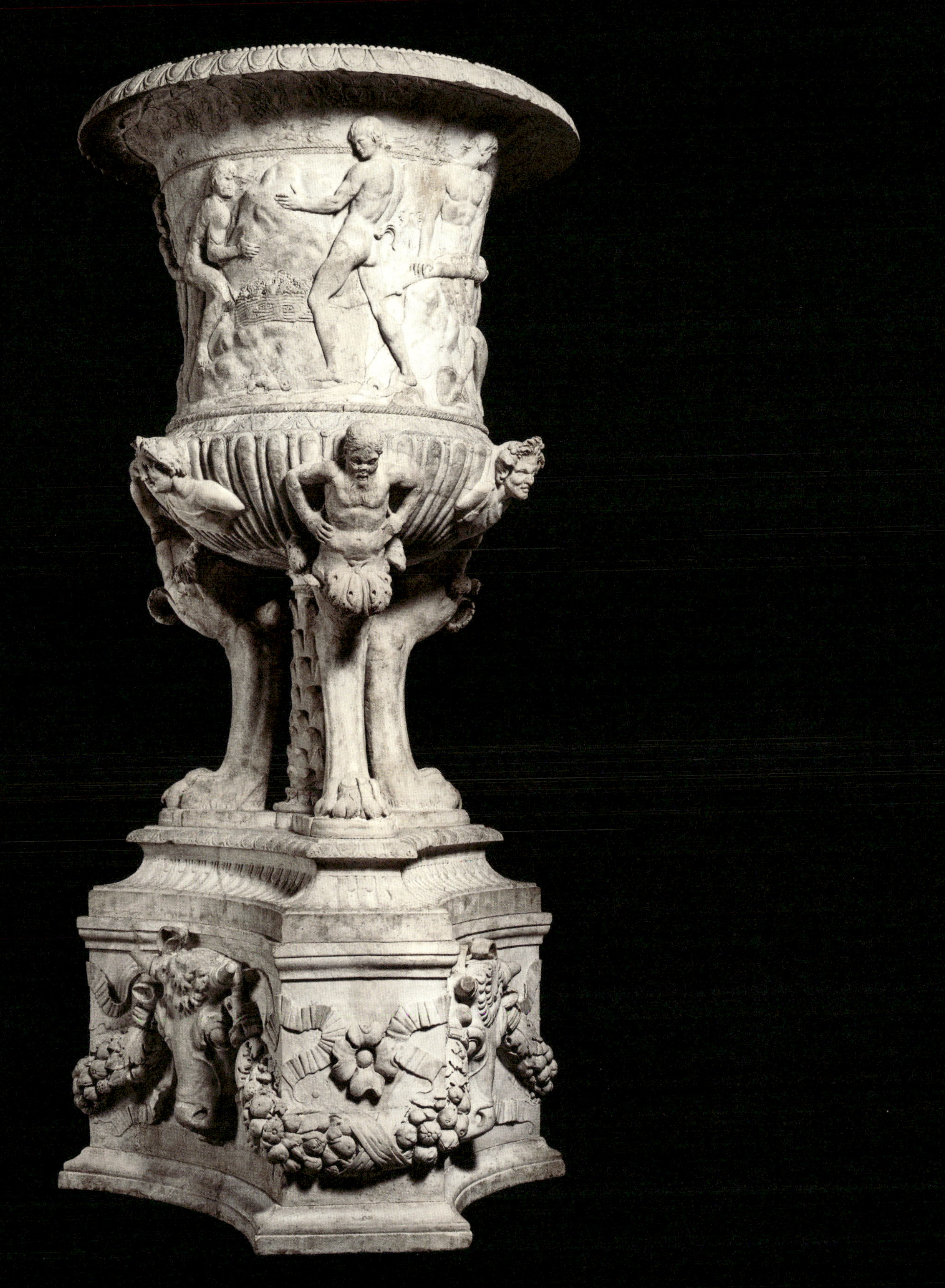

bolstered by first-hand studies of antiquities at the Etruscan sites of Chiusi and Corneto in 1763–64. As with Piranesi's earlier treatises, the elegant prose may have been ghostwritten by some of his learned friends, but the essence of the argument is very much his own.[13] His decorative experiments in the *Diverse maniere* were complemented by the production of six further plates for the *Parere sul'Architettura*, each prepared with exuberant drawings (Fig. 3 and cat. 47), which demonstrated the aesthetic possibilities of combining Egyptian, Etruscan and Roman architecture.

This frenzy of argument and publication was the last great expression of Piranesi's printmaking, which was already declining due to other commitments. In a sensitive portrait made by Angelica Kauffman around 1764–65, he is shown appropriately lost in thought, bowed forward over an album containing some of his published works (Fig. 4). His attention was distracted in 1764–65 by the realization of his dream to become a practical architect. Cardinal Giovanni Battista Rezzonico, nephew of Pope Clement XIII and Grand Prior of the Order of Malta, had commissioned him to restore the order's church of S. Maria del Priorato on the Aventine, for which Piranesi prepared a stately façade ornamented with classical motifs (cat. 45).

Piranesi had also begun to supplement his income by dealing in antique fragments, some of which he combined into constructions that had no archaeological basis beyond his own fantasy (Fig. 5). By 1770 he was employing thirty people in this enterprise, and an associate wrote in frustration that he had 'almost stopped engraving, and is wasting his time dealing in antique marbles'.[14] In fact, Piranesi was still thinking of new publications, and some of his sculptural creations, as well as bona fide antiquities, were transformed into print in his series *Vasi, candelabri, cippi, sarcofagi*, a catalogue of ancient objects and furniture (1778). He also visited Pompeii and Herculaneum several times during the 1770s, producing a sequence of drawings that were never translated into print (cats. 50 and 51). In 1777 he travelled further south to Paestum, where he oversaw the production of large drawings of the Doric temples.

Piranesi fell mortally ill in the following year and died on 9 November 1778, leaving a houseful of drawings and other material, which his son Francesco used to bring his father's final project to completion. Francesco was not alone, however, in continuing Piranesi's legacy: his siblings Laura and Pietro also became printmakers, reproducing and recasting their father's visions of antiquity as part of the family enterprise.

Piranesi's Development as a Draughtsman

Piranesi did not use drawing in the same way as most other printmakers of his age. When asked why he avoided conventional highly finished preparatory studies, which would allow him to transfer compositions easily onto copperplates for etching, his response was typically passionate: 'Can't you see that, if my drawing was finished, my plate would become nothing but a copy; while if, on the contrary, I create the final effects on the copper, I've made it an original?'[15] Like the printmakers who had inspired him as a young man – Rembrandt, Castiglione, Callot and Stefano della Bella – Piranesi continued to reinvent his compositions even in the process of etching,

Nothing was fixed until the plate was printed, and even then, like Rembrandt, he
might go back to make revisions, only to republish the plates later in a new form,
as happened most notably with the *Carceri*, which were reissued in a much reworked
second edition in 1761.

Nevertheless, drawing was a vital part of the creative process in all aspects of
Piranesi's activity, whether as printmaker (cat. 29), restorer (cat. 48), landscapist
(cat. 42), architect (cat. 45) or polemical theorist (cat. 47). From the very beginning
of his career to his last surviving works, we see his drawings acting as spaces for
exploration, experimentation and development. Motifs morph into the basis of a
new sequence of ideas (cat. 15), or act as testaments to works that never found their
finished form (cat. 50). Even more than his printmaking, the drawings show his
increasing graphic confidence and panache.

Ironically, the earliest surviving drawings are precisely the kind of methodical
preparatory works that Piranesi would later abjure (cats. 1 and 2). Inspired by the
conventions of stage design, these are elaborate but implausible spaces, designed to
impress with infinite recessions and arrangements of columns, but surely never
intended to be built. *An antique temple* (c. 1740–42; cat. 1 recto), designed with traditional
single-point perspective, has been only half drawn over neatly ruled chalk lines.
A colonnaded courtyard (c. 1740–42; cat. 2 recto) adopts the *scena per angolo* (two-point
perspective) technique introduced by Ferdinando Bibiena, adding a more ambitious
double-point perspective, but the style of the drawing is much the same, even if the
underlying chalk is more vigorous and exploratory. Piranesi uses neat brown penwork
and grey wash to create his structures; if there is any experimentation, this seems to
be confined to the grey wash marking out the vaults in one drawing, or the decorative
panels on the pilasters in the other. Yet a note of caution is necessary: these are
finished drawings, intentionally restrained.

On the reverse of both sheets, energetic sketches show the young Piranesi in a less
constrained mood. Here, already, it is possible to see how he enthusiastically adapted
motifs from real life into exaggerated fantasies: arches and stairways that recall the
interiors of the Doge's Palace in Venice (cat. 2 verso), or the Scala dei Giganti in the
palace courtyard (cat. 1 verso).

These first drawings clearly show Piranesi's graphic influences coming together.
The more refined studies have a flavour of Canaletto, while the vigorous sketches recall
those of Giuseppe Valeriani (Fig. 6); Piranesi's training had also brought him into
contact with preparatory drawings by the celebrated Andrea Palladio. By the time of
the *Prima Parte*, however, he had developed a style of greater individuality, as seen in
A colonnaded atrium with domes (1740–43; cat. 3), a preparatory drawing for plate 10 of the
series (see Fig. 14). Although the basics of brown ink and grey wash remain, the pen
has a thicker nib and the line is more fluid; ornamentation is added with flicks and dabs
of the pen, as seen in the Corinthian capitals and the decoration of the distant apse.

Characteristically, even though this is the culmination of considerable thought,
Piranesi still allows for the possibility of change, experimenting with a deeper

entablature for the columns on the left-hand side, which would require a taller flight of steps in the centre. Even more characteristically, the final print showed further significant changes, with the apse replaced by a receding series of arches and barrel vaults. Similar vitality is evident in *Alternative designs for a temple* (cat. 6 recto), which is not directly connected to the *Prima Parte*, but clearly dates from the same period. Again, the pen adds darts and spots of ink to give the impression of decoration, but Piranesi uses a darker shade of ink to add a pyramid, triumphal arch and curved colonnade. This use of two different inks, which seems originally to have been purely functional, would become a regular habit in later years, allowing for greater tonal variety and immediately obvious revisions.

When Piranesi returned to Venice in 1745, his drawings had already begun to demonstrate exuberant fluidity. Some of the later preparatory drawings for the *Prima Parte* (cats. 4 and 7) show a lyrical approach in which brown wash, rather than grey, combines with freehand penwork over the very lightest chalk indications. Piranesi had, of course, spent his youth in Venice, and so the graphic language of that region was natural to him. What changed after the return visit was a new sensitivity to tone and

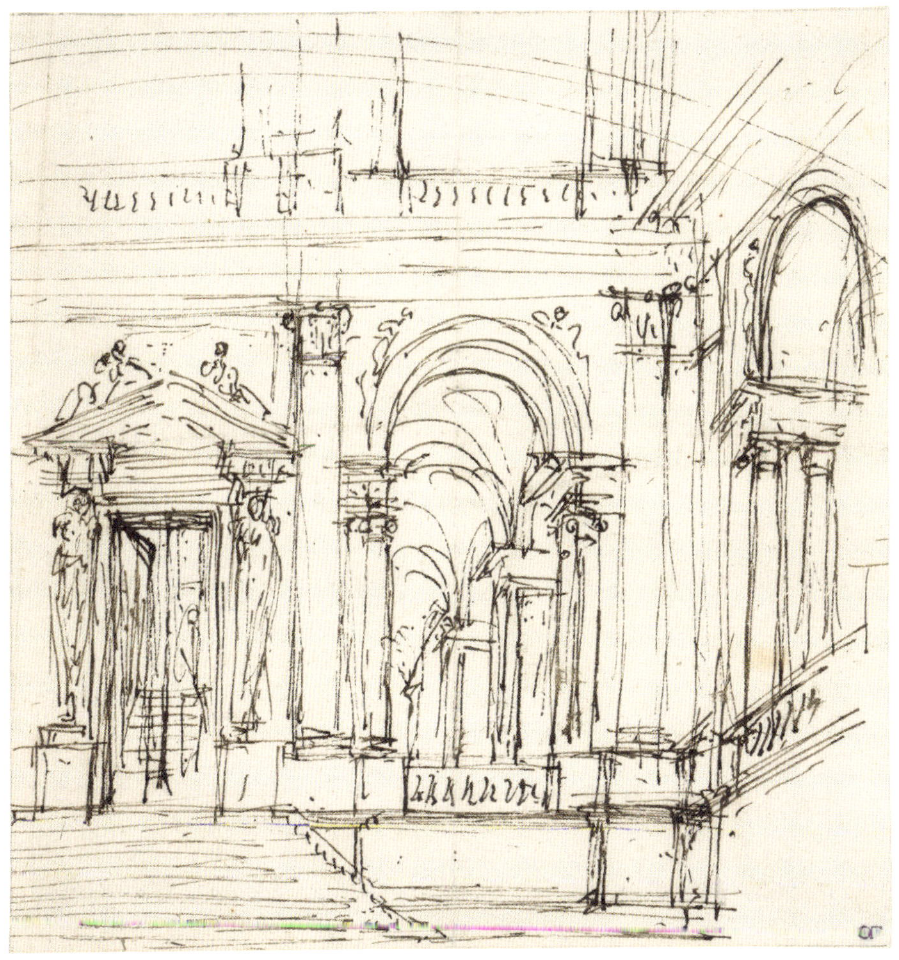

Fig. 6
Giuseppe Valeriani
(*c.* 1708–1761)
*A palace with a pedimented
entrance and arcade*
1728–61
Pen and brown ink
163 × 159 mm (6½ × 6⅜ in.)
1960,0213.2

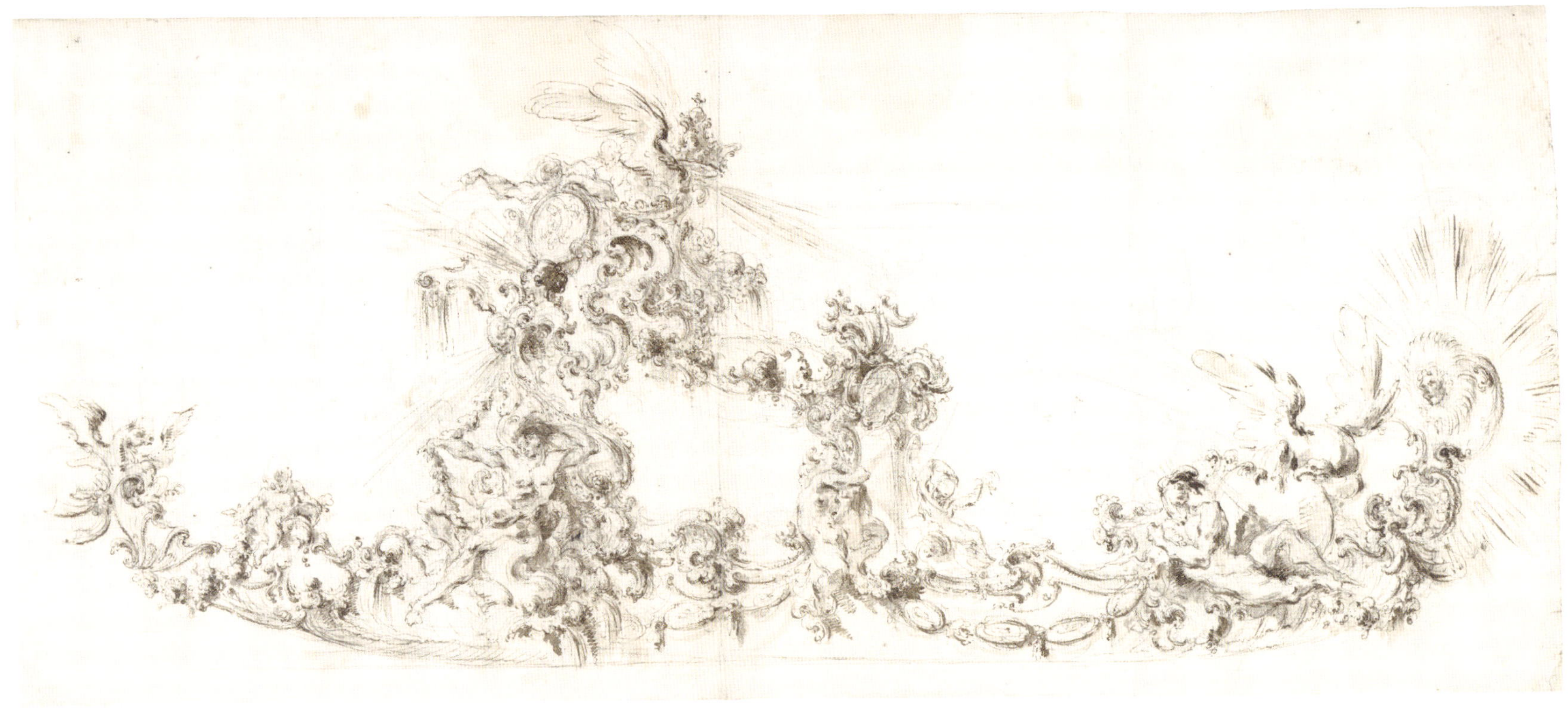

the use of multiple densities of ink and wash to create more dramatic contrasts. Certainly some of this seems to have been inspired by Giambattista Tiepolo, whether or not Piranesi actually worked in his studio. At its most extreme, Piranesi's adoption of the Venetian mode extended to its visual motifs, such as the animated skeletons (cat. 11) of a type that appears in Tiepolo's *Scherzi*, the extraordinarily delicate *Design for a gondola* (Fig. 7), and the *Decorative shell ornament* (Fig. 8).

The ink and wash study *Ancient ruins with monumental urns* (cat. 10) derives from the frontispiece designs in the *Prima Parte* and yet has an airy lightness that marks it as from his Venetian period. It does not yet have the free fluidity of the skeletons and, with its extensive black-chalk underdrawing and spidery quill penwork, appears to date from the beginning of Piranesi's stay, around 1745–46, when he was translating his favourite subjects into a Venetian idiom. From this date onwards, however, his penwork becomes looser and more liquid, while translucent sweeps of light-brown wash help to add tone and to block in spontaneous forms. The Venetian subjects die away in his drawings shortly after his departure, probably because he realized – from the muted commercial success of the *Grotteschi* – that they were of limited appeal in Rome. Instead, he concentrated on applying the lessons he had learned to his architectural fantasies. He began to use red chalk more extensively, sometimes to block in a preliminary composition (cat. 23), but more frequently as a way to enliven the aesthetic of a drawing (cat. 27). Drawings all or mostly in red chalk remain rare in Piranesi's oeuvre, although he did favour this technique in the 1760s and 1770s for preparatory drawings for his large-scale *Vedute di Roma* series (cat. 42).

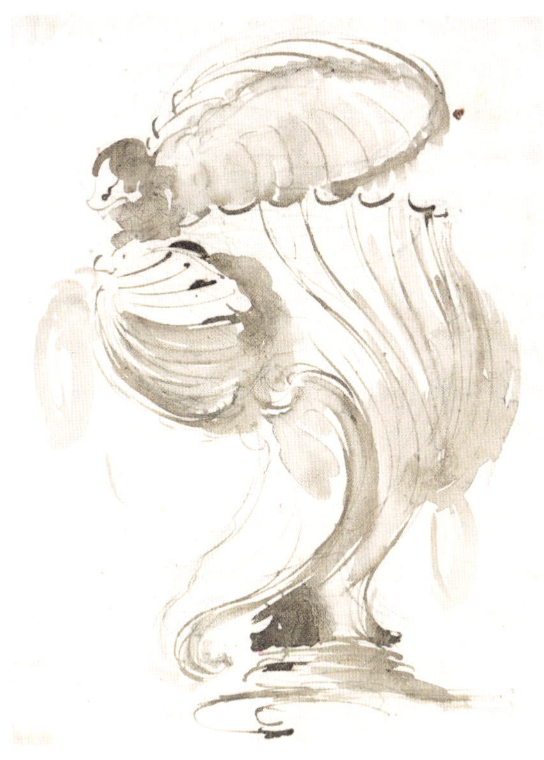

The influence of stage design on Piranesi's compositions remained strong, and it is critical not to overlook the theatrical component of his later work. One significant feature is his concern with framing devices, and two drawings from the late 1740s show how he approached this in different ways. *Interior of an ornate mausoleum* (cat. 18) uses a curtain in grey wash to suggest the revelation of space and to emphasize its theatricality. The space beyond has been worked up from an initial design in lighter brown ink, with a thin nib, into a denser, more dramatic scene with the addition of darker brown ink and sweeps of dark wash. By contrast, the neat symmetry of *A hilltop villa with a monumental staircase* (cat. 19) is undermined by the addition of a tree in dark wash on the left, and another line of wash, with a suggestion of a fountain, in the foreground. These areas of darker wash are probably later additions, introduced in the 1750s when Piranesi had completed his first edition of the *Carceri* and was thinking about the second, more densely worked and dramatic edition. At around this time, he also seems to have mounted many of his earlier drawings, placing them on backing sheets with a ruled-line border, and adding a signature. He constantly revisited and revised earlier drawings, always alert to their potential.

The most self-consciously theatrical of Piranesi's drawings are those related to the *Carceri*, which grew out of an established graphic tradition popularized by the Bibiena family. His increasing use of light to articulate spaces derived from his knowledge of their work. In *A palatial interior* by Francesco Galli Bibiena (Fig. 9) we see a dark foreground with a distant lighter mid-ground, glimpsed beyond a screen of columns –

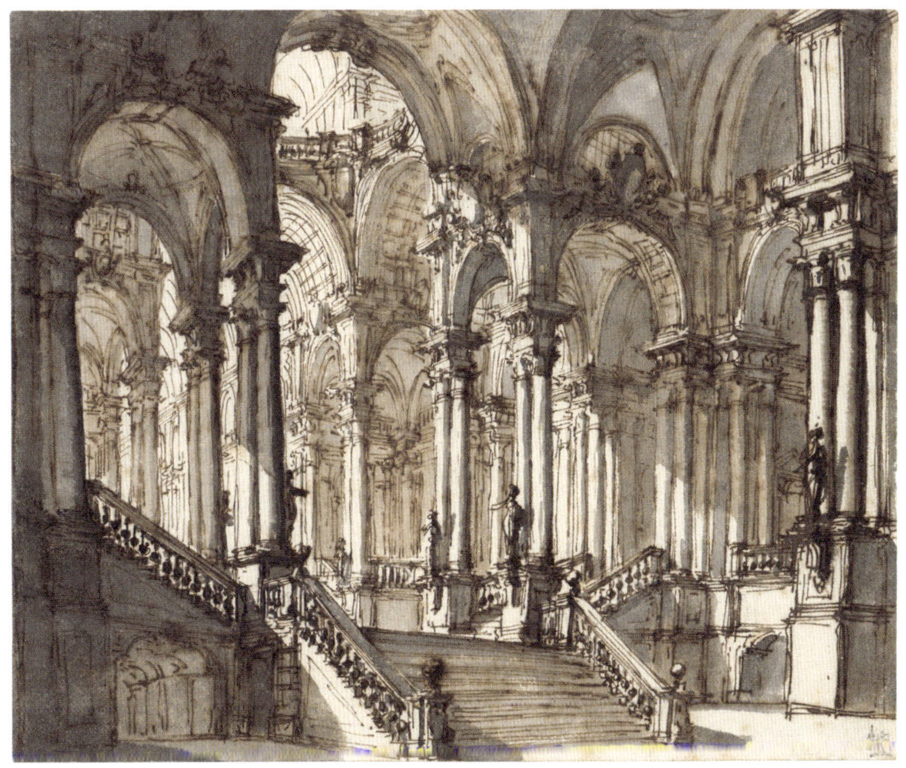

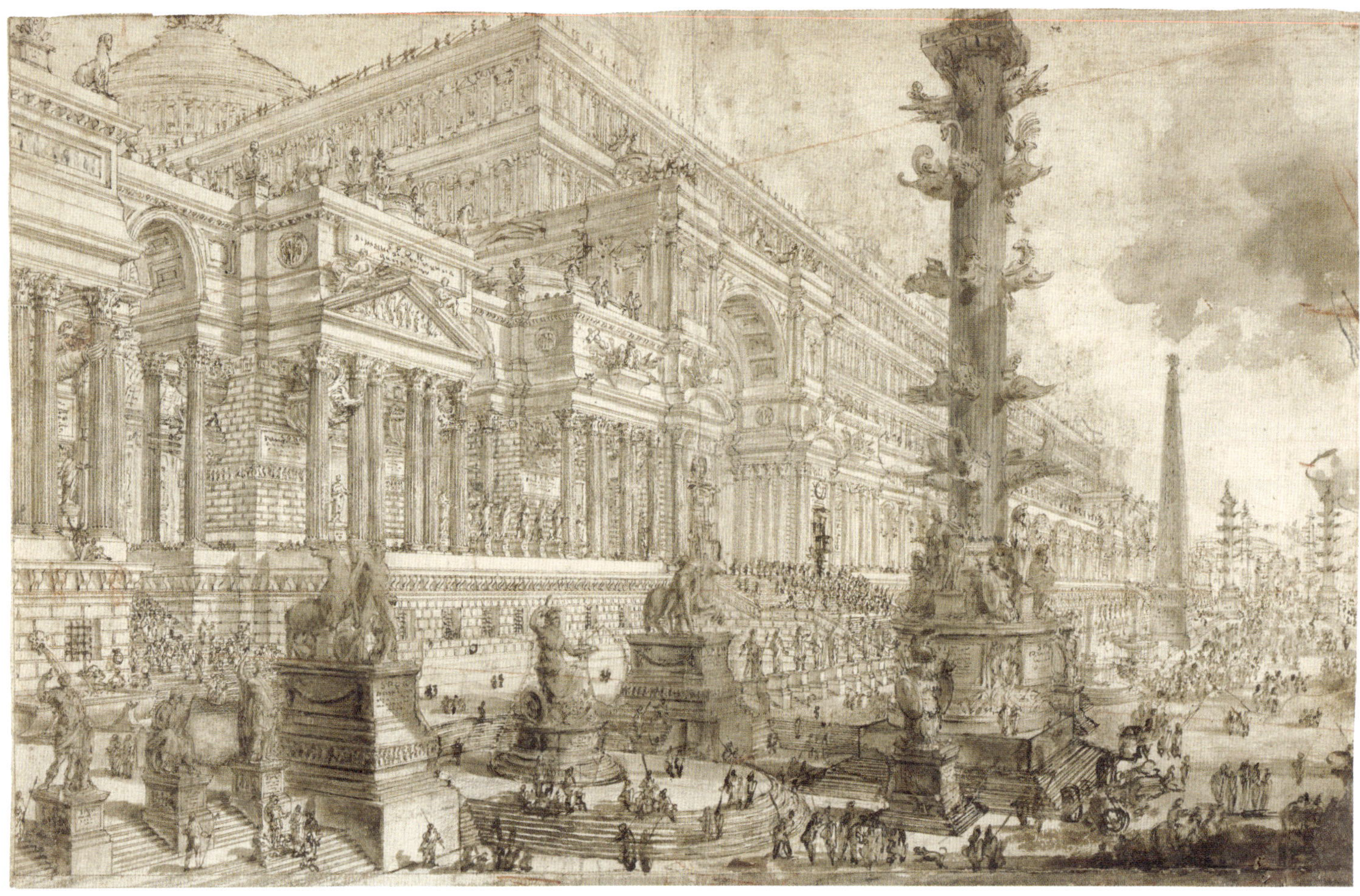

a juxtaposition that Piranesi would use as a way to suggest the vastness of his pictorial spaces, even when the monumental structures were rendered on a small scale (cat. 16).

The enduring influence of the Bibienas' work can also be detected in Piranesi's grandest and most impressive drawing in the British Museum, the preparatory study for one of the frontispieces of the *Antichità Romane*: *The meeting of the Via Appia and the Via Ardentina* (cat. 29). This drawing is striking for its size and its remarkable freedom, not only when compared to Piranesi's earlier drawings, but also when juxtaposed with more polished preparatory studies from the same period, such as that for another of the *Antichità Romane* frontispieces (Fig. 10). It is an exuberant pastiche of classical monuments that never belonged together: the Pyramid of Cestius sits on a rocky crag, while the Capitoline Wolf is tucked away among urns and monuments on the left. Tiny figures exaggerate the monumentality of the scene, and the deliberate theatricality of the drawing is emphasized by the choice of a *scena per angolo* perspective. The vivacity of the draughtsmanship, with its thick, loose penwork and layers of wash, belies the fact that the composition is translated relatively faithfully into the final print (Fig. 11). This was probably not Piranesi's final preparatory drawing (it is

Fig. 10
Architectural fantasy
c. 1740–50
Pen and brown ink, with brown wash, over graphite, perspective lines and details in red chalk
270 × 428 mm (10¾ × 16⅞ in.)
The Morgan Library and Museum, New York

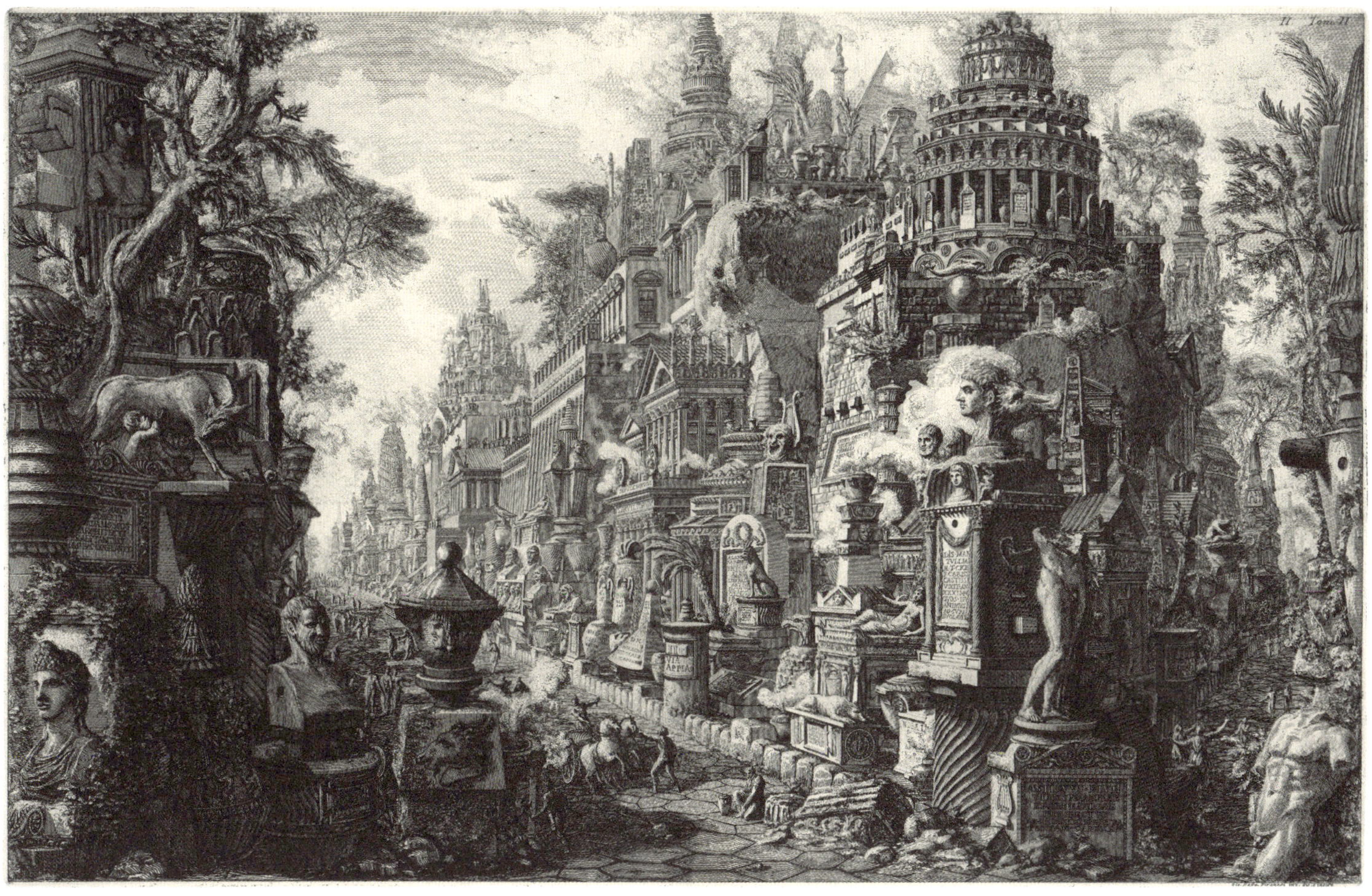

Fig. 11

The meeting of the Via Appia and the Via Ardentina, frontispiece to volume II of the *Antichità Romane*

c. 1756–57

Etching

398 × 637 mm (15¾ × 25⅛ in.)

Rijksmuseum, Amsterdam

likely that he did make a more refined study, similar to Fig. 10), but it demonstrates how expressively he was working even at an advanced stage.

Piranesi's mature work became increasingly broad, his drawings executed with the confidence of an experienced printmaker who was accustomed to working the fine detail directly onto his plates. He did still make more careful drawings, such as *View of the Portico of Gaius and Lucius* (cat. 38), which is related to his *Vedute di Roma* series, but these were the exception rather than the rule, and were probably made only at the very end of a more dynamic and exploratory preparatory process. By the late 1750s and 1760s, Piranesi's drawings were frequently made with thick reed pens, which allowed him to convey dramatic contrasts of tone and structure more easily, and with which he dashed off scribbled hatching on buildings and sky that gives the impression of artistic shorthand (cat. 39). This broad, brisk style is seen at its apogee in his drawings for sculptural reconstructions from the late 1760s and 1770s, which shrug off the use of wash in favour of strong hatching (cat. 48), and which probably served as first thoughts to be worked up more carefully by his assistants.

It is important to note the significance of Piranesi's studio at this late period. The British Museum has only a handful of drawings that show the artist working alongside his assistants, but recent examination of two albums discovered in 2015 at the Karlsruhe Kunsthalle in Germany (whose drawings are similar to others in the Morgan Library's extensive holdings) have revealed a wealth of information concerning his studio practice, especially with regard to the reconstruction of antiquities.[16] Similarly, few drawings from the end of Piranesi's career are in the British Museum's collection, but the collection does include two large studies from the Pompeii sequence, made during the 1770s. Piranesi's authorship of these drawings is less controversial than that of the Paestum series, which were made in the year of his death and probably show the input of several hands,[17] but even in the Pompeii studies there are inconsistences. *View of the Strada Consulare with the Herculaneum Gate in Pompeii* (cat. 50) appears to be entirely in Piranesi's own hand, with confident hatching, thick-nibbed pen and abbreviated, gesticulating figures; but *The Temple of Isis in Pompeii, seen from the rear* (cat. 51) is less clear-cut. One of seven studies of the temple from various angles, the drawing has an underlying stiffness that is most uncharacteristic of Piranesi at this period, and which may indicate the involvement of his son and assistant, Francesco. However, the drawing has certainly been reworked by Piranesi himself, who added the flanking columns and foreground figures, decorative elements, and the rough hatching in the sky. It suggests the complexity of work within the studio at this late stage in Piranesi's life, and the way that he probably engaged Francesco's help to allow him to produce large sequences of drawings in short periods of time.

Until very recently, the British Museum lacked an example of one of Piranesi's signature genres: the independent figure study. Created throughout his career and growing increasingly dynamic, these studies appear to have been drawn for pleasure rather than for a functional purpose: they can rarely be directly related to figures in the etchings and, as such, they are of particular interest in the context of Piranesi's activity as a draughtsman. His unsympathetic early biographer, Bianconi, relates Piranesi's early fascination with drawing beggars on the streets of Rome,[18] and he seems to have continued this tendency by sketching workshop assistants, passers-by and friends, often on fragments torn from letters or proofs of his etchings. In 2019 the Museum was presented with its first Piranesi figure study, *A standing man in profile* (cat. 44 recto), which dates from the mid-1760s and is, characteristically, drawn on the back of a letter. Showing a ragged but typically eloquent figure, it demonstrates the continued appeal of Piranesi's studies and adds a hitherto missing element to the Museum's comprehensive collection of his drawings.

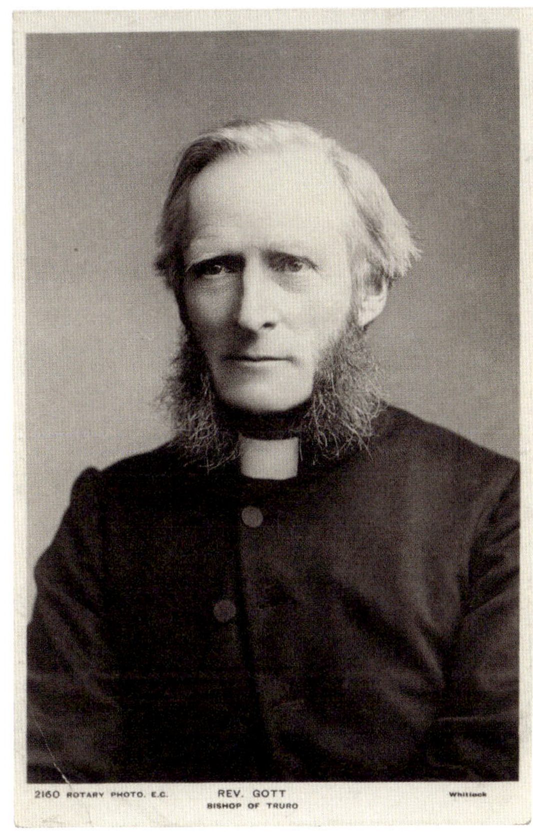

Bishop John Gott and the British Museum Piranesis

In 1908, the British Museum improved its Piranesi collection at a single stroke by purchasing forty-six drawings from the Sotheby's sale of the collection of John Gott (1830–1906), Bishop of Truro (Fig. 12).[19] The provenance is surprising: Gott had a fine library, particularly rich in early English Bibles, but he is not notable for any special interest in the fine arts. Nothing else in his sale explains his ownership of a superb collection of Piranesi drawings. However, archival research carried out in the course of preparing this exhibition suggests that these drawings were inherited by John Gott from his father, William (1797–1863).

William was the son of the industrialist Benjamin Gott (1762–1840), who, in the heat of the Industrial Revolution, transformed his wool mill at Armley in Leeds into the largest factory in the world. Alongside philanthropic spending, Benjamin used his profits to establish his family in the mercantile elite, with a mansion at Armley designed by Robert Smirke, gardens by Humphry Repton, and portraits by Sir Thomas Lawrence. Lawrence had another connection with the family: he had sponsored the sculptor Joseph Gott (1785–1860), one of Benjamin's cousins, to go to Rome, also giving him an introduction to Antonio Canova.[20] Benjamin's sons developed corresponding cultural interests and, although no firm documentation survives, it is highly likely that one of them bought the Gott Piranesis.

William Gott's elder brother, also called Benjamin (1793–1817), embarked on a
Grand Tour in 1814. He travelled from London to Rome, arriving there in February
1817, and afterwards went on to Athens where, in June 1817, he caught a fever and
died. He was initially buried in the Temple of Theseus.[21] During his travels he had
collected a number of Greek sculptures, which passed at his death to his travelling
companion, a Mr Rawson. William Gott bought the marbles back after Rawson's
death in 1845–46, and they remained in the family until Bishop John presented them
to Leeds Museum in 1863–64.[22]

Although there is no record of Benjamin purchasing Piranesi drawings, it would have
been entirely consistent for him to have done so: his marked fascination with classical
antiquities would have made them a natural interest, even without having a cousin active
in artistic circles in Rome. Unfortunately, the only record of his activities focuses on the
sculpture collection now in Leeds, and there is no mention of other aspects of his travels.

Similarly there is no record of William having undertaken a Grand Tour. Perhaps
his brother's death made his parents unwilling to risk another of their children.
Indeed, there is no evidence that he left England at all until he was in his fifties, when
he embarked with members of his family on two European journeys. The carefully
stamped passports remain in the family archives. In 1852 – accompanied by John (the
future bishop), two daughters and a maid – William acquired passes for Sardinia, Milan,
Genoa and Turin, as well as France, Belgium, Austria and the Netherlands. Two years
later, William and his daughters returned to Belgium and the Netherlands but went
north to Denmark instead of south to Italy.[23] It is highly likely that the earlier trip also
included visits to other places in Italy, especially because the elderly Joseph Gott was still
living in Rome. While the family may well have bought the Piranesi drawings during
their travels, in Italy or equally likely in Paris, where the contents of Piranesi's studio
had been taken by Francesco, there are no letters or diaries recording their activities.

The third possibility is that William Gott acquired the drawings in England. An
avid bibliophile (Fig. 13), he was in frequent touch with London agents, who sent him
reports on the most interesting lots coming up for sale. He was fascinated by a variety
of subjects, which corresponded with the strengths of Bishop John's future library:
early English Bibles, Shakespeare and the works of Byron. Inspired by local pride,
he assembled a fine collection of topographical watercolours of Yorkshire, now in
the Hepworth Wakefield Gallery. Yet, in 1860, he was also actively looking out for
a fine copy of works by Piranesi and had set his London agents, the book dealers
T. & W. Boone, on the case.

On 21 July 1860, William Boone reported on five volumes of Piranesi that Gott had
asked him to examine: he felt the binding was too tight and likely to split, but 'should
you have no desire for this particular copy I can supply … a better one, with the […]
Machines and the Magnificenza di Roma, considered the finest of Piranesi's works …
the impressions of the plates as fine as possible the six volumes for £20'.[24] Receiving
a favourable response, Boone wrote again on 24 July asking if he should send all six
volumes for Gott's consideration, and answering a request for advice on a Piranesi

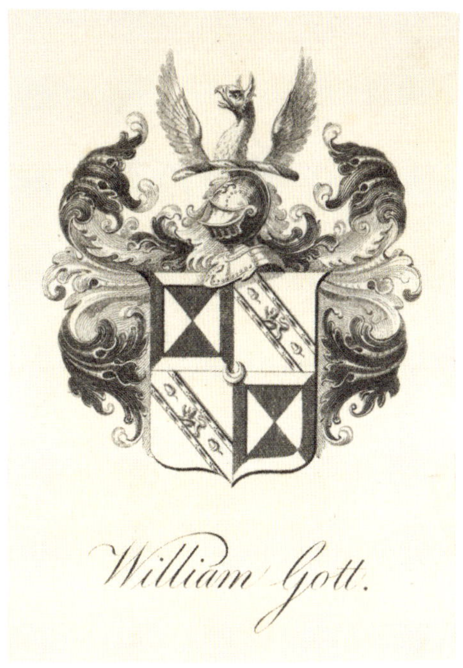

volume that Gott had been offered elsewhere.[25] It is not clear whether Gott decided to go for the six-volume set, but he clearly bought something, because on 30 July Boone asked whether he wanted to have the Piranesi 'and any others that may be ready' sent up, presumably from the binder's.[26] Yet this did not mark the end of Gott's quest for Piranesi, because on 20 October 1860, Boone's brother Thomas wrote with news of another tantalizing offer:

> I have just been offered an extraordinarily fine copy of the books of Piranesi. The Original Roman Impressions, and in the Italian Calf Binding of the period, elaborately gilt, 27 vols folio. This copy was formerly presented to the Margravine of Ansbach and considering the high prices that modern Impressions in new Half Binding have been selling for, I consider the sum of £200 fixed upon this to be very moderate. The present owner is desirous of parting with it only on account of having lately moved into a smaller house. Should you desire some specimen volumes could be sent for your inspection.[27]

No further correspondence survives to establish whether or not Gott was tempted. It is clear, though, that during the 1860s he was actively seeking out fine impressions of Piranesi prints to enrich his library, to illustrate his memories of travelling in Italy in the 1850s, and to accompany the collection of classical sculptures formed by his late brother in the 1810s. It seems likely that, during his quest for Piranesi prints, he was also offered, or acquired, this remarkable group of drawings, which passed to his son Bishop John, and came to form the core of the British Museum's splendid collection.

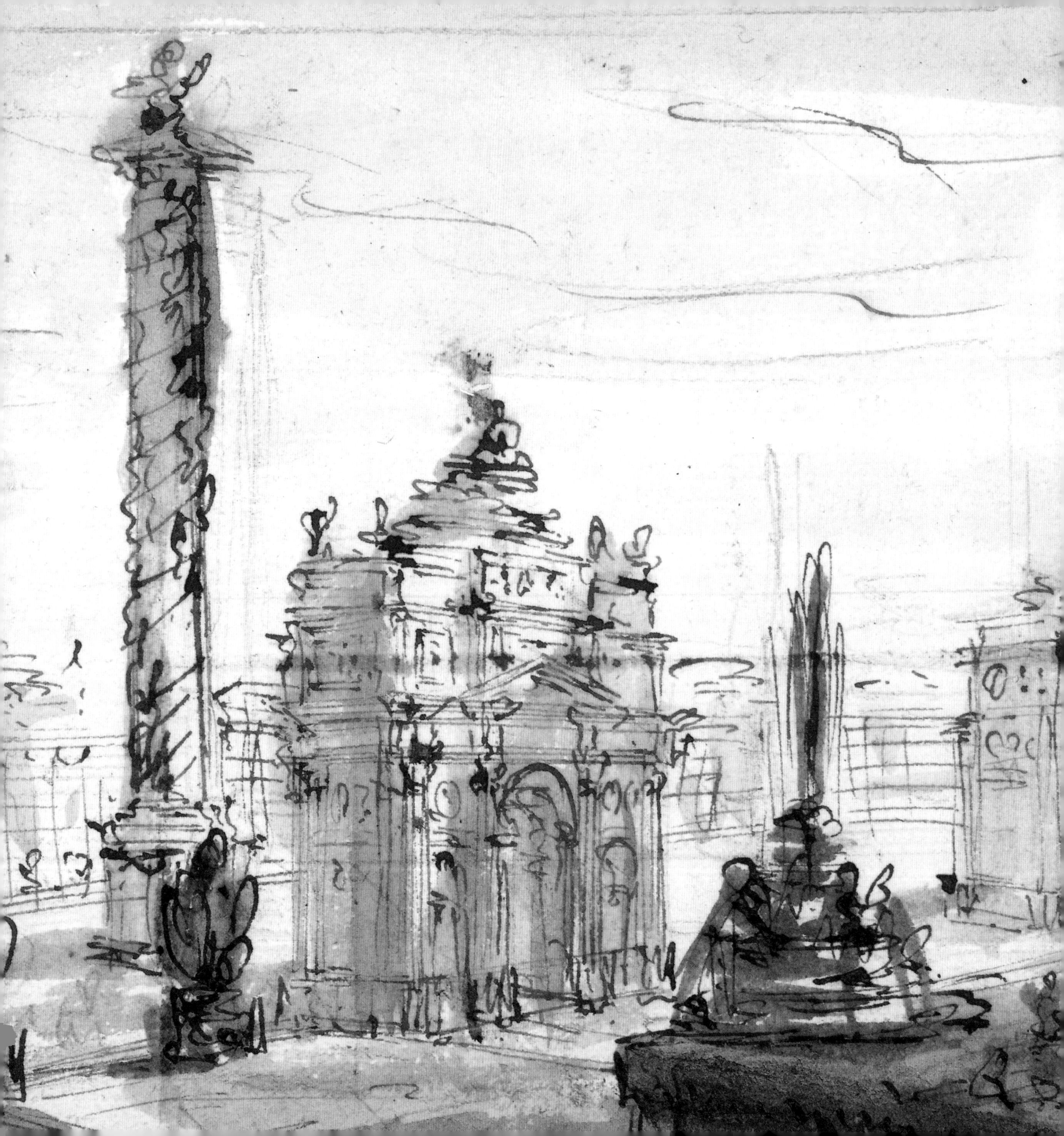

Catalogue

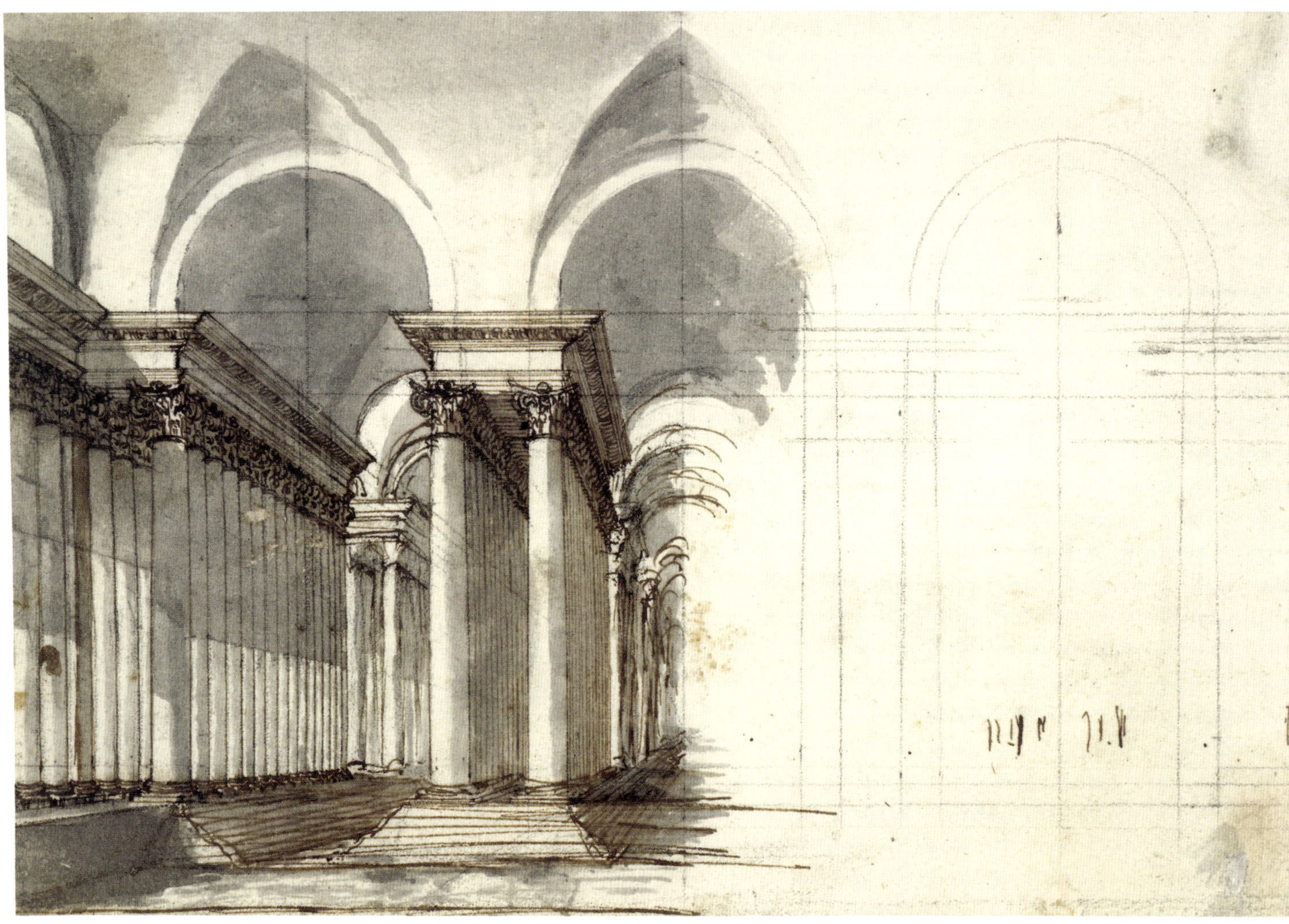

1.

An antique temple (recto); Six architectural sketches (verso)

c. 1740–42

Pen and brown ink, with grey wash, over black chalk (recto); pen and brown ink (verso)

136 × 198 mm (5⅜ × 7⅞ in.)

1908,0616.18

Provenance: Probably William Gott; and by descent to his son, John Gott, Bishop of Truro; his sale, Sotheby's, London, 20 March 1908, part of lot 172

Exhibitions: London 1968, part of no. 18; London 1978, no. 26a; Venice 1978, no. 3; London and elsewhere 2002–4, no catalogue

Literature: Robison 1986a, p. 20, fig. 20

One of the earliest drawings by Piranesi in the British Museum, this probably dates from the period when he moved from Venice to Rome. On the recto the design has been worked up on only half the sheet, revealing carefully ruled black chalk guidelines beneath. The composition would have been traced and flipped in order to complete the design. With single-point perspective and serried ranks of columns, this is probably a design for a stage set: Piranesi seems to be interested in the column as a decorative element to emphasize recession, rather than as a plausibly weight-bearing structure.

The drawings on the verso, far looser and more energetic, show that he was already a confident and instinctive draughtsman. These quick studies are not so different in spirit from the searching, dynamic drawings he would turn to for his first thoughts, or *primi pensieri*, for the rest of his career. The three sketches along the top of the sheet may be first thoughts for *A colonnaded atrium with domes* (cat. 3) and *A colonnaded atrium with a Gothic arch* (cat. 4 recto).

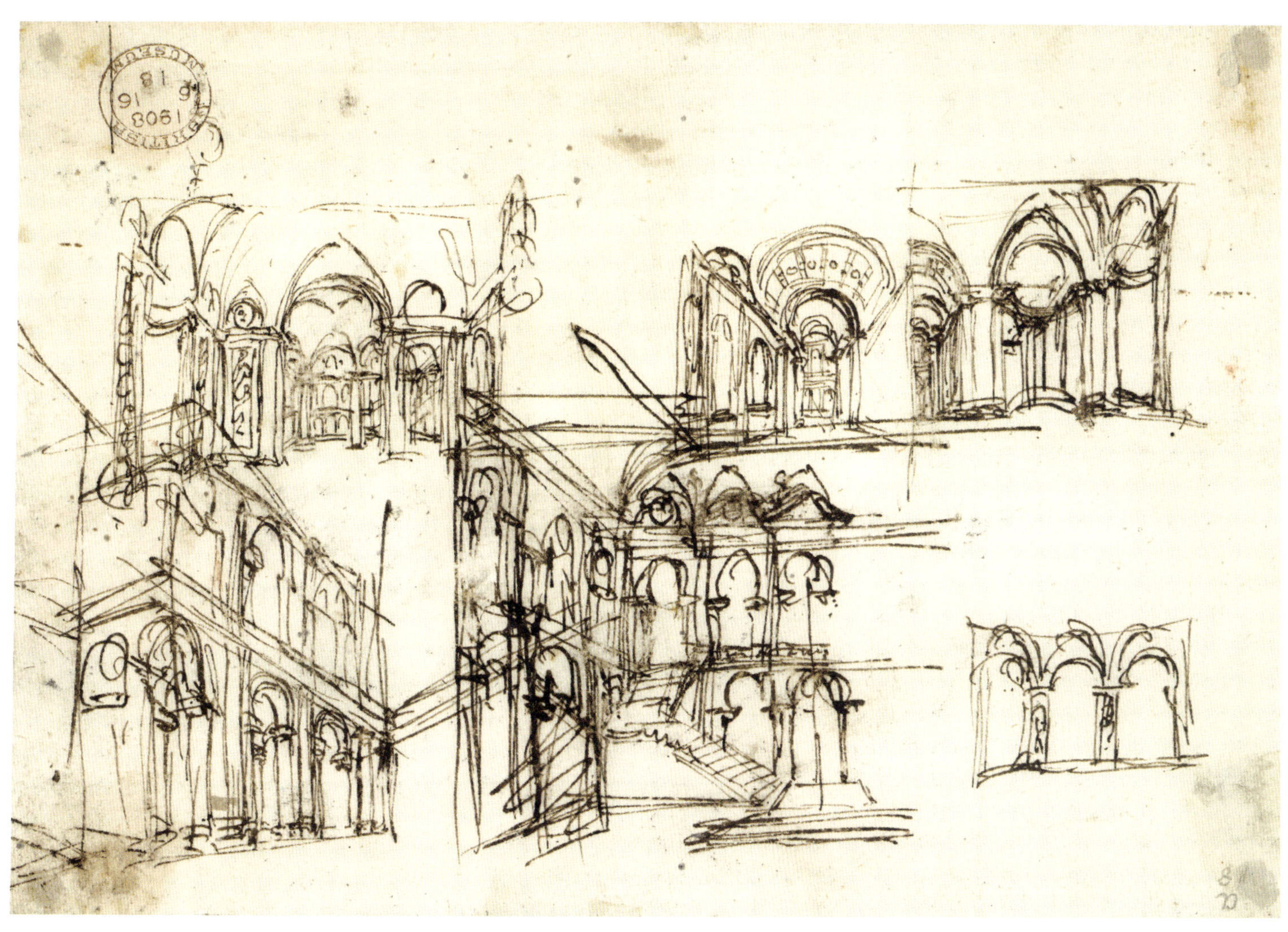

2.

A colonnaded courtyard (recto);
Six studies of colonnades (verso)

c. 1740–42

Pen and brown ink

141 × 212 mm (5⅝ × 8⅜ in.)

1908,0616.19

Provenance: Probably William Gott; and by
descent to his son, John Gott, Bishop of Truro;
his sale, Sotheby's, London, 20 March 1908,
part of lot 172

Exhibitions: London 1968, part of no. 18; London
1978, no. 26b; Venice 1978, no. 2; London and
elsewhere 2002–4, no catalogue

Literature: Thomas 1954, no. 1; Vogt-Göknil
1958, p. 24, fig. 9; Penny 1978, no. 1; Lawrence
2007, p. 142 (text by David Rosand); Nevola
2009, pp. 90–91, fig. 72

While the composition of this drawing
was inspired by the stage designs of the
Bibiena family, it is firmly Venetian in
technique: the combination of brown
ink and grey wash is very similar to
that found in Canaletto's drawings.
The elaborate courtyard on the recto
can be related to the engraving *Gruppo
di Scale* from the *Prima Parte* (1743),[28]
in which the columns are regrouped in
clumps and the flights of steps lowered.
The perspective is also shifted in the print,
so that the central corner is closest to,
rather than furthest from, the viewer,
with arcades receding on both sides,
and the columns are joined by Roman-
style arches.

When planning the present drawing,
Piranesi initially experimented with the
idea of arches, which are still visible in
black chalk at upper centre. The drawing
therefore forms a conceptual point along
the path Piranesi took in adjusting a
concept borrowed from the Bibiena
family to a plainer and more individual
design in his *Prima Parte*.

On the verso, the brisk sketches of
colonnades are annotated with reminders
about the lighting of the scene ('chiaro',
or 'light'; and 'scuro', or 'dark'). Piranesi
was already deeply interested in the way
light could be used to articulate and
dramatize his architectural spaces.

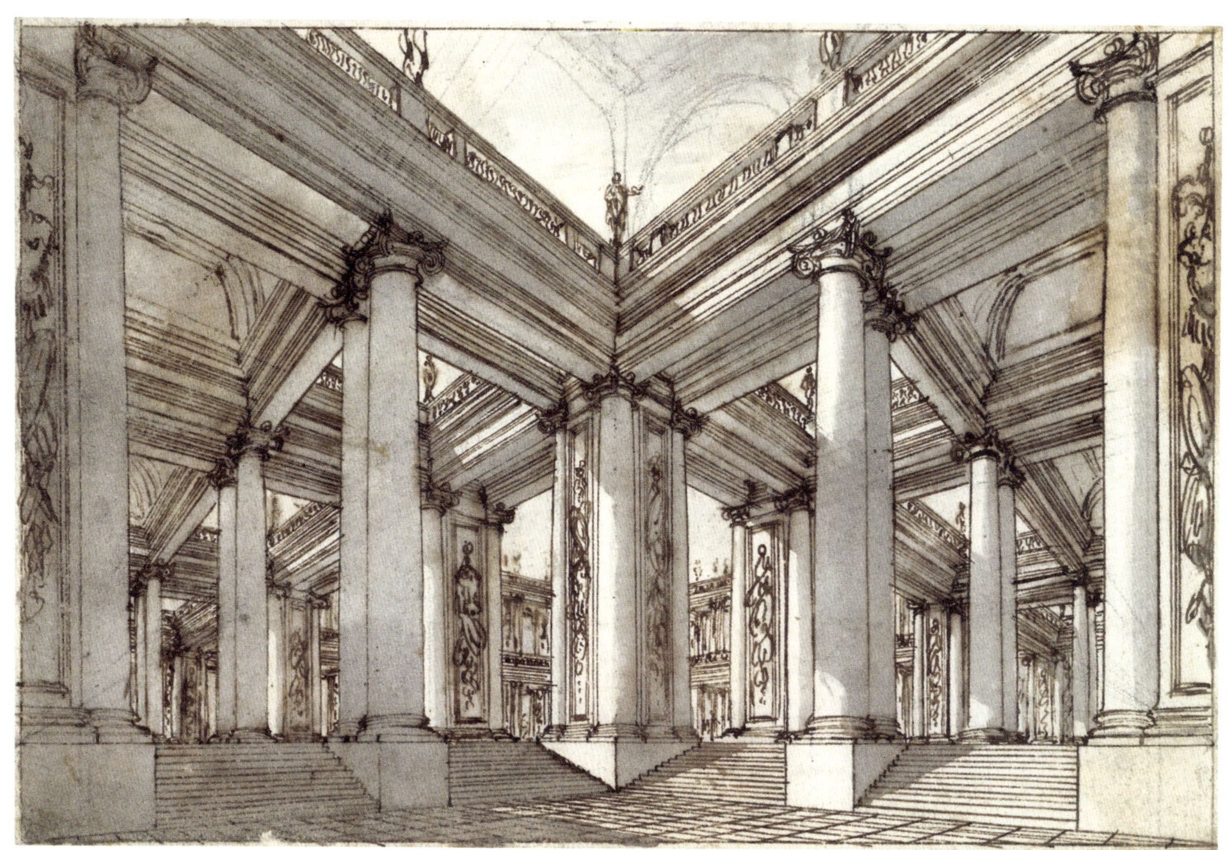

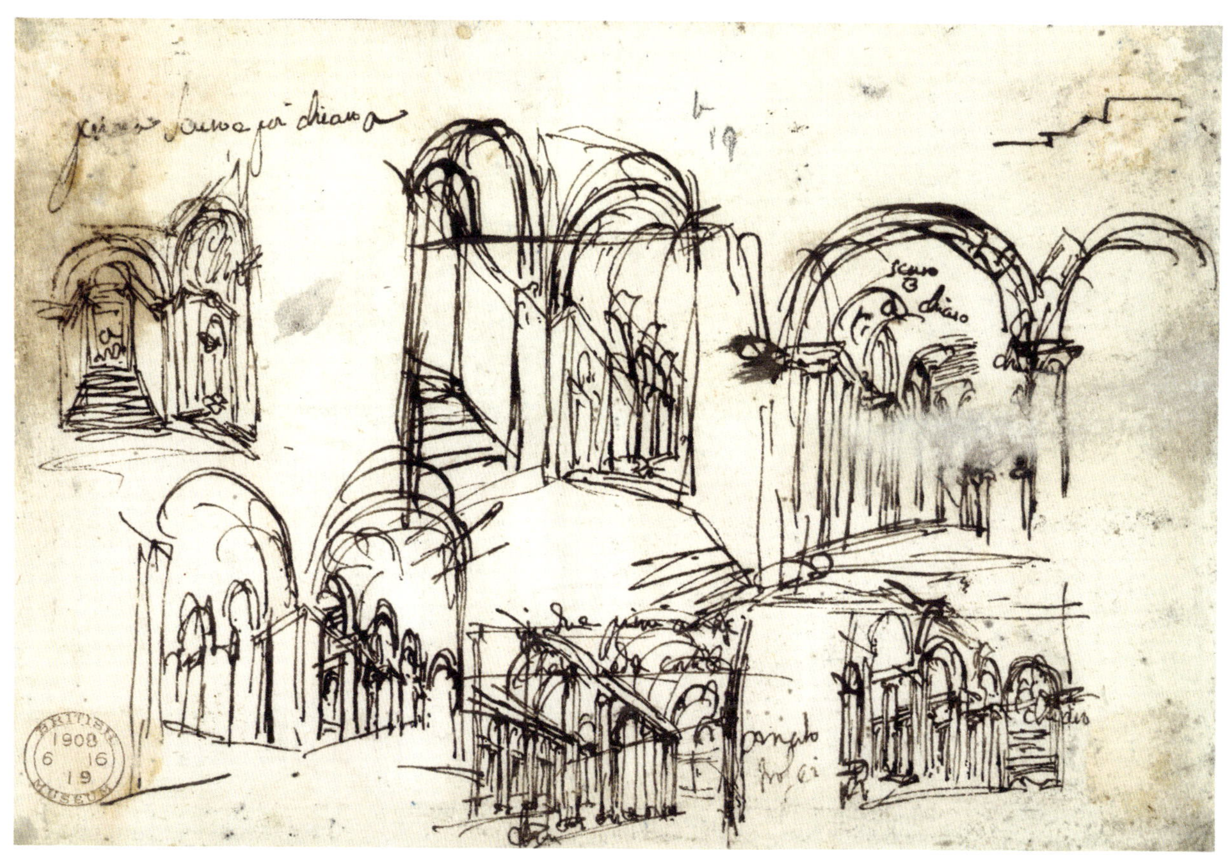

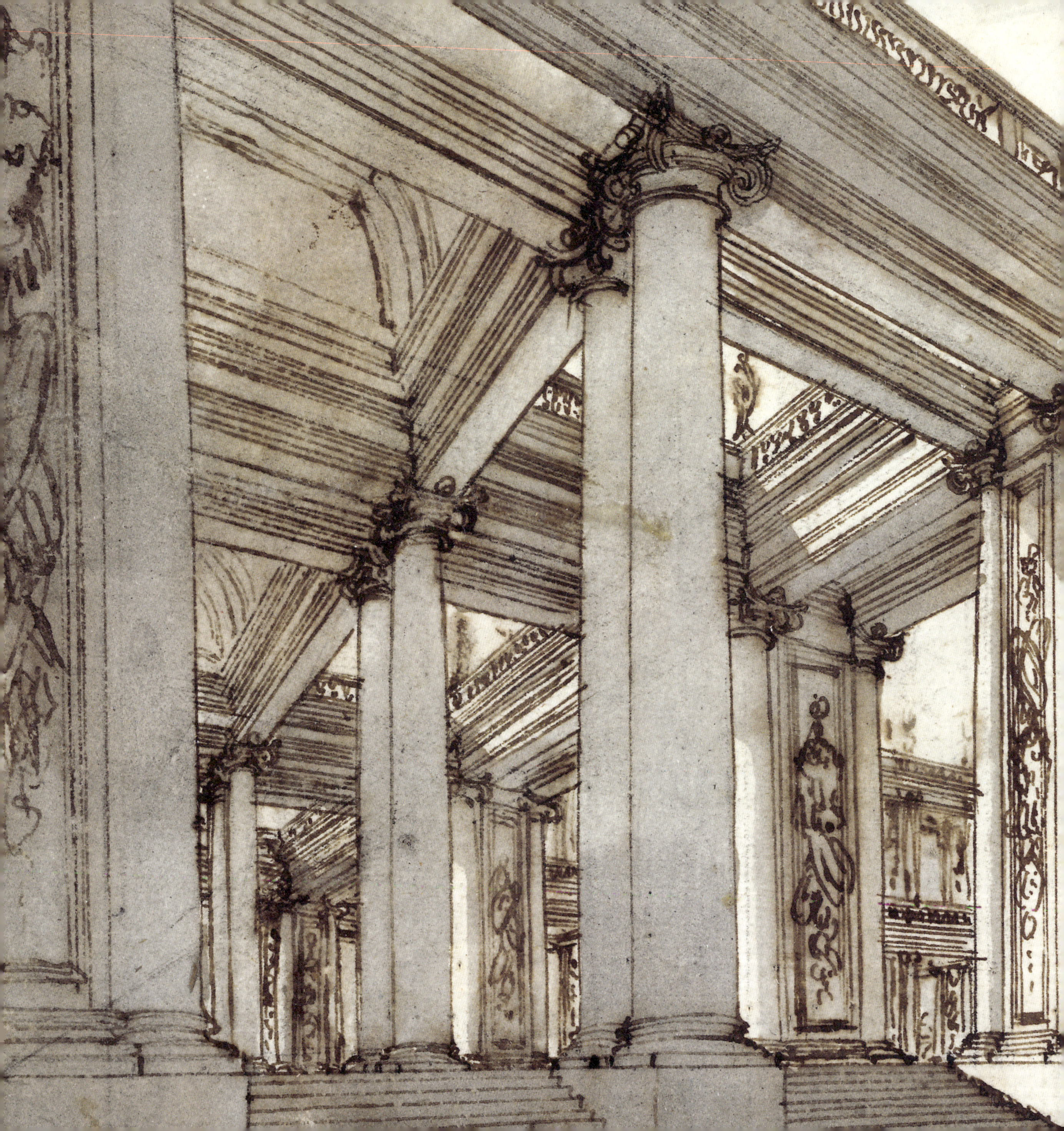

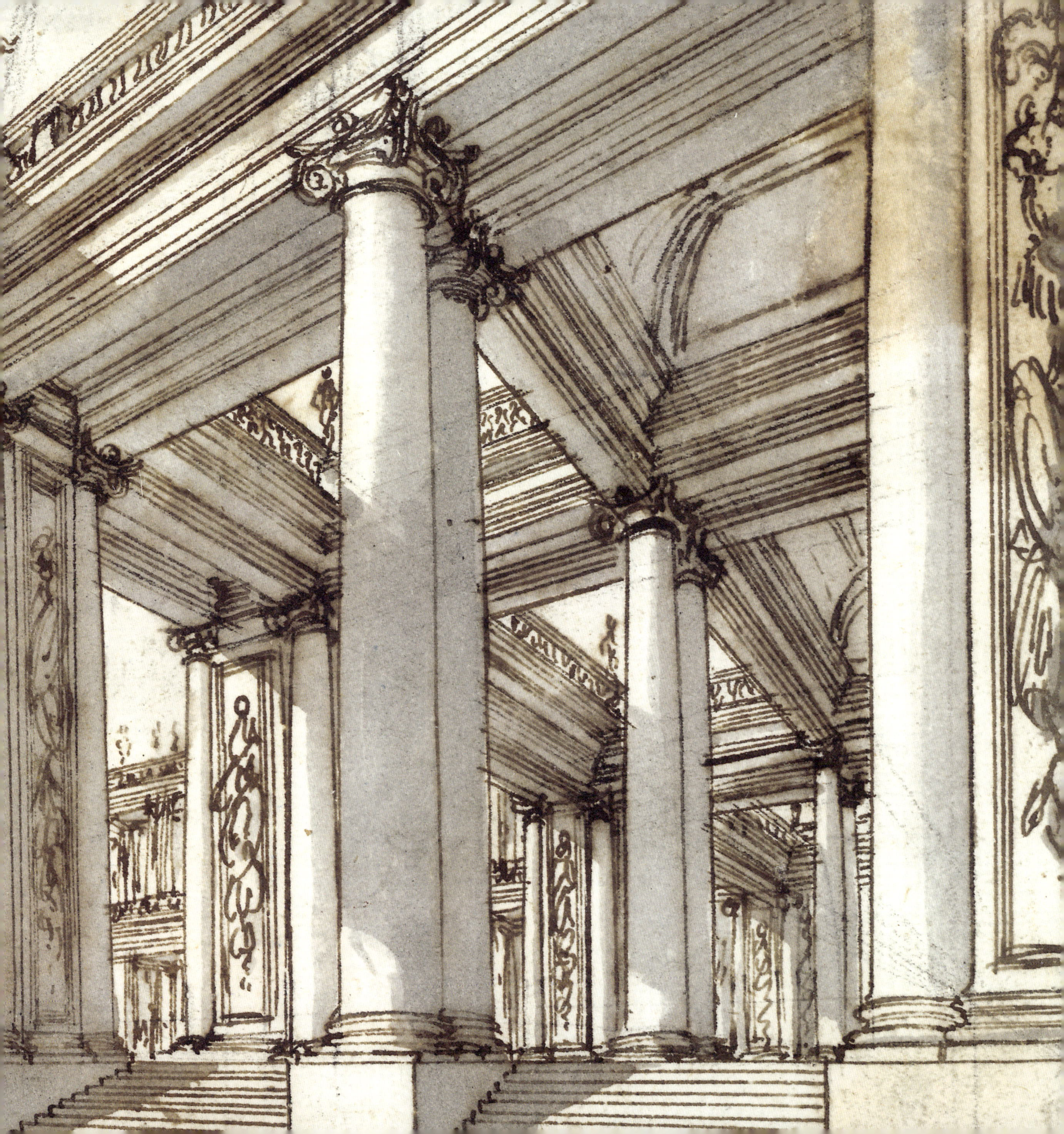

3.

A colonnaded atrium with domes

c. 1740–43

Pen and brown ink, grey wash, over traces
of black chalk
135 × 206 mm (5⅜ × 8⅛ in.)
1908,0616.28

Provenance: Probably William Gott; and by
descent to his son, John Gott, Bishop of Truro;
his sale, Sotheby's, London, 20 March 1908,
part of lot 172
Exhibitions: London 1968, part of no. 18;
Washington 1978, section on the *Prima Parte*,
no. 18; London 1994, no. 263
Literature: Robison 1977, p. 395, fig. 8; Robison
1986a, pp. 18–20, fig. 20 and under no. 11;
Denison et al. 1993, pp. 45–46, under no. 27

This is a preliminary study for *Vestibule of an ancient temple*,[29] plate 10 of the first edition of the *Prima Parte* (1743) (Fig. 14). Its technique, similar to that of cat. 2, recalls Canaletto; the architecture, too, has a Venetian flavour and seems to be based on the interior of Palladio's church of the Redentore. Annotations about the lighting of the scene ('chiaro', meaning 'light') once again testify to the importance that Piranesi placed on this aspect of his work.

Another preparatory drawing for the same print (Fig. 15)[30] shows an earlier stage in the preparatory sequence, in which a central screen of columns is transformed into a recessed apse. The British Museum drawing marks the next stage in the development of the composition, in which the apse is shifted further backwards beyond a bay of colonnades, with the suggestion of a rotunda above. In the final print, the colonnade is extended still more, emphasizing the depth of the pictorial space.

The presence of a curtain at the top of the drawing may indicate that it was produced explicitly as a stage design.[31] However, while there is no doubt that Piranesi was heavily inspired by theatrical designs, a similar curtain appears in the later *Interior of an ornate mausoleum* (cat. 18); it may have been conceived as a form of framing device, rather than an indication of the drawing's function.

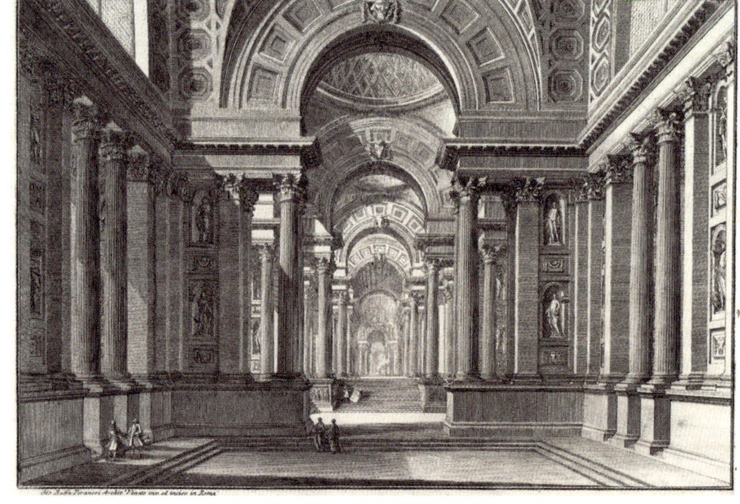

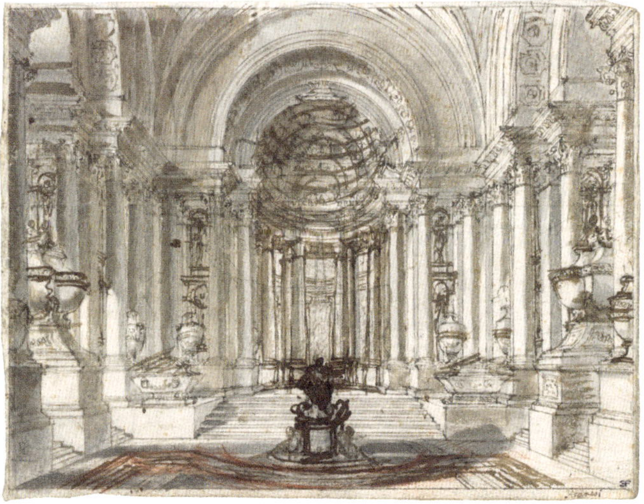

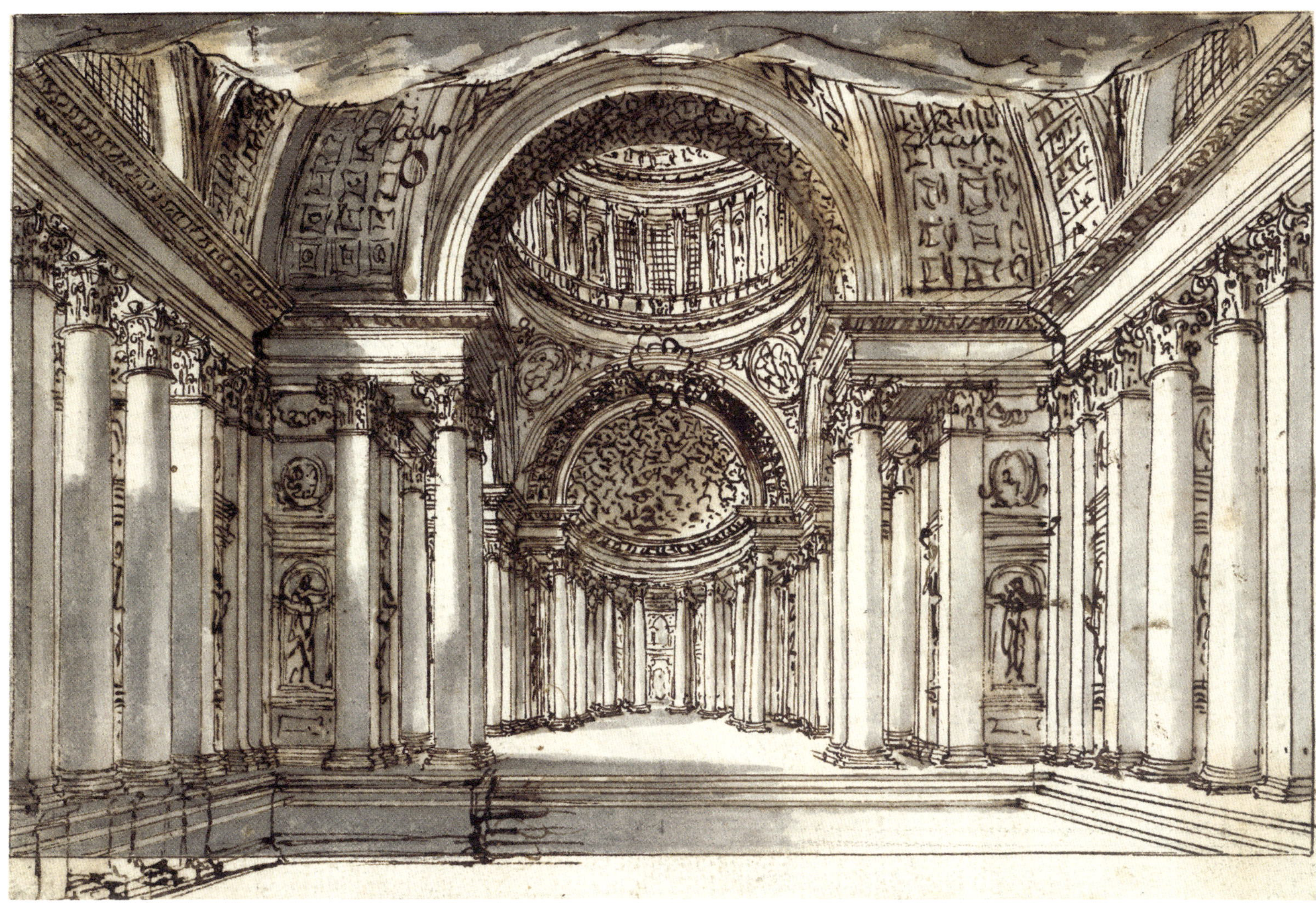

Fig. 14 (opposite, left)

Vestibule of an ancient temple
From the *Prima Parte di Architettura, e Prospettive*
c. 1743
Etching
238 × 355 mm (9⅜ × 14 in.)
Metropolitan Museum of Art, New York

Fig. 15 (opposite, right)

A colonnaded atrium with domes
c. 1740–43
Pen and brown ink and wash, black wash, over black chalk, with overdrawing in red chalk, incised
187 × 246 mm (7⅜ × 9¾ in.)
The Morgan Library and Museum, New York

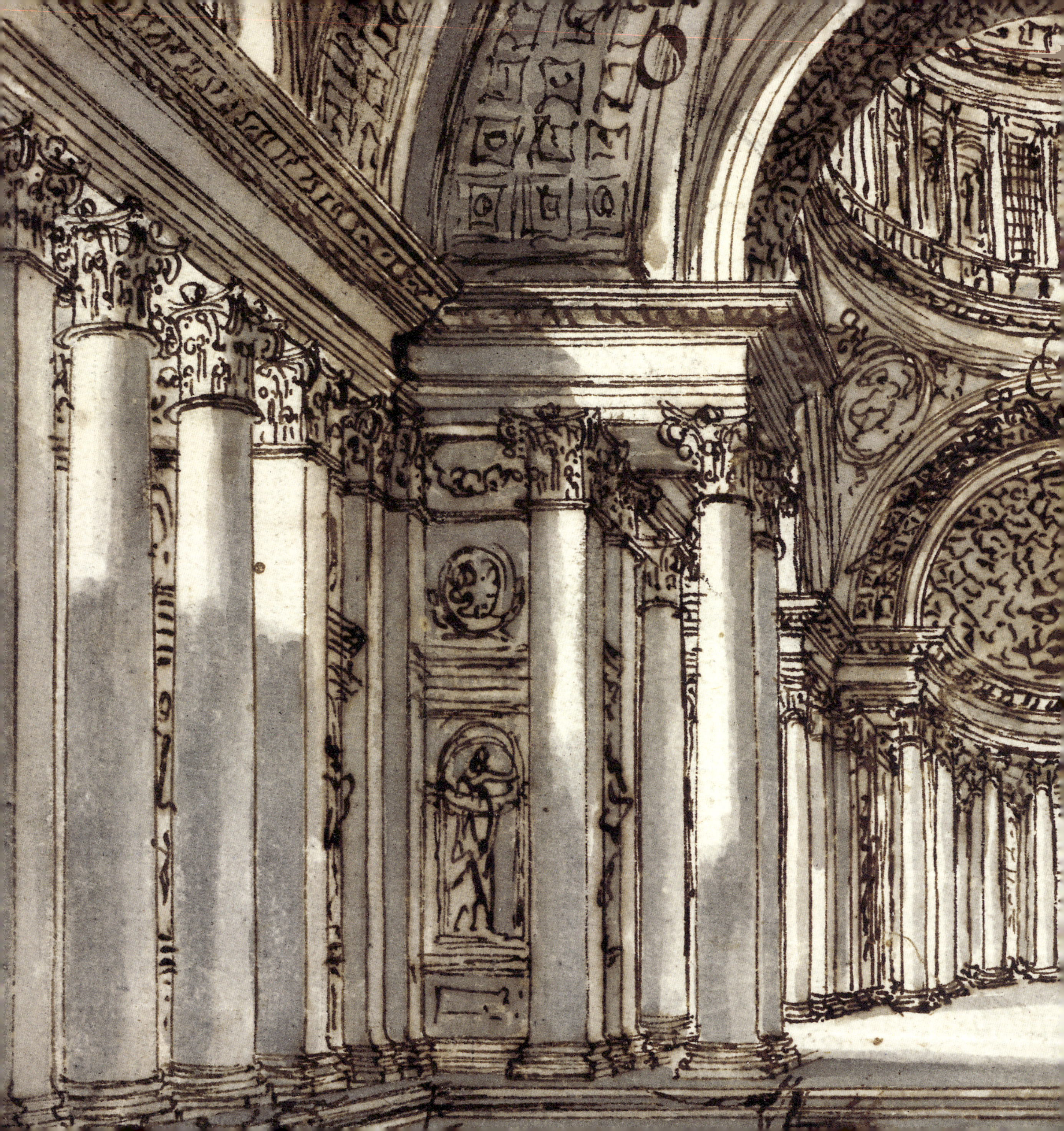

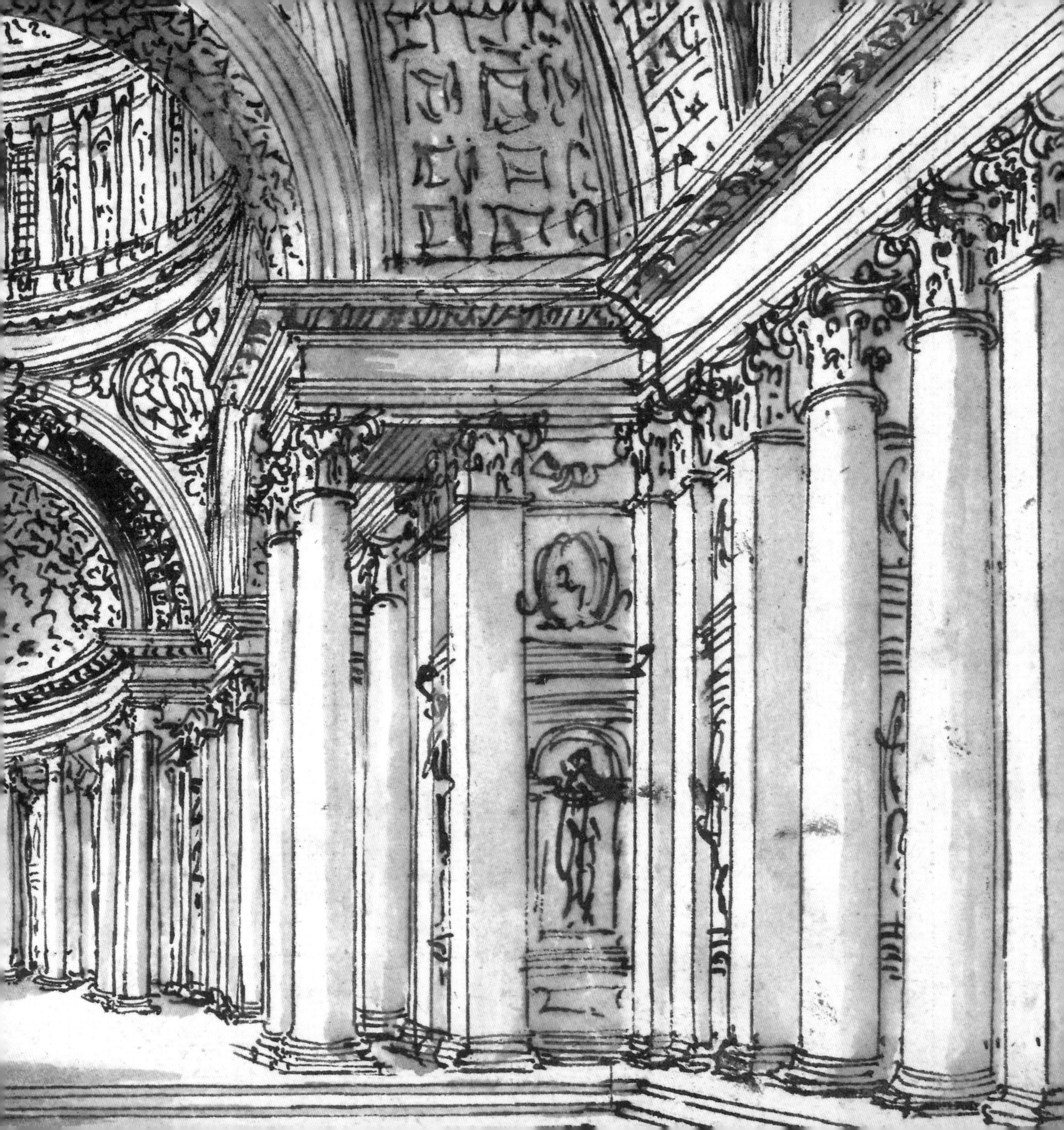

4.

A colonnaded atrium with a Gothic arch (recto); Architectural sketches including a ground plan for a centrally planned Greek cross church (verso)

c. 1742–43
Pen and brown ink, with brown and grey wash, and black chalk (recto); pen and brown ink (verso)
181 × 229 mm (7¼ × 9⅛ in.)
1908,0616.23

Provenance: Probably William Gott; and by descent to his son, John Gott, Bishop of Truro; his sale, Sotheby's, London, 20 March 1908, part of lot 172
Exhibitions: London 1968, part of no. 18; London 1978, no. 32b

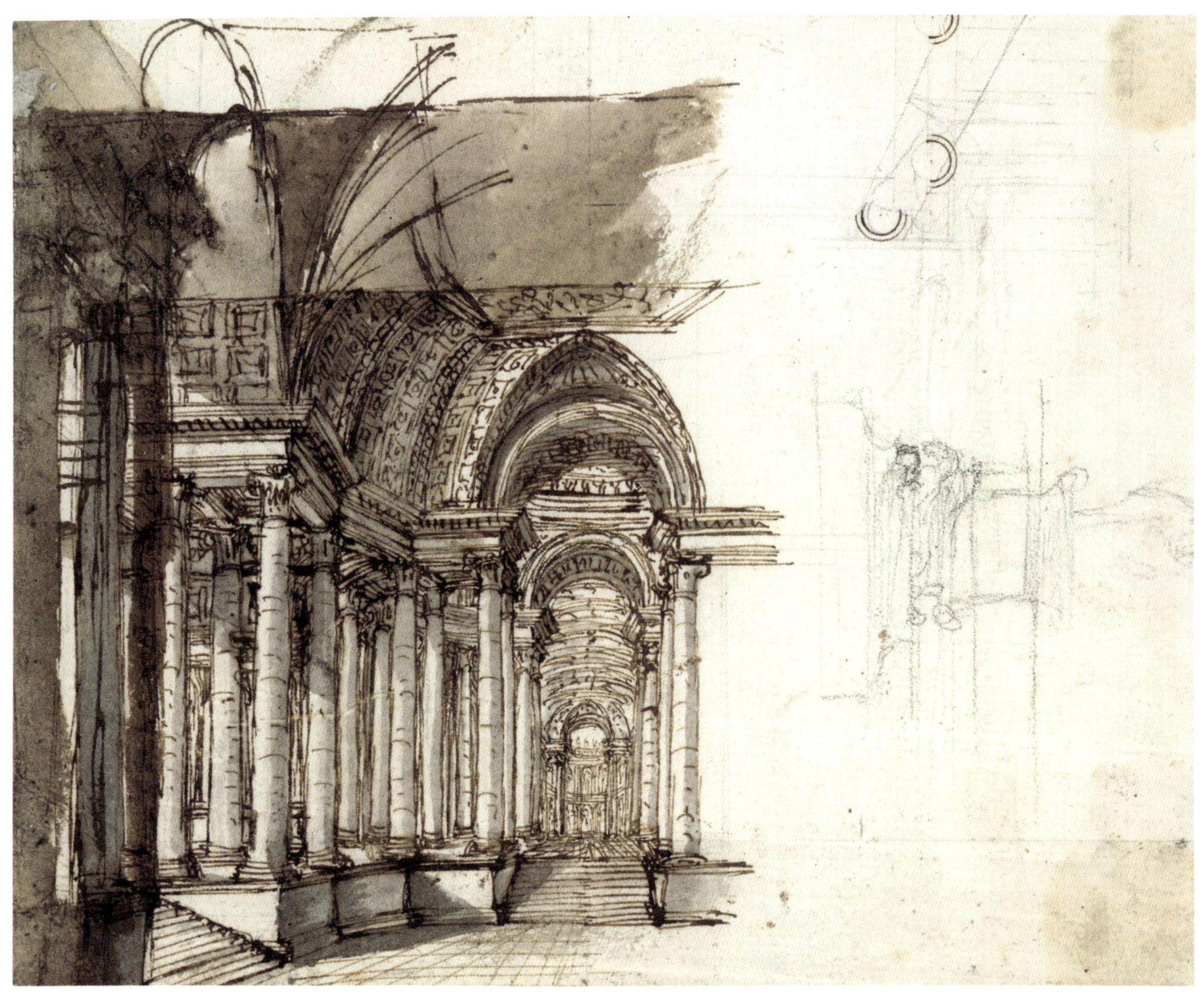

Also dating from the period of the *Prima Parte*, this drawing shows Piranesi exploring further the possibilities of plate 10, *Vestibule of an ancient temple* (Fig. 14). This does not seem to be part of the main preparatory process, but perhaps represents an allied parallel concept. In certain ways this composition is closer to the final print than that of cat. 5 – here the central arcade recedes further into the distance – but the foreground is different, and Piranesi has chosen to use a mixture of rounded and Gothic arches in the central arcade.

The verso of the drawing shows a mixture of architectural details, perhaps the compartment of a ceiling (upper centre), a cornice (upper left) and ground plans (in the lower part of the sheet), where Piranesi explores the idea of a centralized Greek cross church.

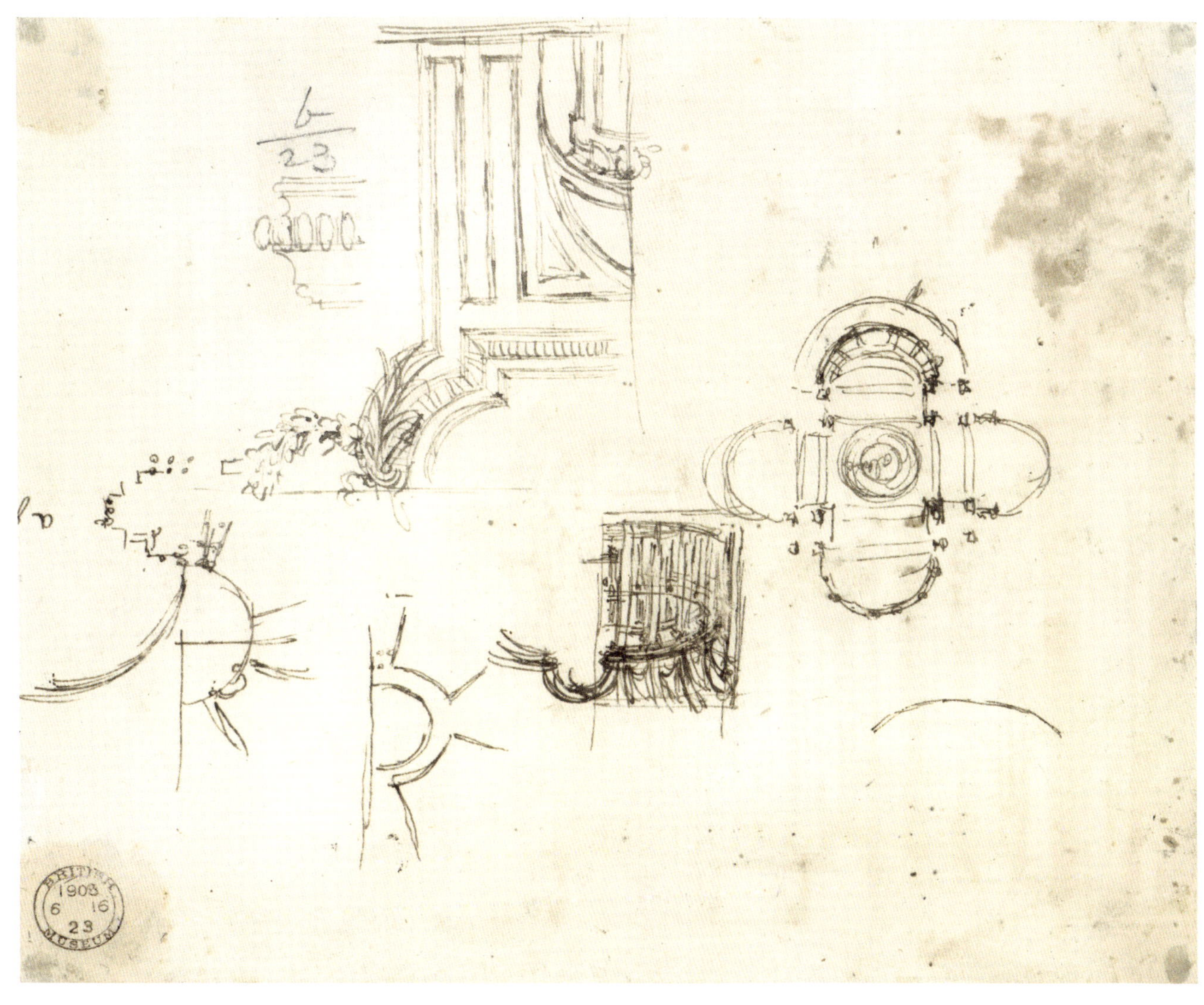

5.

Portico seen from an angle

c. 1741–43

Pen and brown ink, brown wash,
over black chalk
135 × 209 mm (5⅜ × 8¼ in.)
1908,0616.27
Provenance: Probably William Gott; and by
descent to his son, John Gott, Bishop of Truro;
his sale, Sotheby's, London, 20 March 1908,
part of lot 172
Exhibitions: London 1968, part of no. 18;
Washington 1978, section on the *Prima Parte*,
no. 19; London 1994, no. 262
Literature: Robison 1986a, p. 14, fig. 6

This is a development of Piranesi's early works influenced by stage design, transforming them into more complex exercises in perspective. The building is placed on an angle, following the Bibiena family's principle of the *scena per angolo*, and the underlying black chalk lines that plot the two vanishing points are rougher and less precise than in cats. 1 and 2. The composition is a rare example of symmetry in Piranesi's works, which were rapidly shifted off-centre to create more dynamic and challenging designs.

The drawing may have been inspired by a print from Ferdinando Galli Bibiena's treatise *L'Architettura Civile*.[32] While it is not a direct preparatory drawing for the *Prima Parte*, the British Museum sheet may represent a first thought for the complex colonnaded building in plate 14, *Foro antico Romano* (Fig. 16).[33]

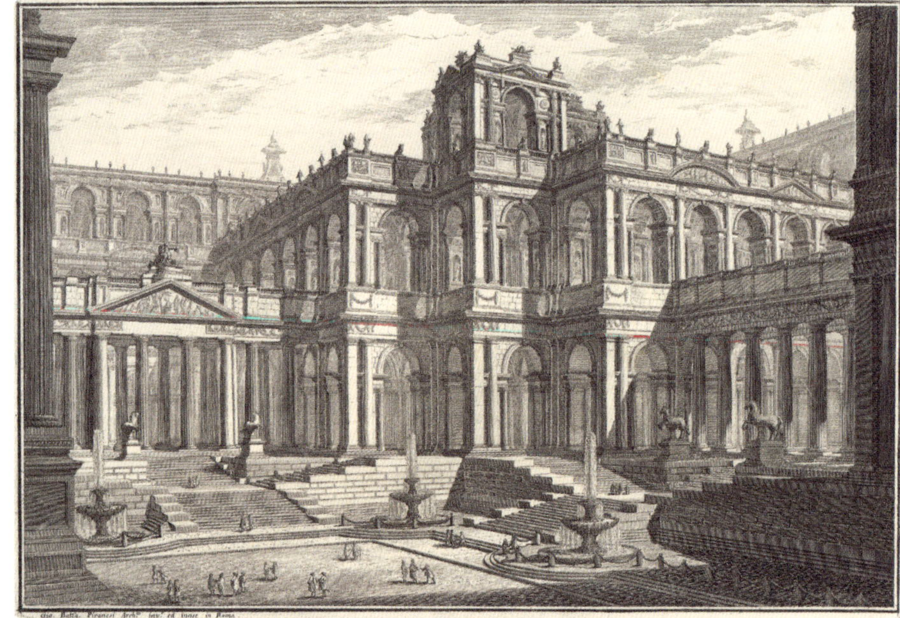

Fig. 16
Foro antico Romano
From the *Prima Parte di Architettura, e Prospettive*
c. 1743
Etching
243 × 360 mm (9⅝ × 14¼ in.)
Metropolitan Museum of Art,
New York

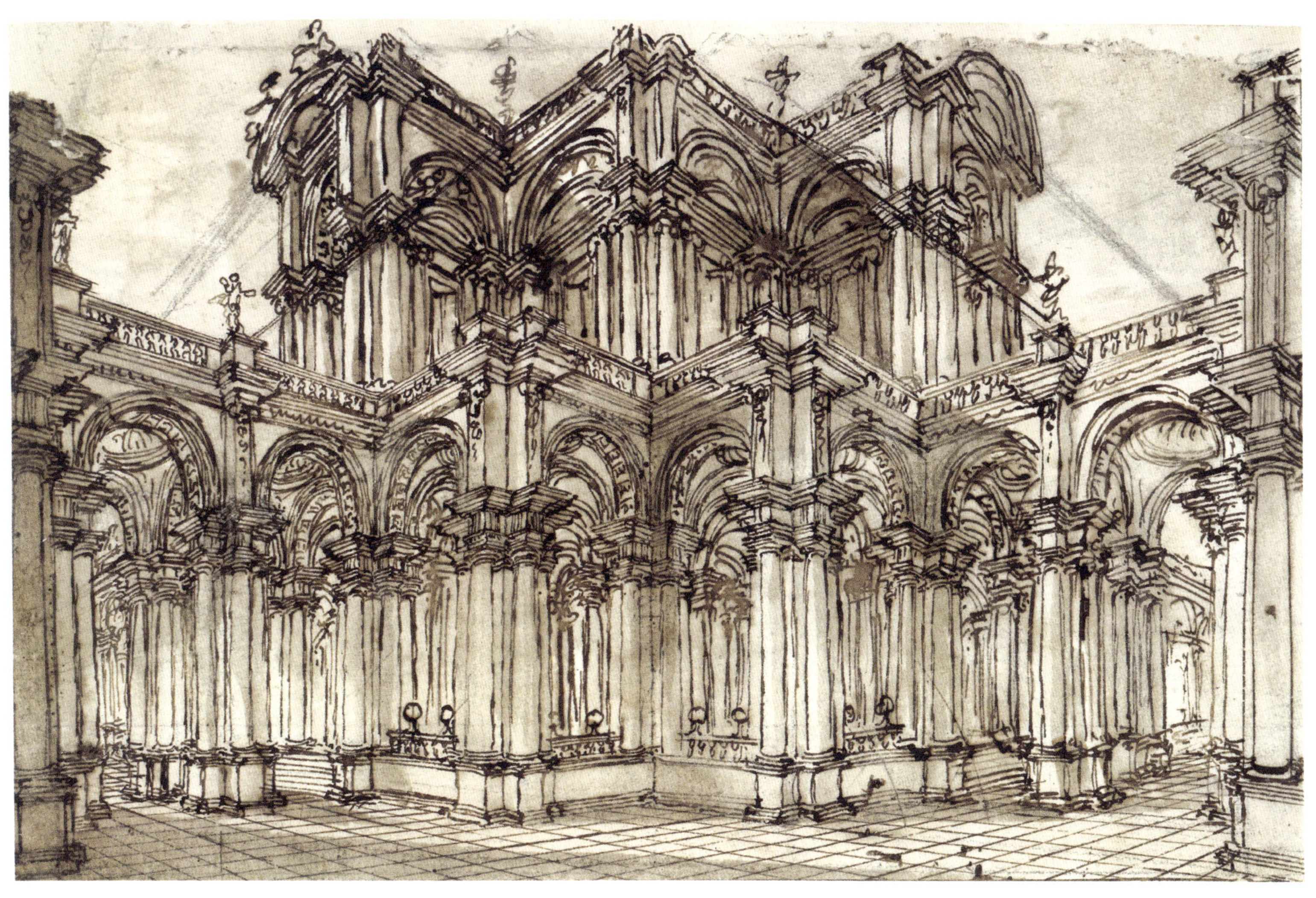

6.

Alternative designs for a temple (recto); Study of a colonnade (verso)

c. 1742–43

Pen and brown ink, with grey wash, squared
for transfer in black chalk (recto); pen and
brown ink, over black chalk (verso)
136 × 208 mm (5⅜ × 8¼ in.)
1908,0616.22

Provenance: Probably William Gott; and by
descent to his son, John Gott, Bishop of Truro;
his sale, Sotheby's, London, 20 March 1908,
part of lot 172
Exhibitions: London 1968, part of no. 18;
London 1978, no. 32a

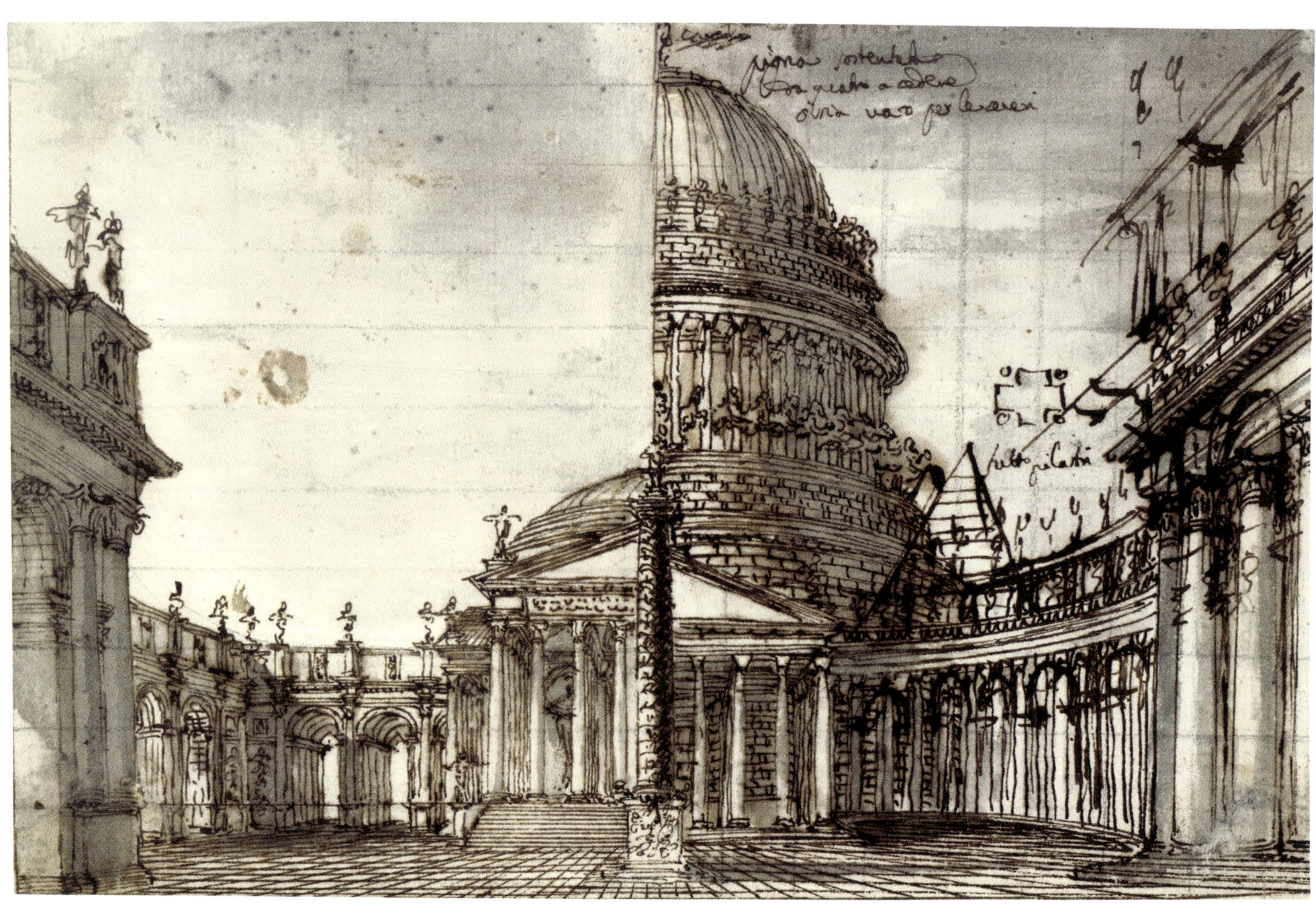

No related print is known, but stylistically this drawing must date from the same period as the *Prima Parte*. It shows two variations on the design of a domed building, probably a church or temple. That on the left is based on the lower dome of the Pantheon and is accompanied by a rectangular colonnade; another study of a very similar structure is in the Morgan Library.[34] The variation on the right appears to be inspired by St Peter's, and on this side of the sheet Piranesi has added further details in darker, untidier ink: a pyramid, inspired by the Pyramid of Cestius; a triumphal arch; and a curved colonnade, probably based on Bernini's oval piazza in front of St Peter's.

The rougher drawing on the verso appears to take the idea of a curved colonnade further, adding a flight of steps and showing how the right-hand end of the arcade curves towards the viewer. Notes and calculations on both sides of the sheet make it abundantly clear that, even if this started out as a polished design, it rapidly became a working drawing.

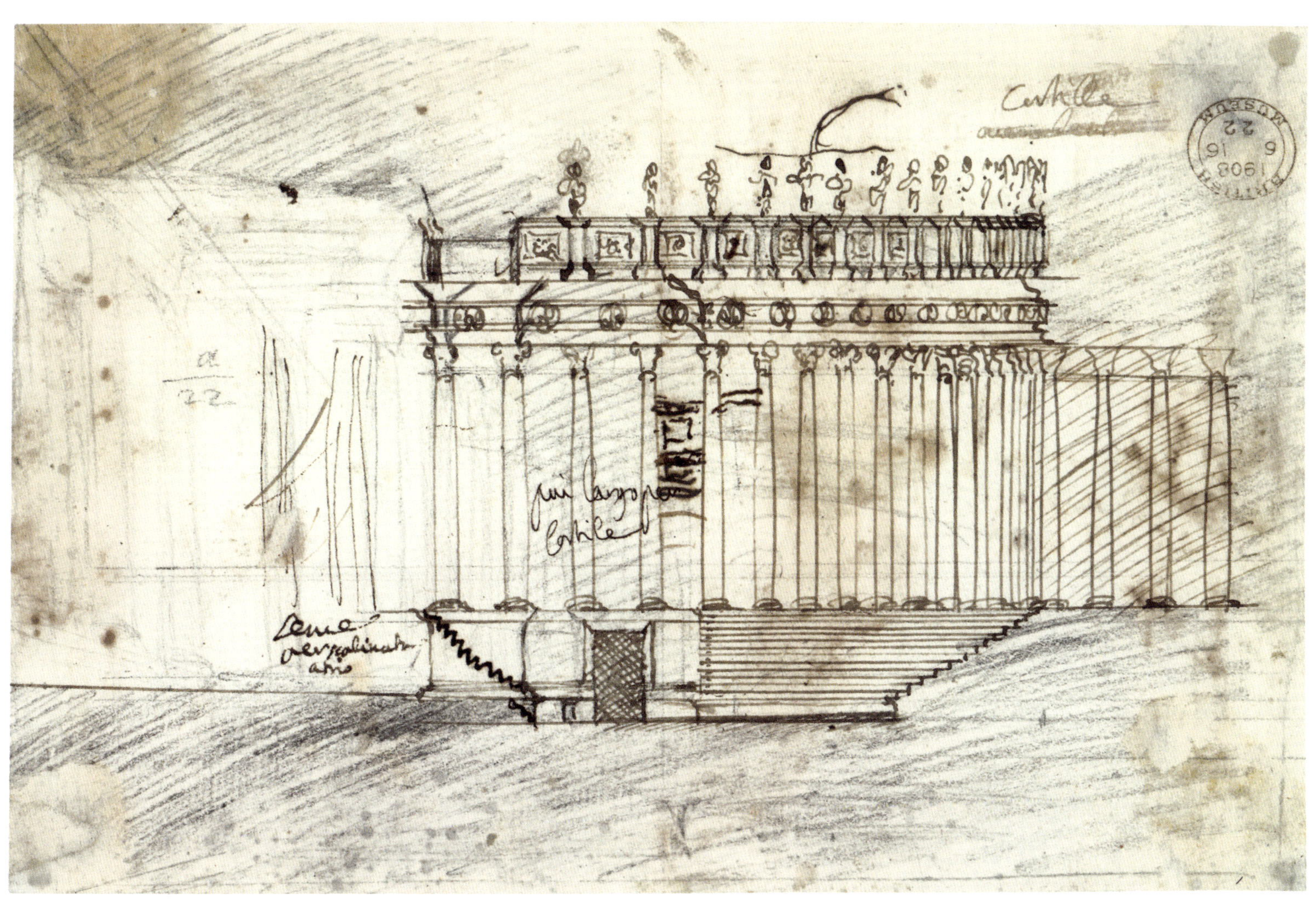

7.

An atrium with Doric columns (recto); A ground plan for a church (verso)

c. 1742–43

Pen and brown ink, brown wash, over traces of
black chalk (recto); pen and brown ink (verso)
160 × 214 mm (6⅜ × 8½ in.)
1908,0616.30

Provenance: Probably William Gott; and by
descent to his son, John Gott, Bishop of Truro;
his sale, Sotheby's, London, 20 March 1908,
part of lot 172
Exhibitions: London 1968, part of no. 28;
Washington 1978, section on the *Prima Parte*,
no. 22
Literature: Robison 1977, pp. 395–96, fig. 10;
Robison 1986a, pp. 19–20, fig. 21 and under
no. 13

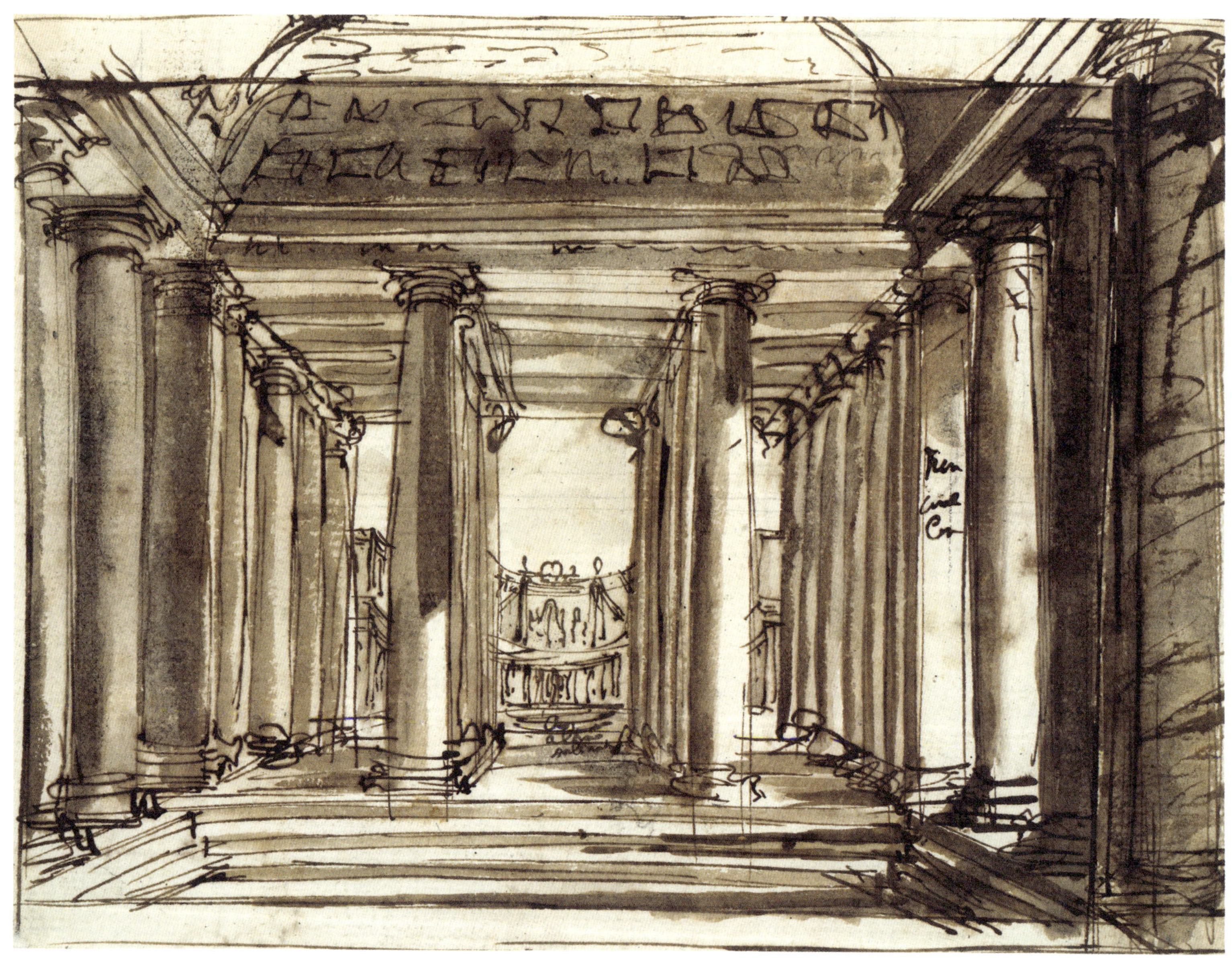

This is a preliminary study for plate 12 of the first edition of the *Prima Parte* (1743).[35] The fluidity of pen and wash shows Piranesi's increasing confidence as a draughtsman, suggesting that this was one of the later drawings for the series. This idea is supported by the fact that the drawing relates very closely to the composition of the print, which is not the case with the British Museum's other *Prima Parte* studies.

The ground plan shown on the reverse of the drawing has not been identified, but it may be the same building as that shown on the recto.[36] Certainly both structures have a distant curved wall viewed through ranks of columns, and Piranesi seems to have marked out on the ground plan the point from which the drawing is made, complete with sight-lines. This is fascinating testimony to Piranesi's maturing sense of architectural space, as he fluently transforms a conceptual design into the ground plan of a plausible structure.

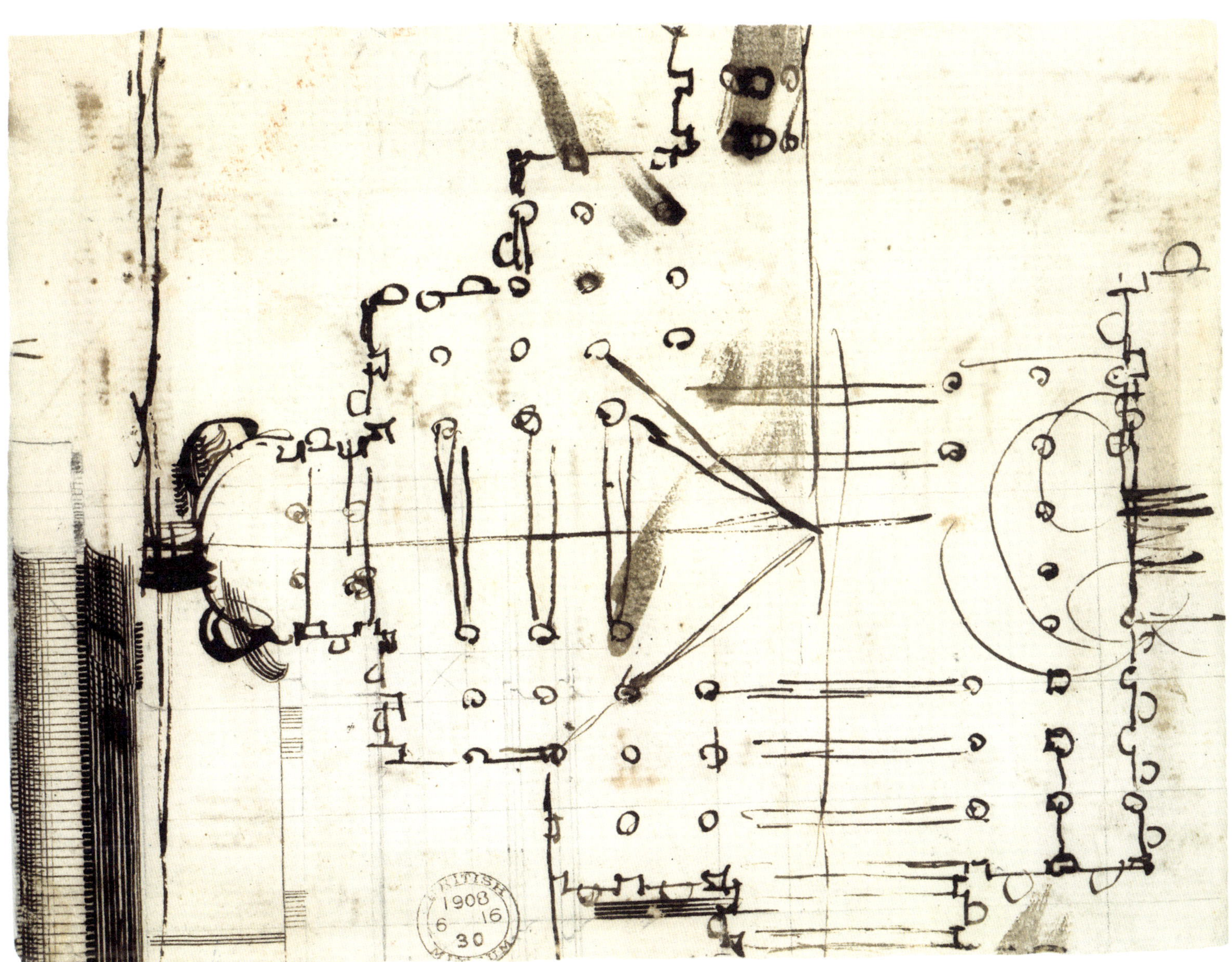

8.

The Hospital of Santo Spirito

c. 1742–44

Pen and brown ink, brown wash,
over black chalk

121 × 109 mm (4⅞ × 4⅜ in.)

1908,0616.29

Provenance: Probably William Gott; and by
descent to his son, John Gott, Bishop of Truro;
his sale, Sotheby's, London, 20 March 1908,
part of lot 172

Exhibitions: London 1968, part of no. 28

Literature: Sørensen 2001, p. 430, note 7

This is a preparatory study[37] for one of
Piranesi's early etchings of Roman views
for the *Varie Vedute di Roma Antica e Moderna*,
produced in collaboration with various
other artists (Fig. 17 shows the print
of the same view). On the verso of
the sheet (not pictured) are some light,
illegible sketches. The dating of the
series is not clear, as prints were issued
throughout the 1740s, but there are
stylistic commonalities with Piranesi's
drawings for the *Prima Parte*, suggesting
a date before his return to Venice.

This sheet shows only half the
composition: a preparatory study for
the right-hand half of the print is in one
of Piranesi's sketchbooks in Modena.[38]
The black chalk underdrawing was
probably made on the spot, allowing
Piranesi to capture the complex space
of this Roman square.

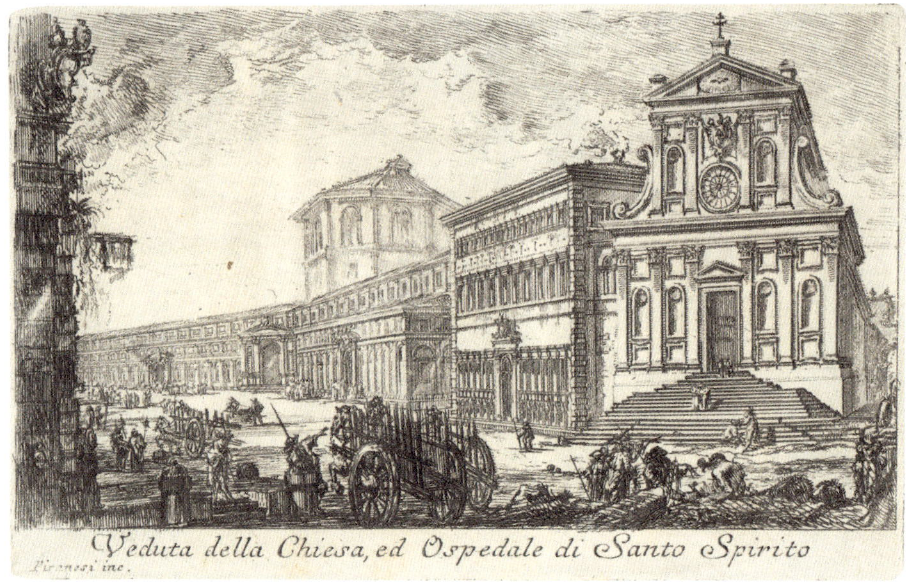

Fig. 17
*View of the Church and
Hospital of Santo Spirito*
1741–48
Etching
122 × 198 mm (4⅞ × 7⅞ in.)
2001,0729.38

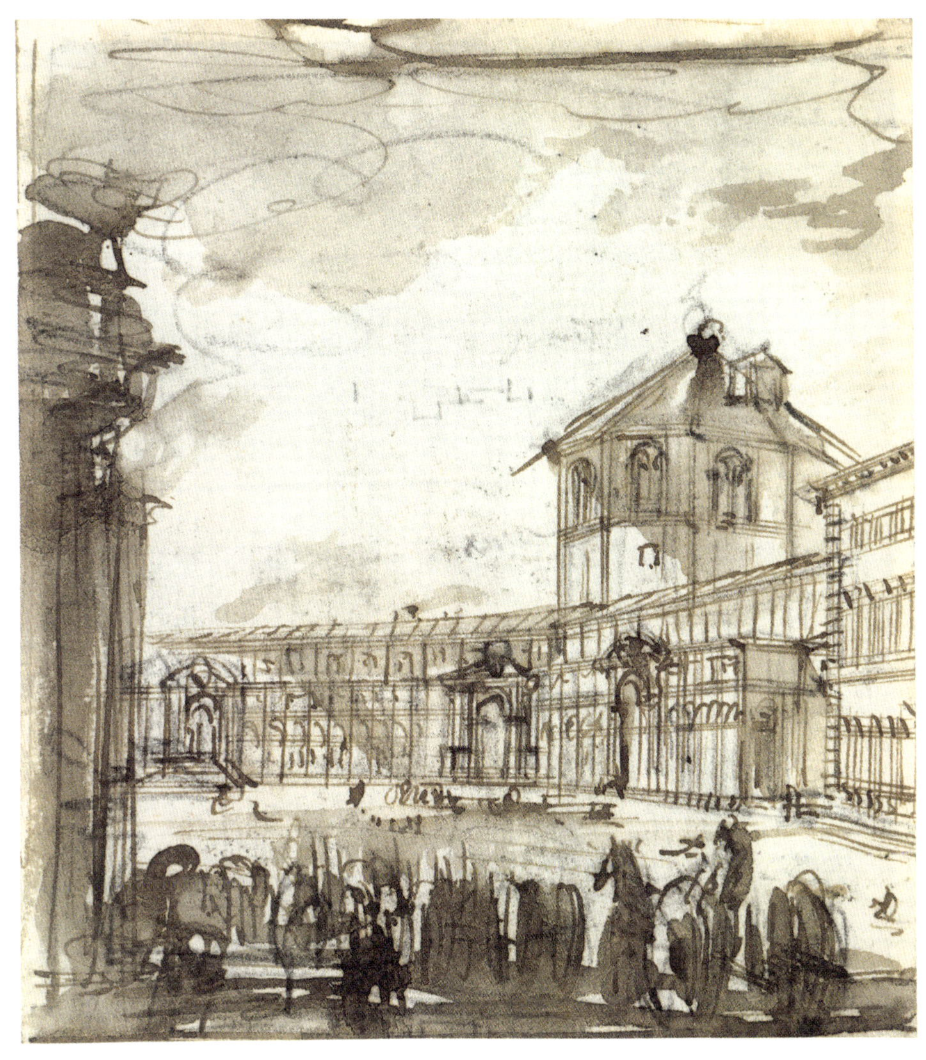

9.

A circular atrium with a baldacchino

c. 1744–49

Pen and brown ink

219 × 123 mm (8⅝ × 4⅞ in.)

1908,0616.3

Provenance: Probably William Gott; and by
descent to his son, John Gott, Bishop of Truro;
his sale, Sotheby's, London, 20 March 1908,
part of lot 172

Exhibitions: London 1968, part of no. 27

Stylistically similar to the rough sketches
on the backs of cats. 1 and 2, this drawing
is nevertheless difficult to date, as Piranesi
continued to work in a similar style for
the rest of his career. In the 1968 British
Museum exhibition, it was suggested that
the drawing could have been based on
a design by Filippo Juvarra for Act III,
Scene 4, of Filippo Amadei's opera
Teodosio il Giovane (published in 1711).
The connection to the opera seems to be
generic, but there is a strong flavour of
Juvarra's style in the draughtsmanship.
The composition may be an unused idea
for the *Prima Parte*, but in fact there is a
striking connection to a later drawing
(cat. 36), which is linked to Piranesi's
Crossing of St Peter's, a print in the
Vedute di Roma. The present drawing
is dominated by three arches, but is
spatially ambiguous in its placement
of the baldacchino, or canopy.

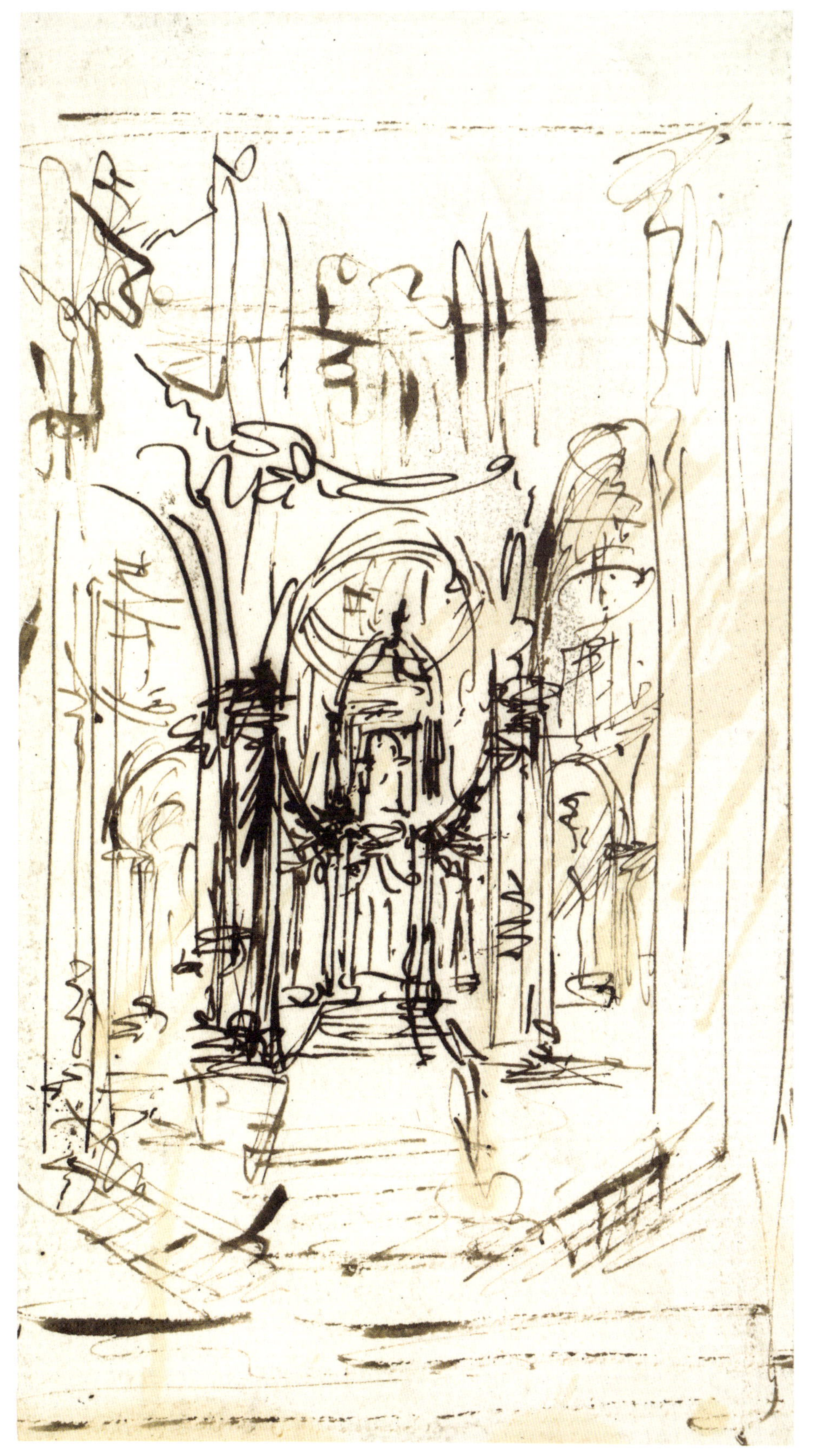

10.

Ancient ruins with monumental urns

c. 1745–46

Pen and brown ink, brown wash, over black
and some red chalk

254 × 183 mm (10 × 7¼ in.)

1908,0616.36

Provenance: Probably William Gott; and by
descent to his son, John Gott, Bishop of Truro;
his sale, Sotheby's, London, 20 March 1908,
part of lot 172
Exhibitions: London 1968, part of no. 19;
Washington 1978, section on the *Prima Parte*,
no. 45
Literature: Robison 1986a, p. 23, fig. 25,
and under nos. 1 and 16; Nevola 2009,
pp. 174–76, fig. 147

This has been connected to the *Prima Parte*,[39] as motifs recur from that series, especially from plate 5 and the title plate from the sixth edition. However, the similarities are generic rather than specific, and the connection simply shows that Piranesi was occupied with revisiting certain themes at this particular period. It can also be linked loosely to *The Tomb of Nero*, one of the plates from the *Grotteschi* (*c.* 1748), while the sarcophagus resembles that of Marcus Agrippa, which Piranesi etched in his *Vestiggi d'Antichi Edifici* just after his return to Rome from Venice.[40]

The use of untouched white paper for highlights and the thin translucent layers of wash support the idea that this dates from Piranesi's time in Venice, when he was influenced by the drawings of the Tiepolo family, but the underlying penwork has a scratchiness that may date it to the earlier part of his stay in the city. The handling is certainly not as free and confident as in works such as *A frontispiece design with two skeletons in front of a tomb* (cat. 11), which was probably produced at the very end of his Venetian sojourn. The nervous flickering of the drawn line in the present drawing suggests that Piranesi had been studying the prints of Castiglione, whose bristling etched line would also influence his own printmaking style.

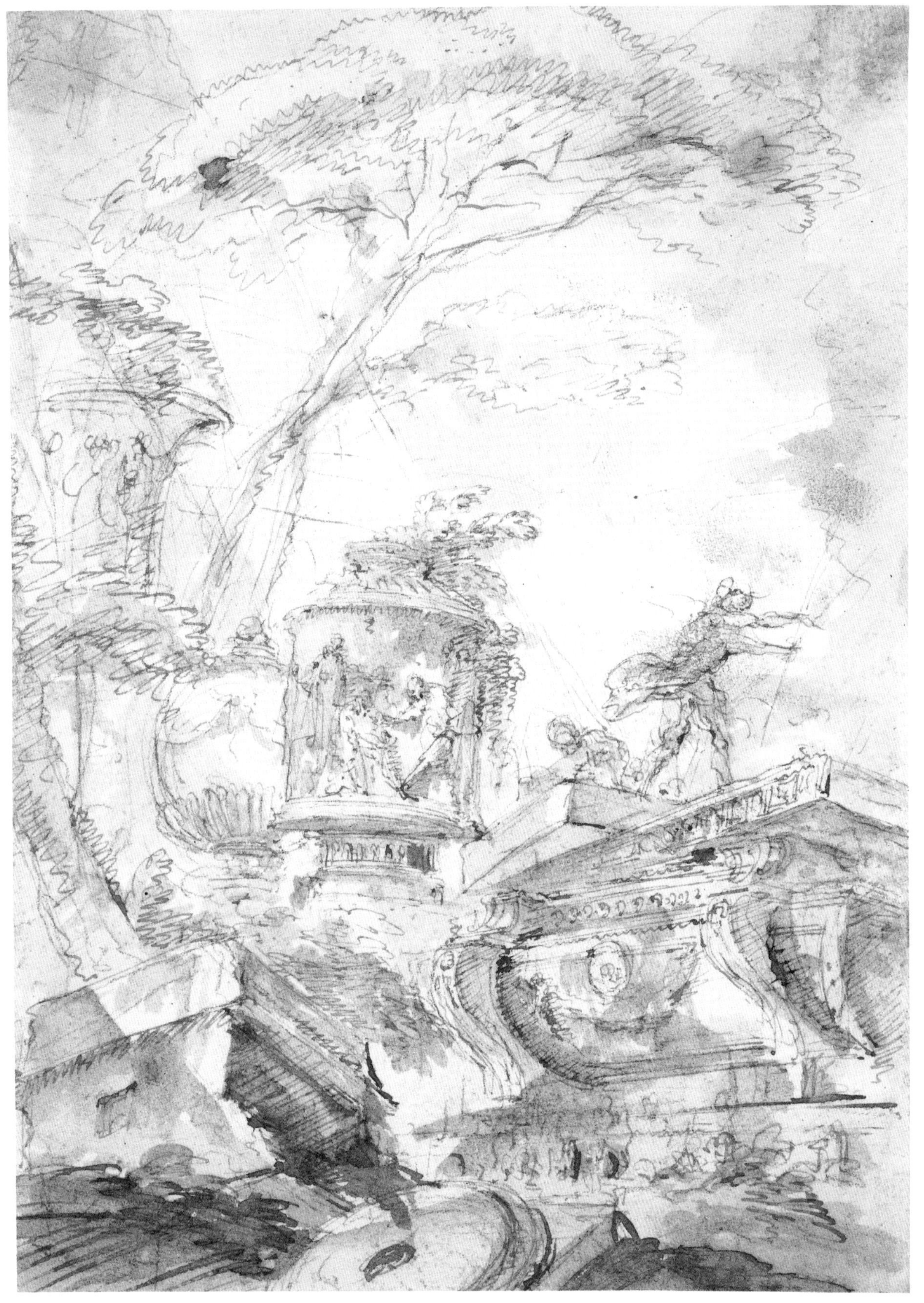

11.

A frontispiece design with two skeletons in front of a tomb

c. 1746–47

Pen and brown ink, brown wash,
over black chalk

279 × 197 mm (11 × 7⅞ in.)

1908,0616.37

Provenance: Probably William Gott; and by
descent to his son, John Gott, Bishop of Truro;
his sale, Sotheby's, London, 20 March 1908,
part of lot 172

Exhibitions: London 1965, no catalogue; London
1968, part of no. 19; London 1972, no catalogue;
London 1978, no. 8; Venice 1978, no. 10;
Cologne, Zurich and Vienna 1996–97, no. Z-19
Literature: Thomas 1954, no. 13; Scott 1975,
p. 15, fig. 10; Penny 1978, no. 9; Robison 1986a,
p. 56, note 50; Nevola 2009, pp. 164–65,
fig. 134

The most Venetian of Piranesi's drawings
in the British Museum, this design was
undoubtedly inspired stylistically by his
knowledge of Giambattista Tiepolo's
graphic work. The macabre subject can
be linked to Tiepolo's *Scherzi* but may
also suggest Piranesi's familiarity with the
skeletons that appear on Roman Baroque
tomb monuments, particularly those
sculpted by Bernini for Urban VIII and
Alexander VII in St Peter's.[41] It cannot
be directly connected to a print, although
the tablet at upper left suggests it may
have been conceived as a frontispiece.
Thematically it can be associated with
Piranesi's *Grotteschi*, particularly the
plate known as *The skeletons* (Fig. 18).[42]
Drawings in a similarly fluid Venetian
style include *The Adoration of the Magi*
in the Ashmolean Museum, Oxford,
Decorative shell ornament (Fig. 8) and
Design for a gondola (Fig. 7), both in the
Morgan Library.

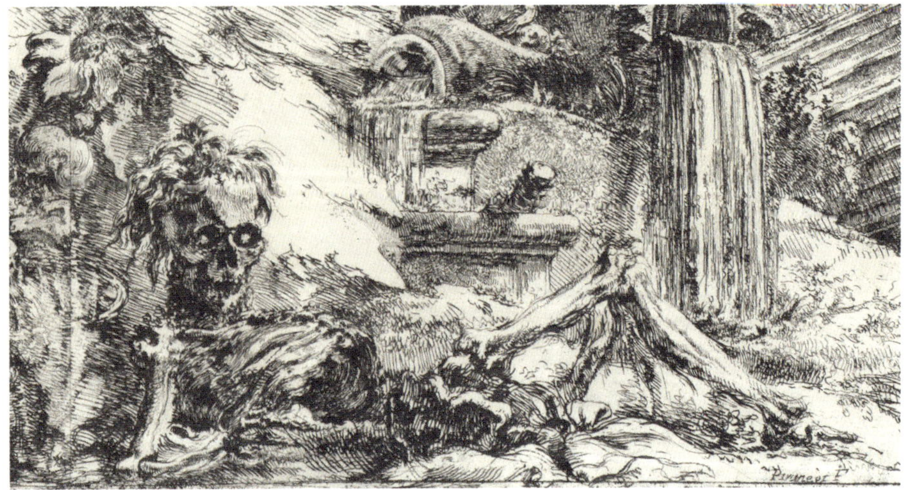

Fig. 18
Detail from *The skeletons*
From the *Grotteschi*
c. 1748
Etching with engraving, drypoint
and burnishing
390 × 540 mm (15⅜ × 21⅜ in.)
Metropolitan Museum of Art,
New York

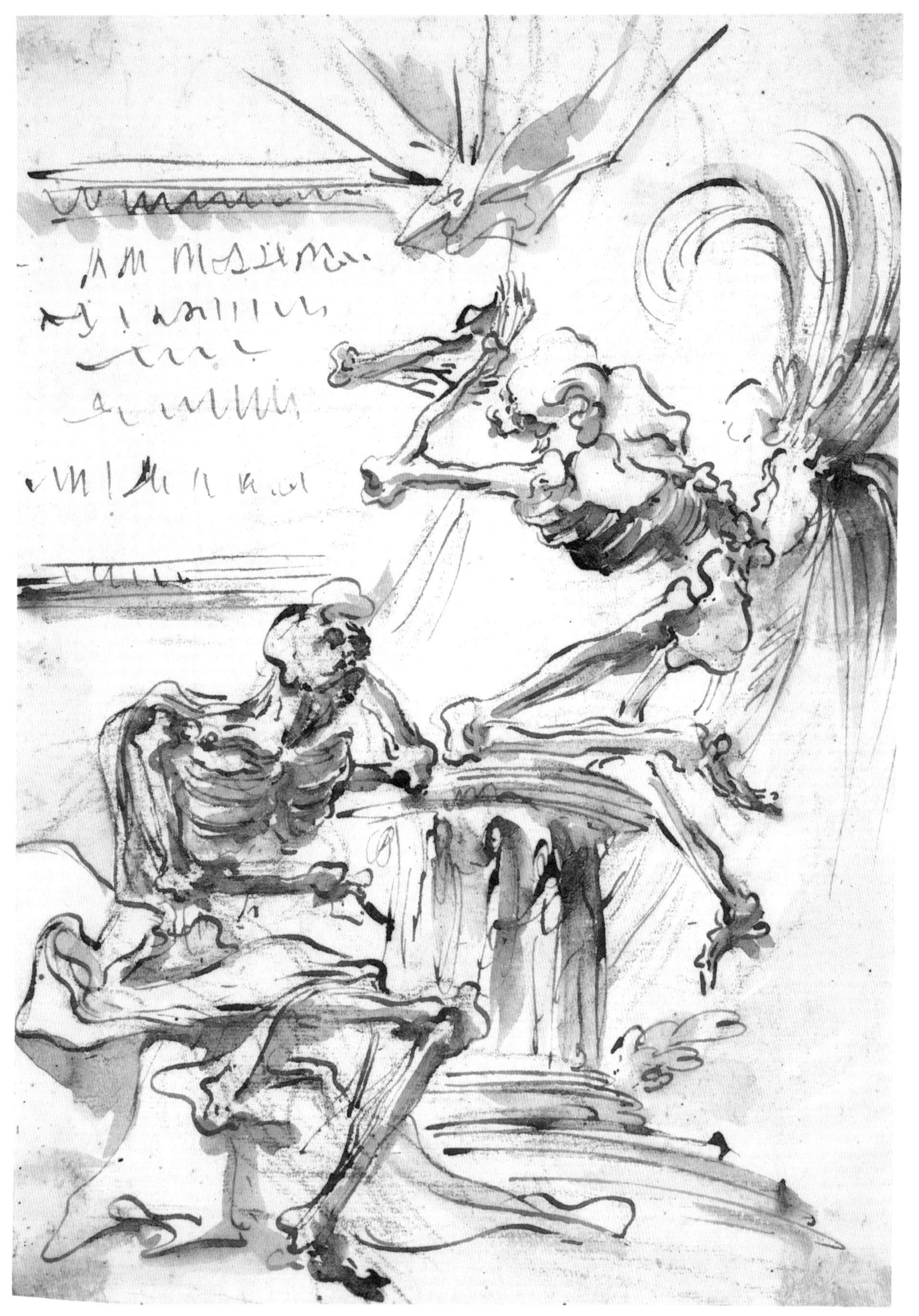

12.

An architectural fantasy with
a bridge and a rotunda

c. 1747–49
Pen and brown ink, with brown wash
and red chalk
164 × 224 mm (6½ × 8⅞ in.)
1908,0616.7
Provenance: Probably William Gott; and by
descent to his son, John Gott, Bishop of Truro;
his sale, Sotheby's, London, 20 March 1908,
part of lot 172
Exhibitions: London 1968, part of no. 23;
London and elsewhere 2002–4, no catalogue
Literature: Thomas 1954, under no. 18

This drawing is very close in style and
technical detail to *Architectural fantasy
with arch and domes* in the Hamburger
Kunsthalle (Fig. 19), there dated to *c.* 1745
and perhaps representing an early stage
in the planning of the *Carceri*. The aesthetic
idiom still looks very Venetian with its
loose, fluid penwork and thin veils of
wash. The circular structure in the
drawing appears to be built within an
interior, with a barrel vault running
around its outside, viewed from beneath
the arch of an imposing bridge pierced
with an oculus. The strange viewpoint
and the oculus are features that recur
frequently in the *Carceri* and other prints
of the late 1740s and early 1750s, and the
combination of a circular building with
bridges and vaulting recurs in *The round
tower*, plate 3 of the first edition of the
Carceri (1749). Cat. 15 is a comparable
drawing, both in style and composition.

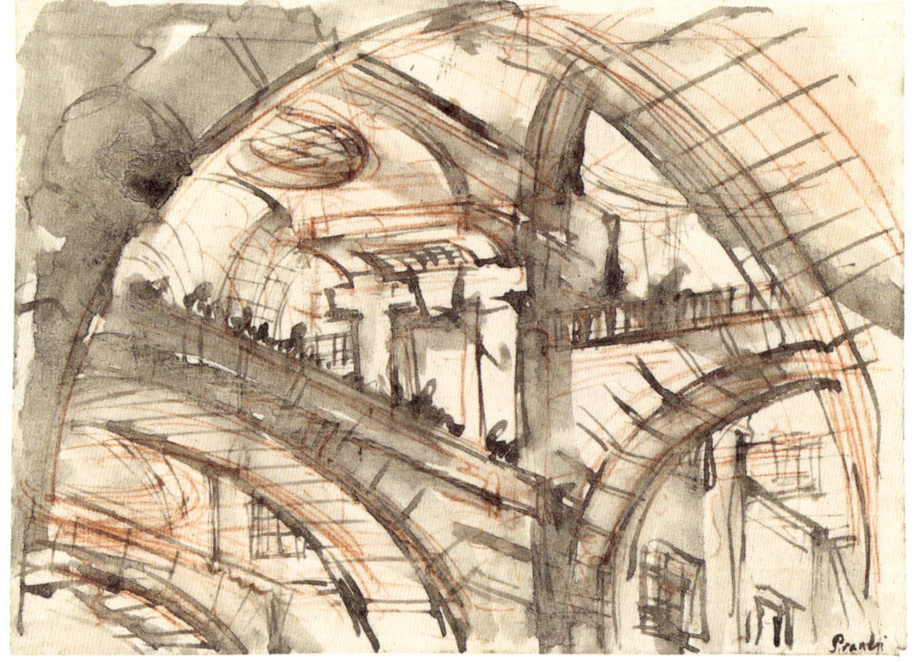

Fig. 19
*Architectural fantasy with arch
and domes*
c. 1745
Pen and brown ink over red
chalk and brown wash
182 × 255 mm (7¼ × 10⅛ in.)
Hamburger Kunsthalle,
Kupferstichkabinett

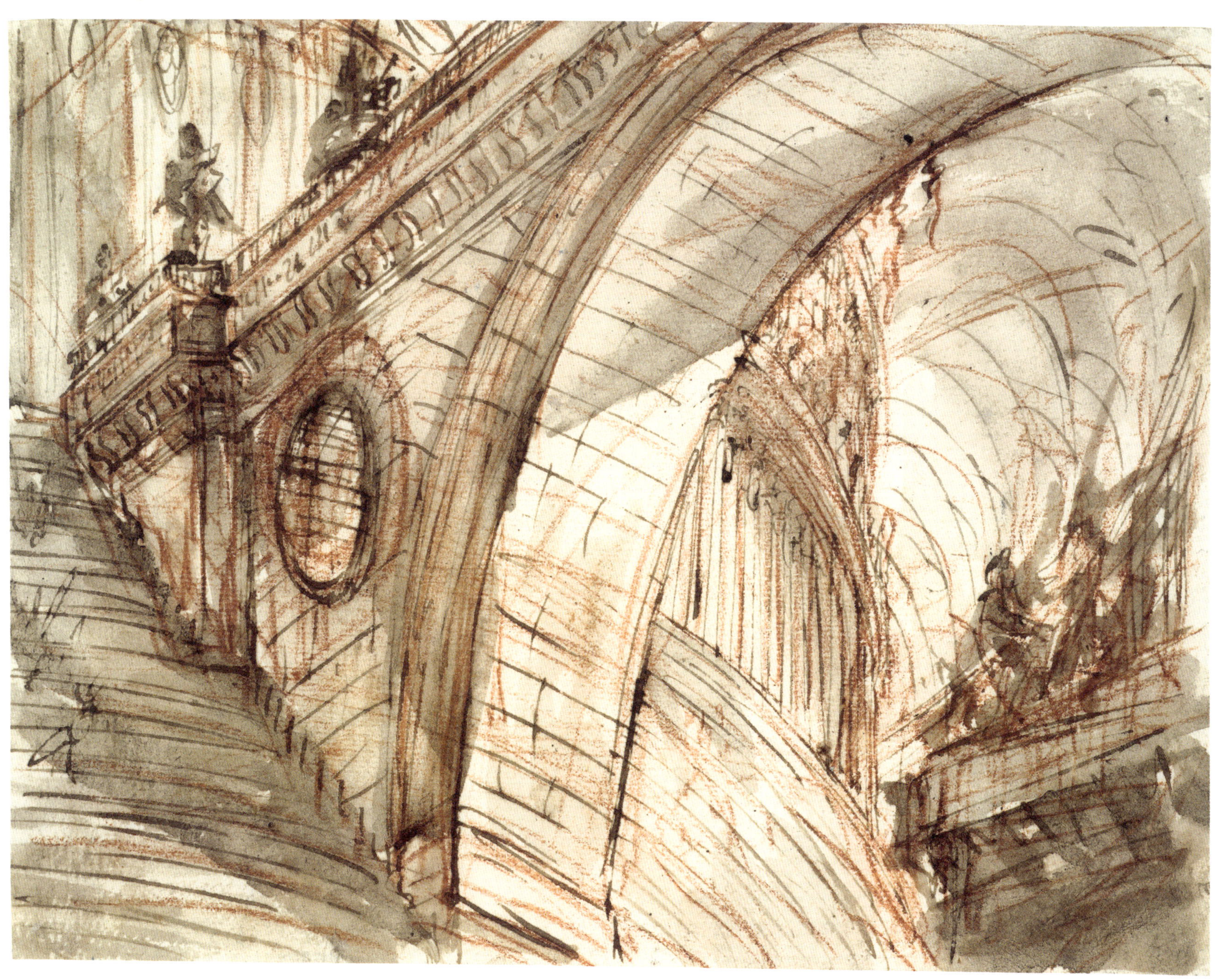

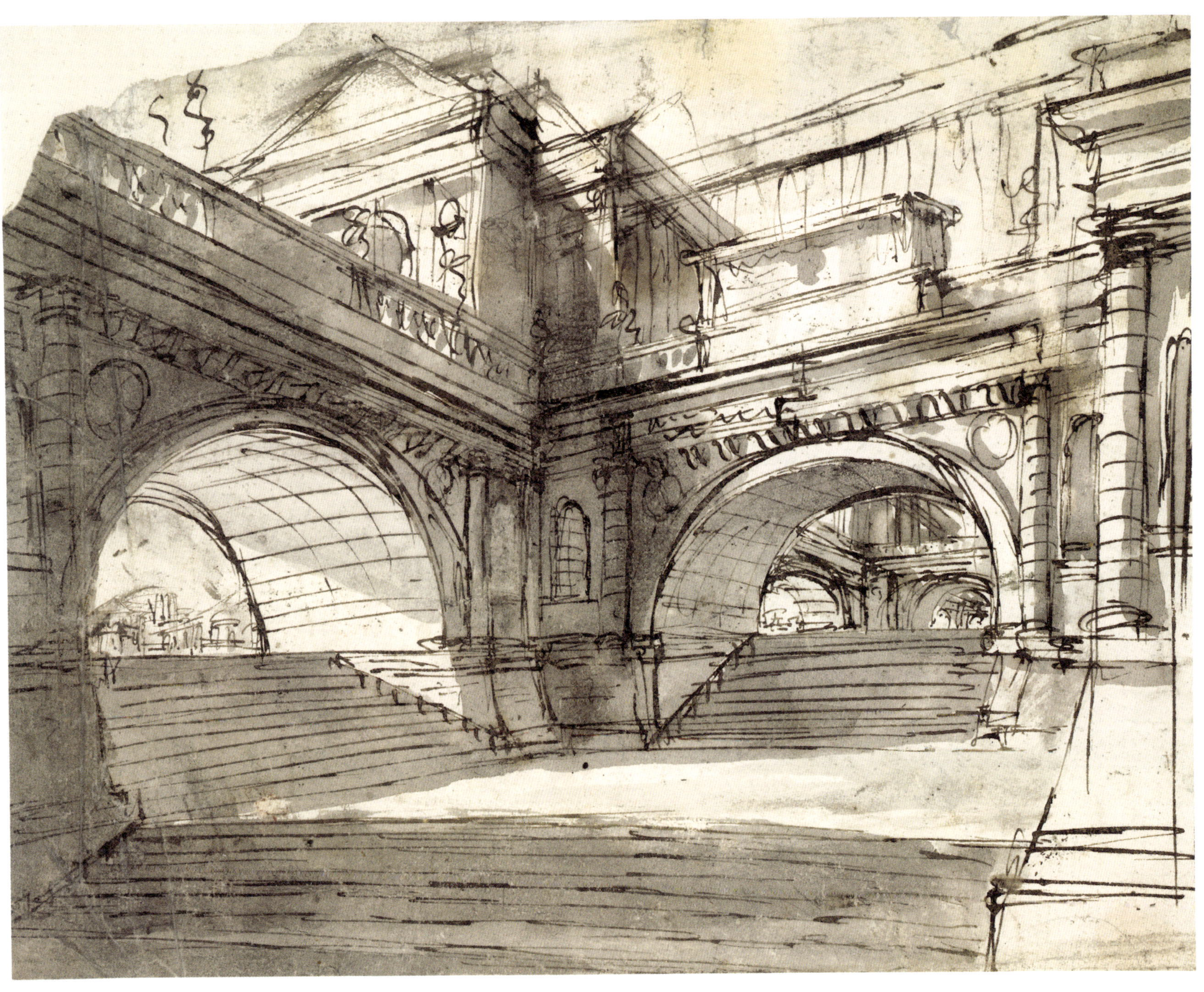

Exterior with flights of steps under low arches

c. 1747–49

Pen and brown ink, with brown wash, upper left corner made up

258 × 331 mm (10¼ × 13⅛ in.)

1908,0616.40

Provenance: Probably William Gott; and by descent to his son, John Gott, Bishop of Truro; his sale, Sotheby's, London, 20 March 1908, part of lot 172

Exhibitions: London 1968, part of no. 32

Although the 1968 British Museum catalogue dated this to 1750 or later, the drawing appears to be slightly earlier in style. The simplicity of the composition recalls the *Ponte magnifico* of the *Prima Parte* (1743; Fig. 20), and the combination of low viewpoints looking up beneath the arches of bridges can be linked to post-Venetian drawings such as cat. 15. The composition seems to be a development from cat. 12, showing a more sophisticated and convincing flow of space glimpsed through the arches. It demonstrates Piranesi's growing fascination with the creation of complex spaces, which would come to fruition as he devised the *Carceri* series.

14.

Architectural fantasy with monuments, sculpture and ruins

c. 1747–50
Pen and brown ink, with brown wash, over
red and black chalk, the upper left corner made
up, the left part redrawn over an added piece
of paper
253 × 460 mm (10 × 18⅛ in.)
1908,0616.41
Provenance: Probably William Gott; and by
descent to his son, John Gott, Bishop of Truro;
his sale, Sotheby's, London, 20 March 1908,
part of lot 172
Exhibitions: London 1968, part of no. 32
(as *Capriccio on the Appian Way*); London
and elsewhere 2002–4, no catalogue
Literature: Thomas 1954, under no. 26;
Bettagno 1978, under no. 21

This *capriccio* of Roman architecture
brings together many different
monuments and seems to be an early
thought for the *Antichità Romane*. While it
foreshadows the grandiose composition
of *The meeting of the Via Appia and the Via
Ardentina* in volume II (cat. 29), it is closest
in composition to *The Circus of Mars*,
the frontispiece to volume III. The
style, with thin pen lines and light wash,
gone over with darker layers of wash,
is comparable to drawings that Piranesi
made in and shortly after his second
time in Venice (see particularly cat. 10,
in which the treatment of the trees is
especially similar). The left-hand side of
the composition has been redrawn on a
piece of paper that Piranesi added over
the original sheet, presumably because he
was dissatisfied with his first design. The
mixture of antique elements, including
columns and obelisks, also foreshadows
his fantasy forums, in which similar
juxtapositions appear (see cats. 24 and 25).

The figures here, unlike those in *The
Hospital of Santo Spirito* (cat. 8), have shrunk
to become miniature forms, which help
to emphasize the dizzying monumentality
of Piranesi's fictive worlds. This would
become a recurring and characteristic
feature of his mature work.

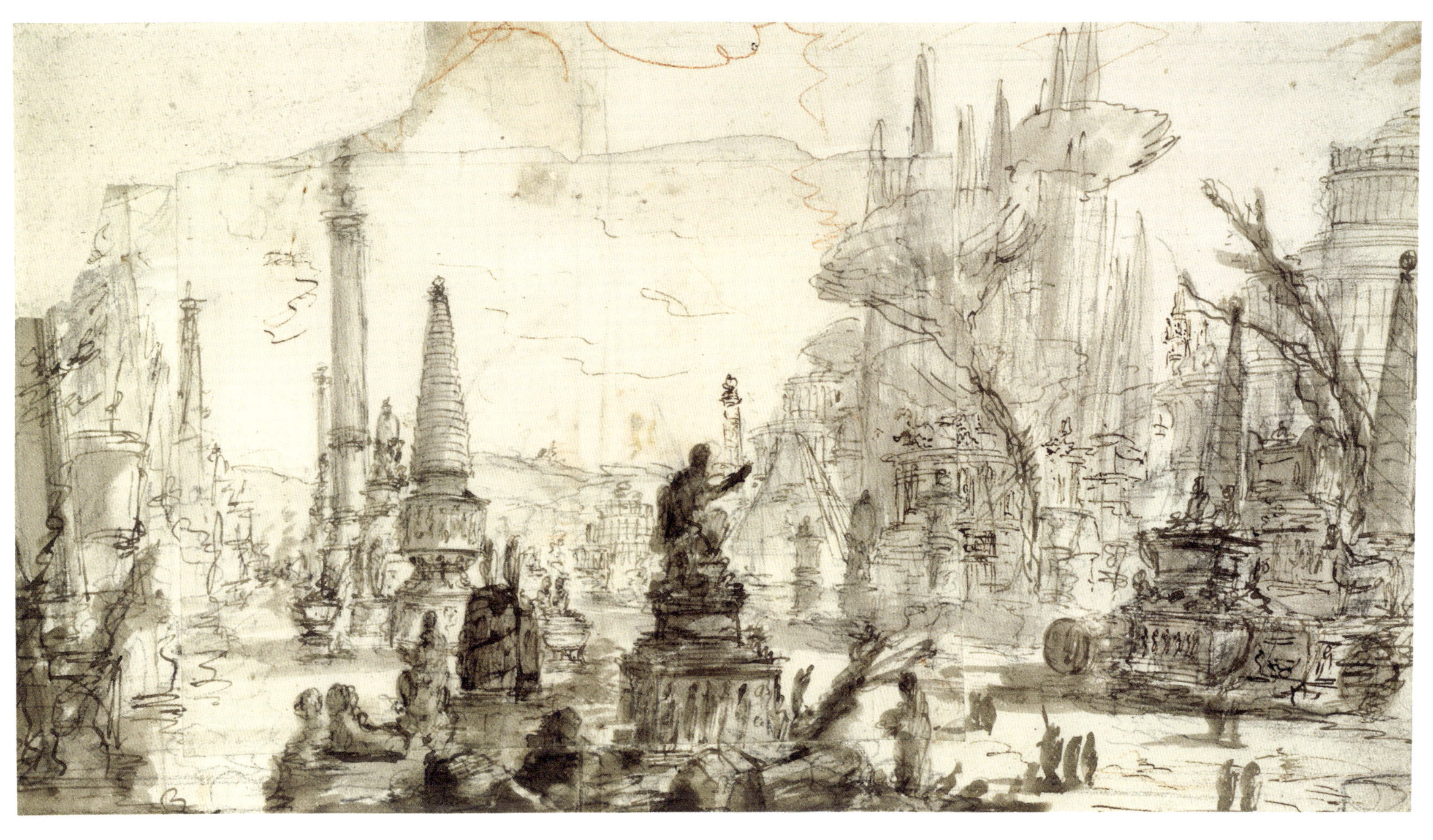

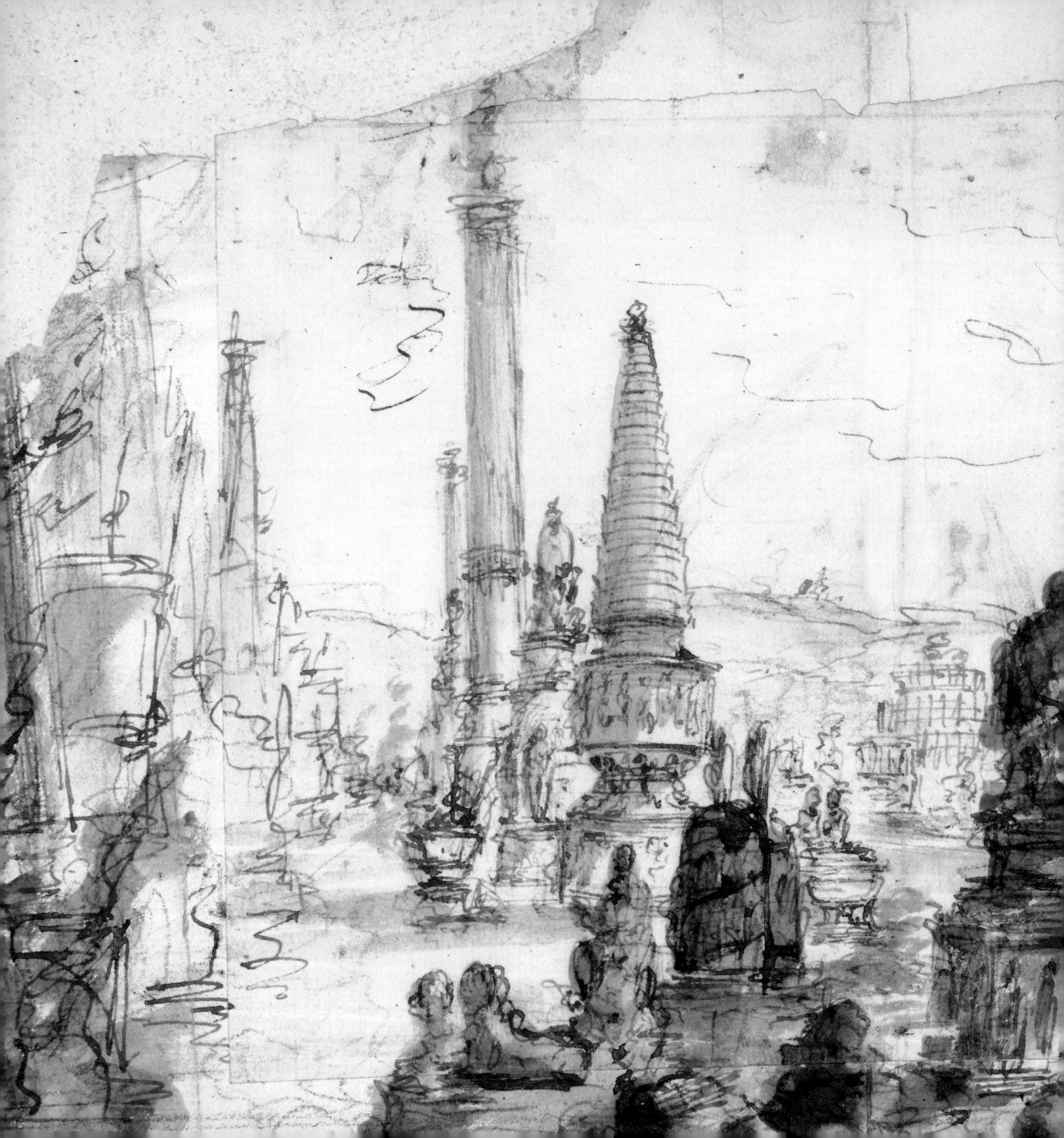

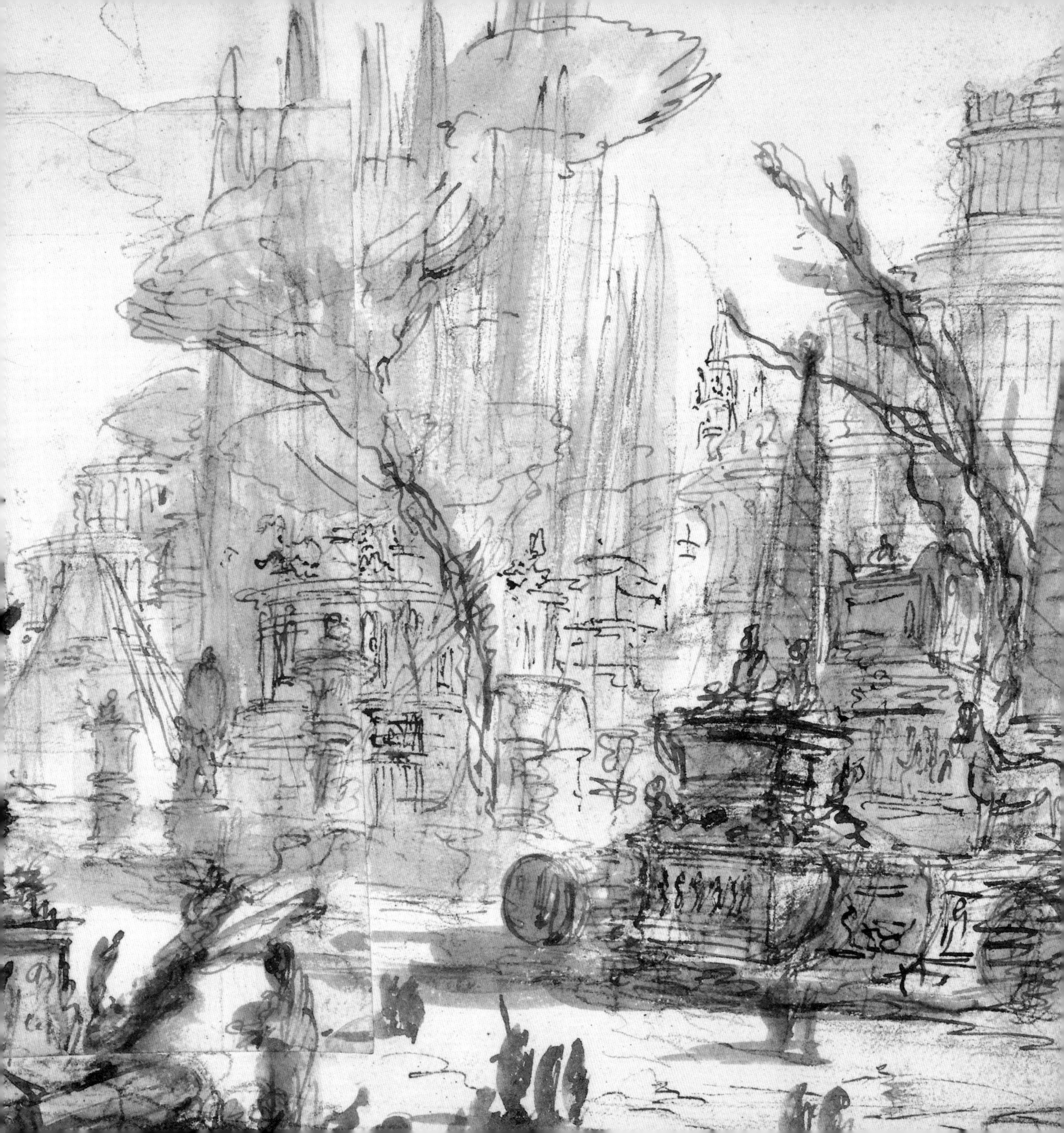

15.

A monumental vaulted interior viewed from beneath an arch

c. 1747–50

Pen and brown ink, brown wash, over red chalk

162 × 224 mm (6½ × 8⅞ in.)

1908,0616.20

Provenance: Probably William Gott; and by descent to his son, John Gott, Bishop of Truro; his sale, Sotheby's, London, 20 March 1908, part of lot 172

Exhibitions: London 1968, part of no. 23; Rome, Dijon and Paris 1976, no. 148; London 1978, no. 193a; Washington 1978, section on the *Carceri*, no. 13; Sheffield 1988, no. 19; London and elsewhere 2002–4, no catalogue

Literature: Hind 1922, p. 23; Thomas 1954, no. 18; Seckler 1962, fig. 15; Bacou 1974, p. 41; Scott 1975, fig. 65; Robison 1986a, p. 39, fig. 45, and under no. 37; Gavuzzo-Stewart 1999, p. 84, fig. 44; Lawrence 2007, p. 32 (text by J. Wilton-Ely)

This fascinating drawing occupies a space firmly between the extravagant palatial interiors of Piranesi's earlier scenographic drawings and the *Carceri* (1749–50). The motif of a grand space seen from beneath an arch is developed from Piranesi's *Ponte magnifico*, a plate from the *Prima Parte* (1743) (Fig. 20; see also cat. 42), but in this drawing the viewpoint is shifted so that both bridge and background are seen at an oblique angle. Although the structure remains elaborate, with a sculptural group crowning the central parapet of the bridge in the mid-ground, the framing devices foreshadow those of the *Carceri*, especially the ragged standards or trophies blocked in with wash at lower left.

Piranesi would rework this drawing into a more austere space, complete with bars, cranes and oculi, for his etching *Arch with a shell ornament*, plate 11 of the *Carceri*. The connection between drawing and print is most obvious in the first edition of the *Carceri*, where the framing devices remain very similar, but the monument in the centre of the bridge is scratched out. Extensive reworking of the plate after 1761, however, makes later editions of the print very different.

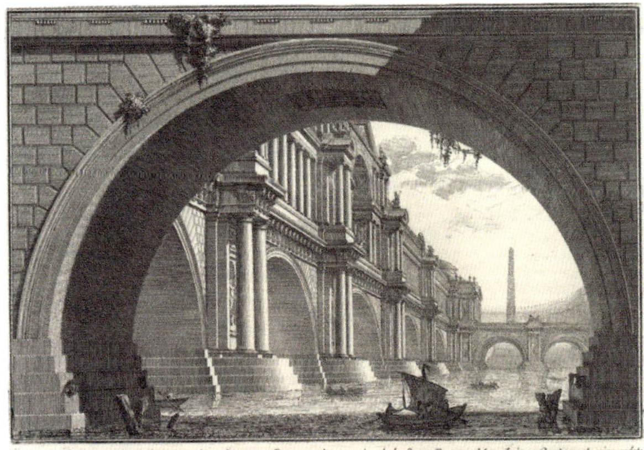

Fig. 20
Ponte magnifico
From the *Prima Parte di Architettura, e Prospettive*
c. 1743
Etching
238 × 358 mm (9⅜ × 14⅛ in.)
Metropolitan Museum of Art, New York

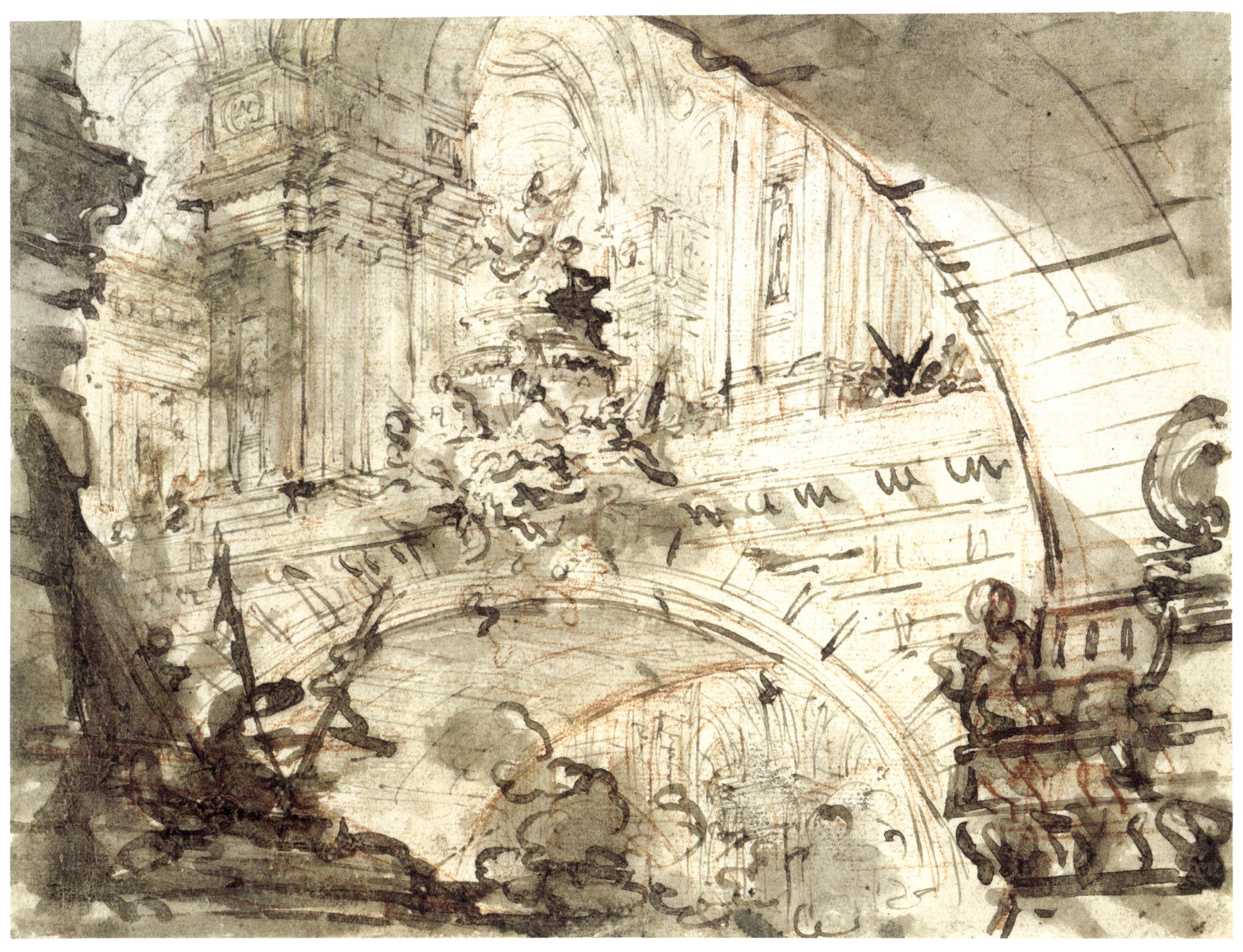

16.

A palace beside a canal with two figures in a boat

c. 1747–50
Pen and brown ink, and brown wash,
over black chalk
128 × 88 mm (5⅛ × 3½ in.)
1908,0616.12
Provenance: Probably William Gott; and by
descent to his son, John Gott, Bishop of Truro;
his sale, Sotheby's, London, 20 March 1908,
part of lot 172
Exhibitions: London 1968, part of no. 22
Literature: Vasari Society 1912–13, no. 11;
Thomas 1954, no. 5; Scott 1975, fig. 71

Probably dating from just after Piranesi's
return to Rome from Venice, this retains
a sense of *capriccio* as well as displaying
a Venetian interest in the juxtaposition
of water and architecture, with the
attendant play of shimmering light on
stone surfaces. However, it shows the
addition of darker washes and denser
tones that became more prevalent in
Piranesi's draughtsmanship from the
late 1740s onwards.

The drawing is comparable to a sheet
in the Hamburger Kunsthalle (Fig. 21),
although that may be very slightly earlier,
retaining as it does a more translucent
sense of wash. Both drawings experiment
with the use of obliquely angled arches
giving onto more monumental spaces
beyond, foreshadowing the spatial
playfulness of the *Carceri* but still focusing
on elegant and extravagant architecture.
This is a particularly good example
of how Piranesi was able to suggest
magnificent spaces even when working
on a very small scale.

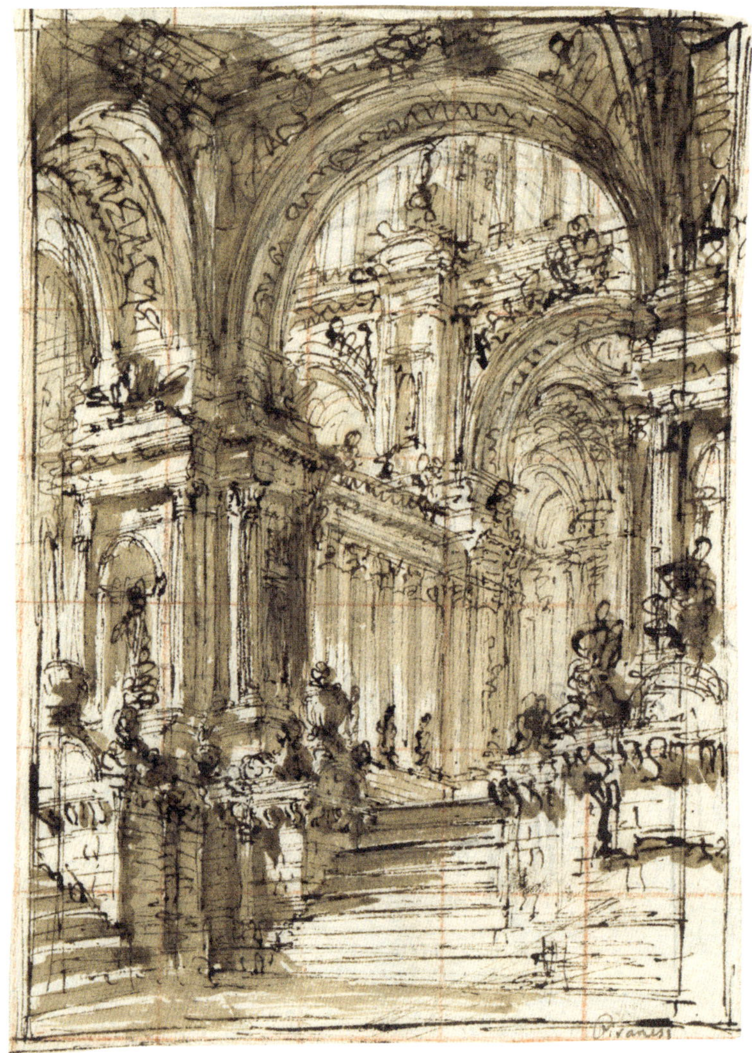

Fig. 21
Imaginary reconstruction of
a royal atrium
c. 1747–50
Pen and brown ink, over black
pencil and brown wash, with
a red chalk frame
149 × 108 mm (5⅞ × 4⅜ in.)
Hamburger Kunsthalle,
Kupferstichkabinett

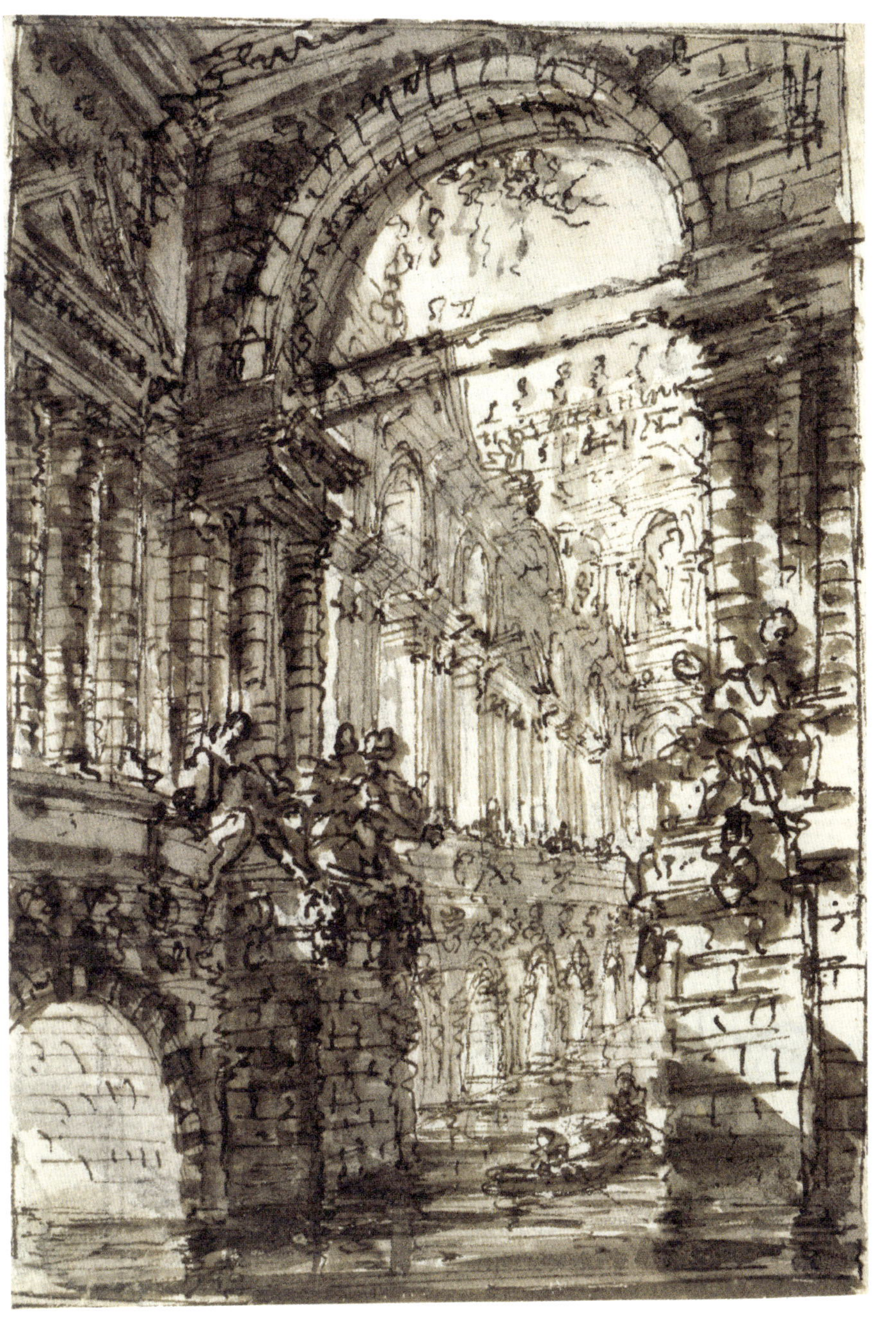

17.

A fortified building with a well

c. 1747–50

Pen and brown ink, and brown wash,
over black chalk, the left corners made up
119 × 165 mm (4¾ × 6½ in.)
1908,0616.14
Provenance: Probably William Gott; and by
descent to his son, John Gott, Bishop of Truro;
his sale, Sotheby's, London, 20 March 1908,
part of lot 172
Exhibitions: London 1968, part of no. 22
Literature: Vasari Society 1912–13, no. 13;
Corfiato 1951, pl. 55; Thomas 1954, under no. 5

This drawing is probably datable to
shortly after Piranesi's return to Rome
from Venice, and related to his first ideas
for the *Carceri* series. It is particularly
close in spirit to that series, with its use
of different levels, its low viewpoint, the
geometrical flight of steps and the use
of strange framing devices that resemble
cranes and gallows. The crenellated
building has a strangely forbidding,
medieval quality, which is also closer
to the *Carceri* than to Piranesi's more
classical structures from his other
publications. The heavy dark wash in
the foreground was probably added later,
over the finer original pen lines beneath.
It may have been added in the late 1750s,
at a point when Piranesi was revisiting
his ideas connected with prisons in
preparation for the reissue of the
second version of the *Carceri* (1761).

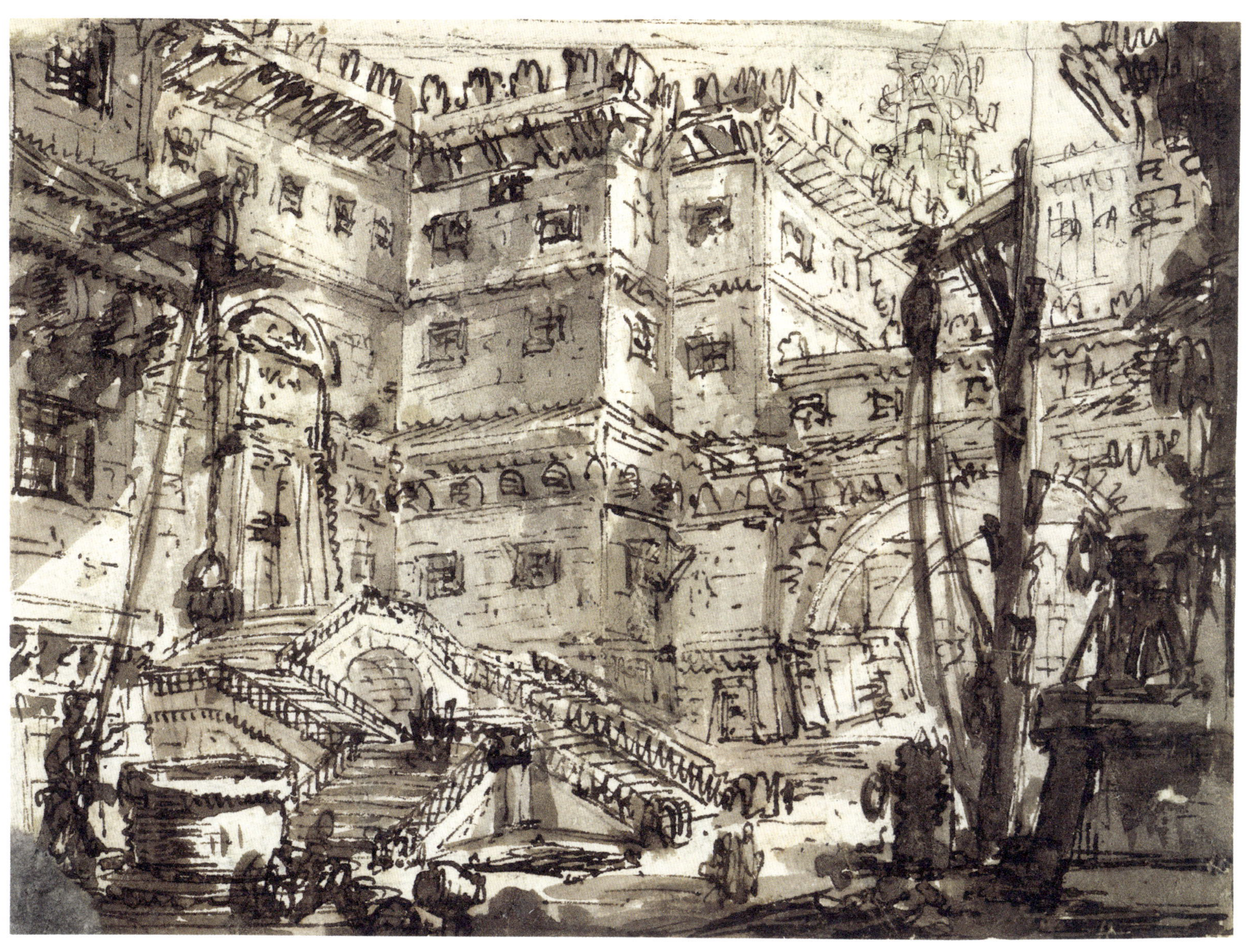

18.

Interior of an ornate mausoleum

c. 1748–52
Pen and two shades of brown ink, brown
and grey wash, over black chalk and touches
of red chalk, partly squared in black chalk,
on the artist's mount with later foil strips
signed 'Piranesi' (lower right, partly obscured
by later foil strip)
186 × 241 mm (7⅜ × 9½ in.)
1900,0824.134
Provenance: Bequeathed by Henry Vaughan
Exhibitions: British Museum 1968, part of no. 21

Dating from shortly after Piranesi's return
to Rome from Venice, this shows how
his early scenographic drawings were
beginning to evolve, in the late 1740s,
into more elaborate fantasy interiors.
Black-chalk underdrawing is covered
with light-brown penwork, which adds
the structure and finer details such as
the ornamental plaques on the wall,
and is followed by brown wash to give
tone and shadow, and to add the figures.
It is noticeable that these figures are still
on a human scale, rather than being
reduced to the tiny scale of the figures
in Piranesi's later works. Revisions have
been made, perhaps some time later, in
darker ink, which emphasizes the details
on the columns and adds a rotunda in
the more distant part of the structure.
These additions may date from the period
at which Piranesi mounted this drawing
and added his signature at lower right.

Piranesi's interest in ornament was
increasing at this period, and the interior
hints at his later Roman structures with
their elaborate mixture of decorative
motifs. The presence of a curtain in grey
wash at the top of the drawing indicates
the continuing theatricality of his work
and adds movement and drama to an
otherwise static scene.

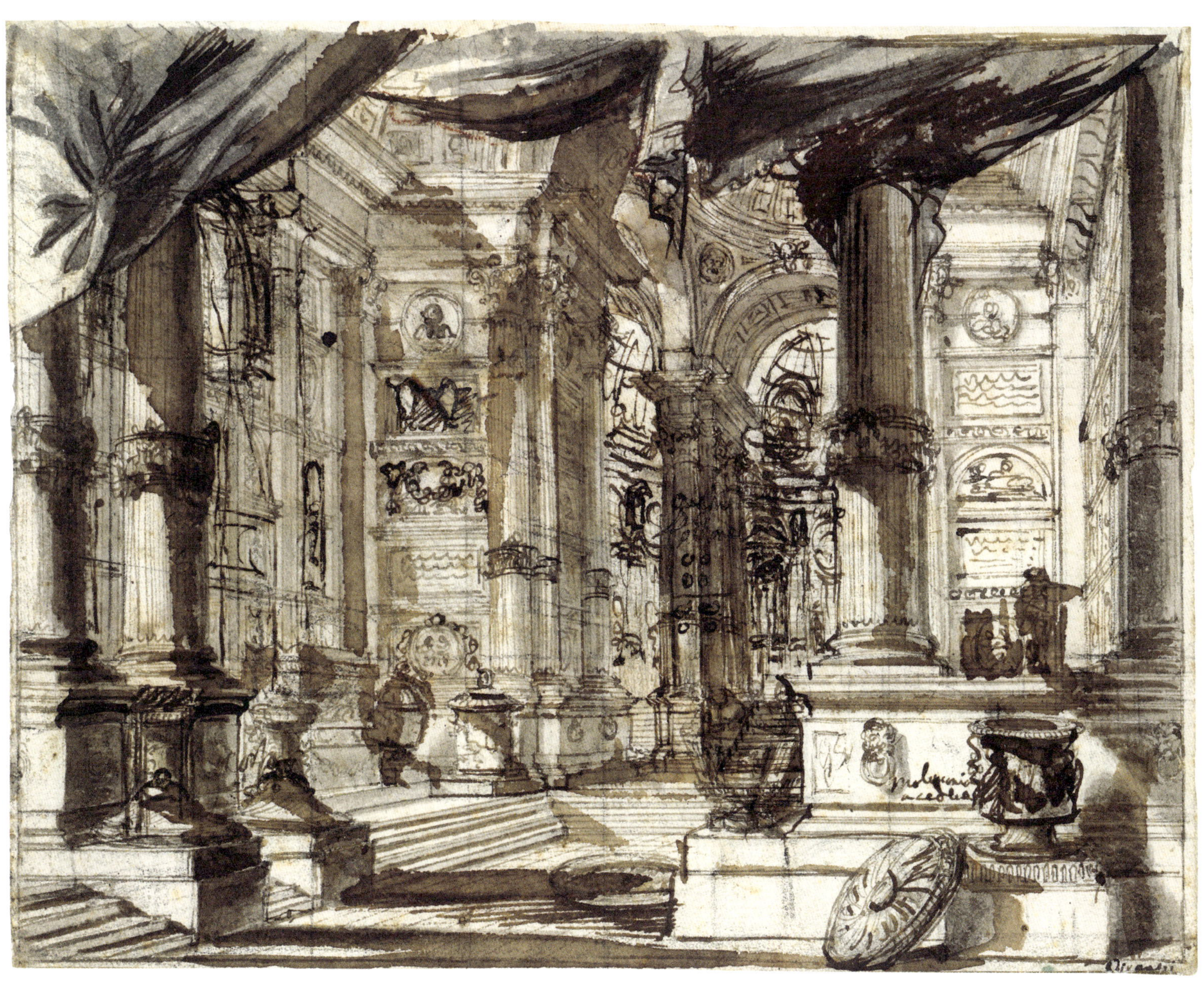

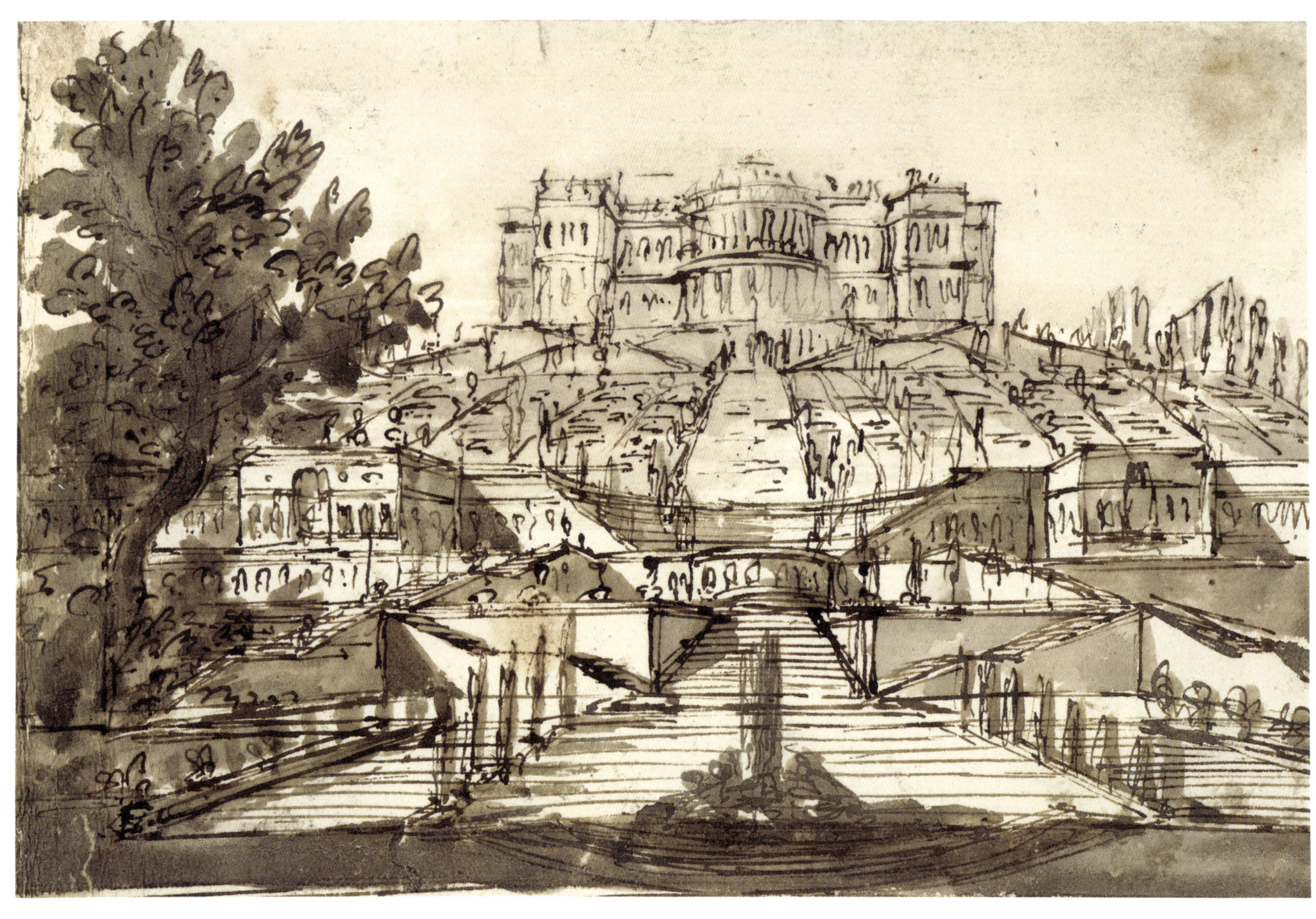

19.

A hilltop villa with a monumental staircase

c. 1748–52

Pen and brown ink, and brown wash

163 × 249 mm (6½ × 9⅞ in.)

1908,0616.1

Provenance: Probably William Gott; and by descent to his son, John Gott, Bishop of Truro; his sale, Sotheby's, London, 20 March 1908, part of lot 172

Exhibitions: London 1968, part of no. 28

An early example of Piranesi's exterior fantasies showing forums or grand palaces, this drawing probably dates from around 1750 – a time when the fluidity of his Venetian period was starting to be tempered by the darker tones of his mature drawings. The terraced sequence of steps and gardens may have been inspired by a real building, such as the ancient temple of Fortuna Primigenia at Palestrina in Lazio, or the Villa d'Este at Tivoli, but Piranesi uses reality as a jumping-off point for an architectural *capriccio*. He has added the tree on the left and the fountain or monument in the centre foreground in darker wash, helping to create a dark frame to lead the eye beyond to the bright and grandiose structures that form the main part of the image.

This dark wash, like that in cat. 17, may date from the late 1750s, as it is most uncharacteristic for this earlier period. The reworking of earlier studies is indicative of the central and dynamic importance of drawing in Piranesi's creative thinking, but it can make firm dating of his graphic oeuvre extremely challenging. The almost abstract fountain appears as an addition in other *capricci* from around the same date, such as cat. 22.

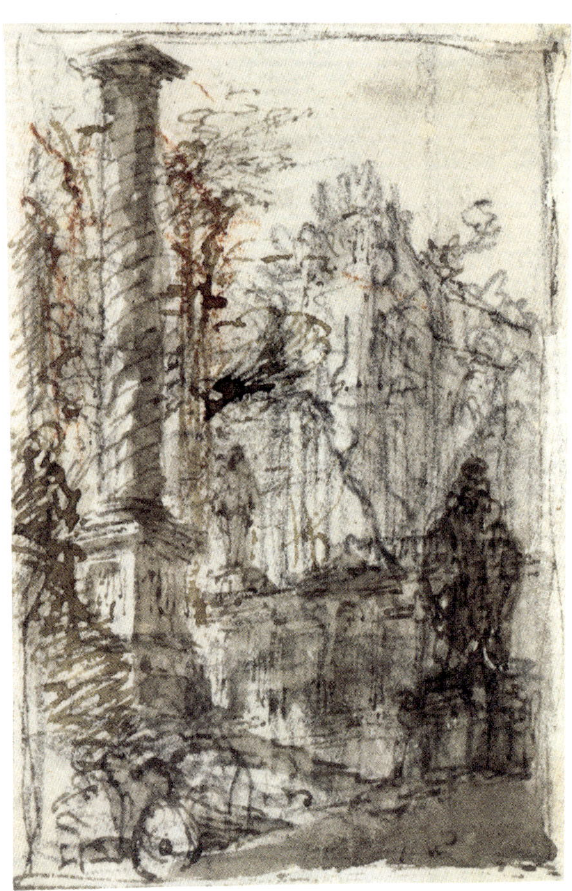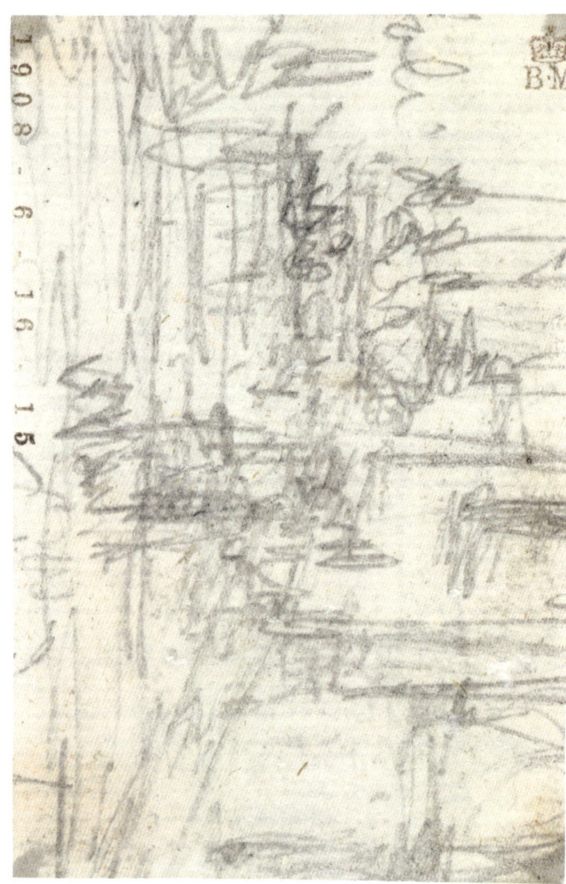

20.

Architectural scene with a column (recto); Illegible sketch (verso)

c. 1748–52

Pen and grey-brown ink, with grey-brown wash, over black and red chalk (recto); black chalk (verso)

83 × 54 mm (3⅜ × 3 in.)

1908,0616.15

Provenance: Probably William Gott; and by descent to his son, John Gott, Bishop of Truro; his sale, Sotheby's, London, 20 March 1908, part of lot 172

Exhibitions: London 1968, part of no. 24

Piranesi was capable of working on an extremely small scale, and these two diminutive sheets (cats. 20 and 21) show him exploring *capricci* themes in swift, functional studies. Very loose black-chalk underdrawing is refined with touches of grey wash and, in the case of the exterior scene, enlivened with touches of red chalk. This appears to be a variant of the exterior *capricci* inspired by Roman forums (see cats. 24 and 25 for further examples of this type), while the other drawing shows an interior with obelisks flanking a flight of steps.

It is difficult to date these drawings, but the style fits with that of Piranesi's work from the late 1740s or early 1750s, when he was exploring similar juxtapositions of motifs in larger drawings. The inclusion of the obelisks is an early example of an Egyptian reference in a drawing, indicating that Piranesi was beginning to expand his notions of architectural history, even if these particular obelisks take a conical form, which is not historically correct.

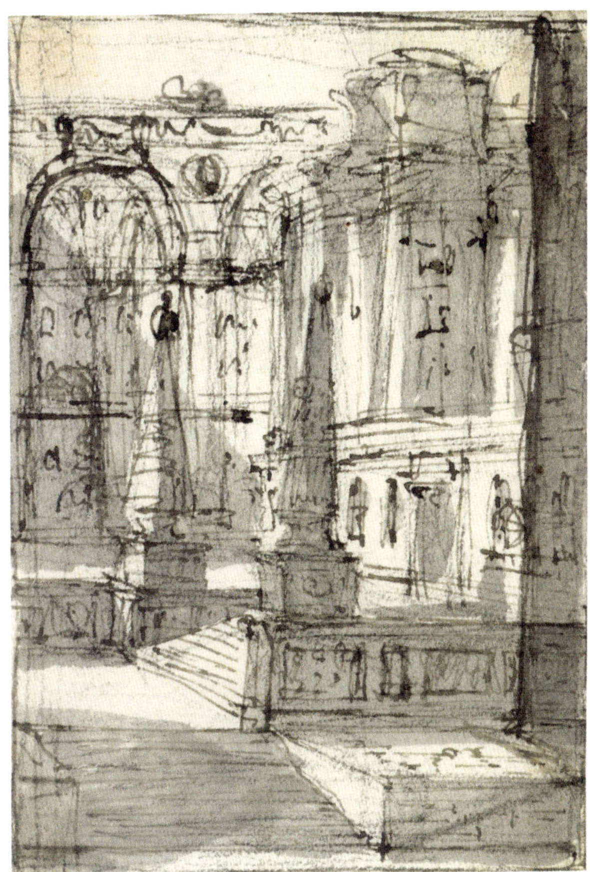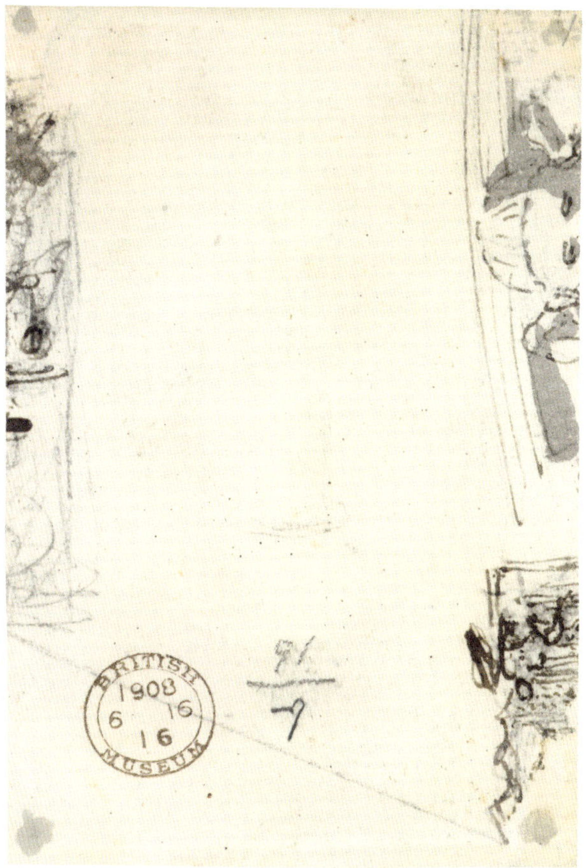

21.

A staircase flanked by obelisks (recto); Fragmentary sketches (verso)

c. 1748–52

Pen and brown ink, with grey wash, over black chalk (recto and verso)

111 × 76 mm (4⅜ × 3 in.)

1908,0616.16

Provenance: Probably William Gott; and by descent to his son, John Gott, Bishop of Truro; his sale, Sotheby's, London, 20 March 1908, part of lot 172

Exhibitions: London 1968, part of no. 24

See cat. 20 for caption

22.

A grand columned palace with triumphal arches

c. 1748–52
Pen and brown ink, and brown wash,
over black chalk
78 × 127 mm (3⅛ × 5 in.)
1908,0616.13
Provenance: Probably William Gott; and by
descent to his son, John Gott, Bishop of Truro;
his sale, Sotheby's, London, 20 March 1908,
part of lot 172
Exhibitions: London 1968, part of no. 22
Literature: Vasari Society 1912–13, no. 12;
Thomas 1954, under no. 5

This extravagant palace seems to be
a development from the *Foro antico
Romano*, plate 14 of the *Prima Parte* (1743;
Fig. 16), which established the idea
of a magnificent structure formed from
conjoined rectangular blocks with several
storeys of columned arcades. Powerfully
drawn in ink and wash, this drawing has
the confidence of the years around 1750
and is comparable in style to Piranesi's
early *Carceri* drawings. The fountains in
dark-brown wash in the foreground are
similar to those in cat. 19 and seem, like
those, to be more expressive additions
emphasizing the original framing
elements. They were probably added
towards the end of the 1750s.

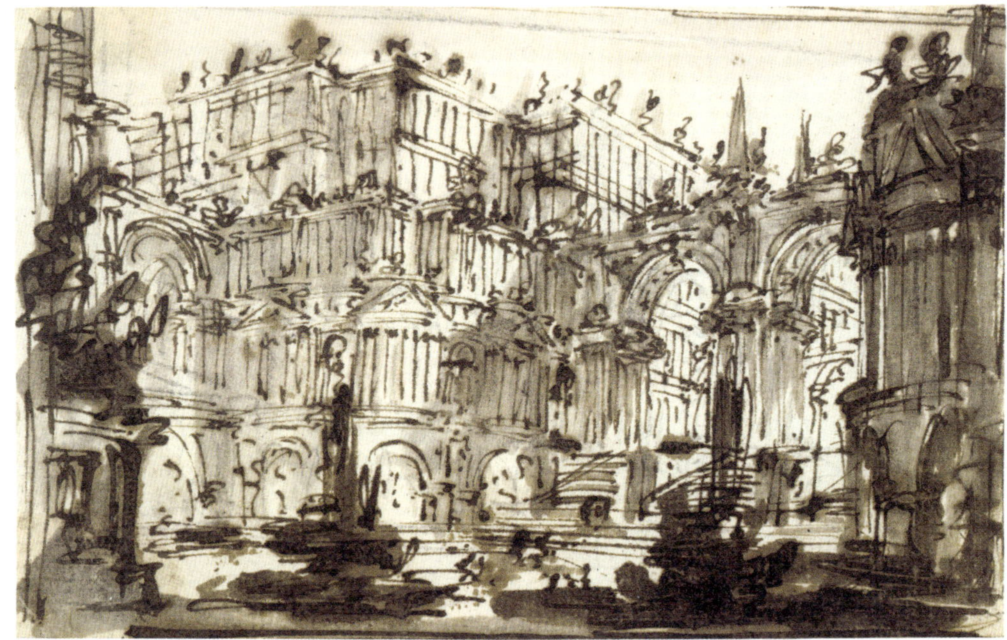

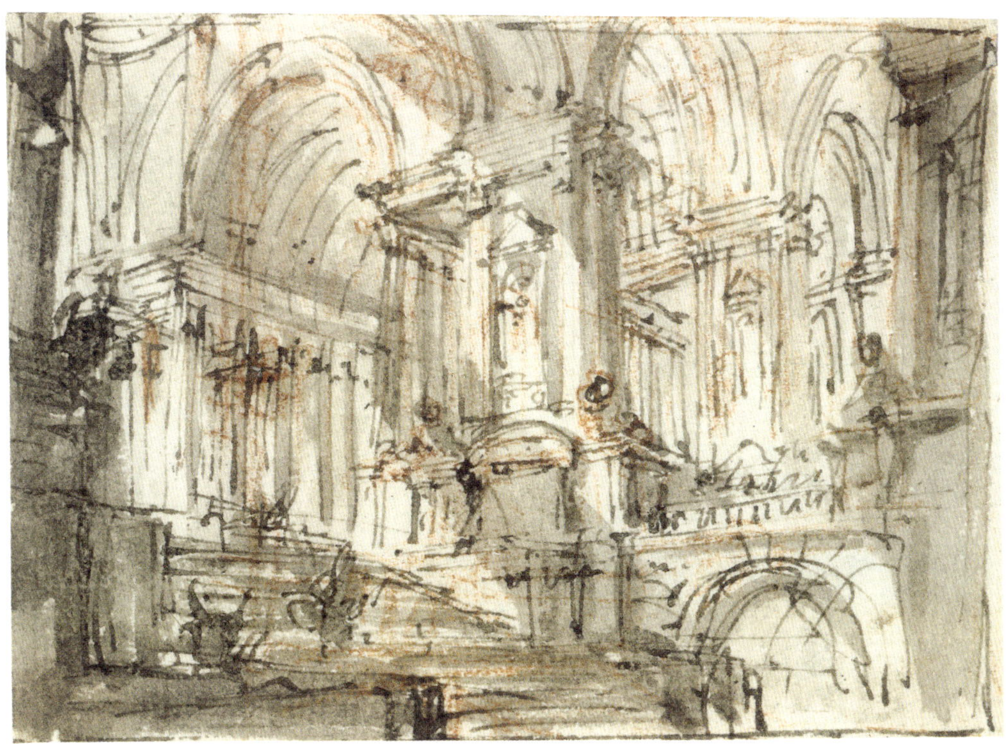

Interior of a vaulted building

c. 1748–55

Pen and brown ink, brown-grey wash, red chalk

76 × 106 mm (3 × 4¼ in.)

1908,0616.9

Provenance: Probably William Gott; and by descent to his son, John Gott, Bishop of Truro; his sale, Sotheby's, London, 20 March 1908, part of lot 172

Exhibitions: London 1968, part of no. 22; Rome, Dijon and Paris 1976, no. 145; London 1978, no. 42a; Cologne, Zurich and Vienna 1996–97, ex-catalogue; London and elsewhere 2002–4, no catalogue

The combination of red chalk with loose penwork and light layers of wash links this drawing to the period just after Piranesi's return to Rome from Venice in 1747 (see cat. 12 for a comparable drawing of this date). Despite the tiny scale, Piranesi manages to evoke the vast recessions of a palatial hall, framing the drawing with darker layers of wash at the edges, with a sensibility that remains distinctly theatrical. While this grows out of his early scenographic-style drawings, the interest in vast spaces glimpsed through and behind other structures parallels his work on the *Carceri*, which began in the late 1740s.

The drawing seems to belong to the period when Piranesi was turning away from the elaborate interiors of his first prints, and thinking about the darker, more complex spaces of his prison sequence (see cat. 15 for another drawing that seems to date from the same period).

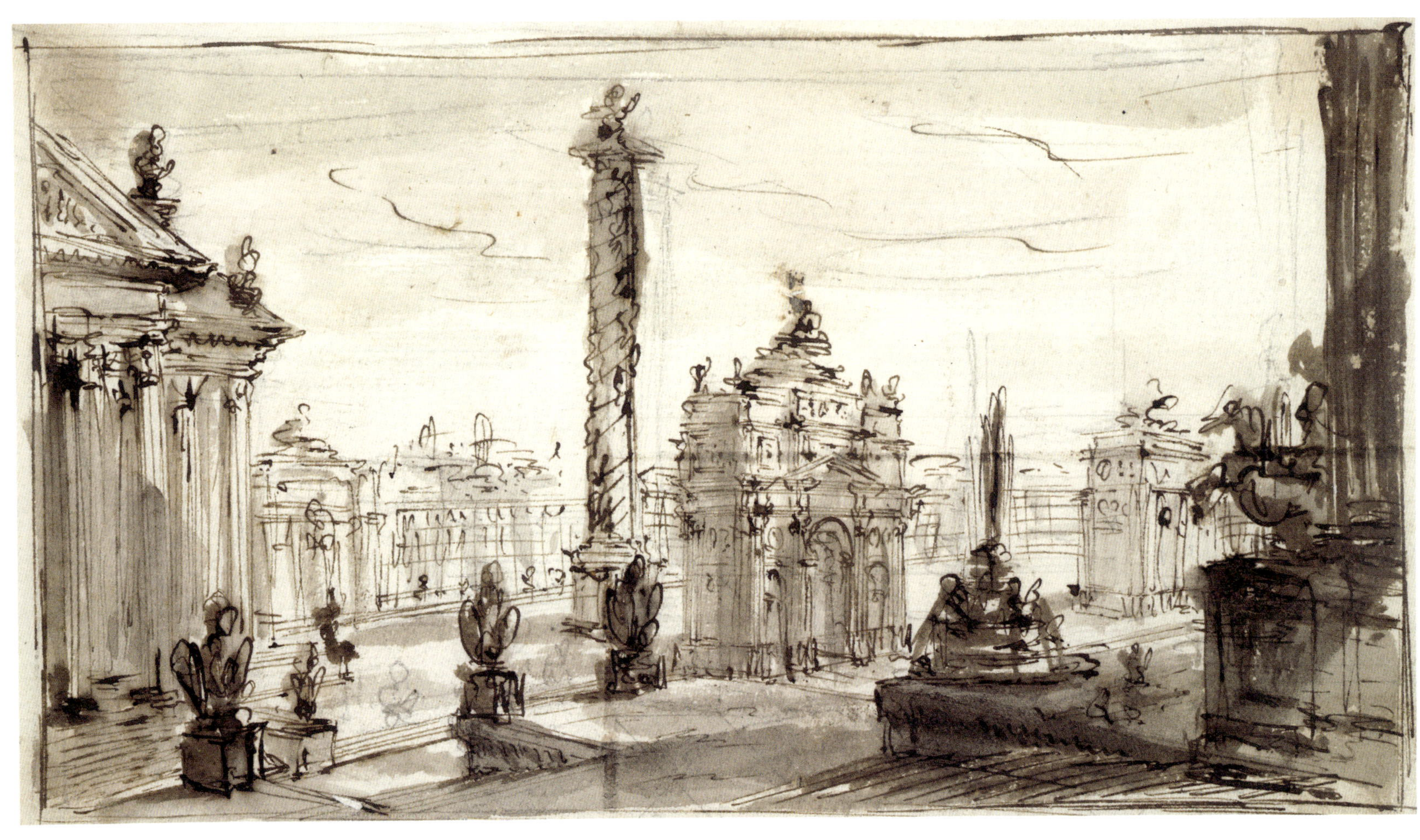

24.

View of a forum with two triumphal arches and a column

c. 1748–52

Pen and brown ink and brown wash,
over black chalk

155 × 280 mm (6⅛ × 11⅛ in.)

1908,0616.2

Provenance: Probably William Gott; and by descent to his son, John Gott, Bishop of Truro; his sale, Sotheby's, London, 20 March 1908, part of lot 172

Exhibitions: London 1968, part of no. 28

One of several drawings of Roman forums or squares probably made in the late 1740s or early 1750s (see also cat. 25), this is perhaps a development of the early *capriccio* of the *Campidoglio antico*, which was plate 10 in the *Prima Parte* (Fig. 22). Piranesi creates a bizarre space in which grandeur is prized over legibility. The central triumphal arch appears to have a column directly behind it, thus frustrating its intended purpose, and neither of the two arches leads anywhere – they have apparently been included as monuments rather than functional objects. Grandiose buildings surround the square, while a fountain and trophies have been added in darker wash in the foreground to create a *contre-jour* effect (i.e. with the foreground backlit). This was an increasingly popular feature of Piranesi's compositions at this period.

This drawing cannot be linked directly to any print, but it foreshadows the more dramatic juxtapositions of Roman monuments that would come to fruition in the magnificent *Meeting of the Via Appia and the Via Ardentina* (cat. 29).

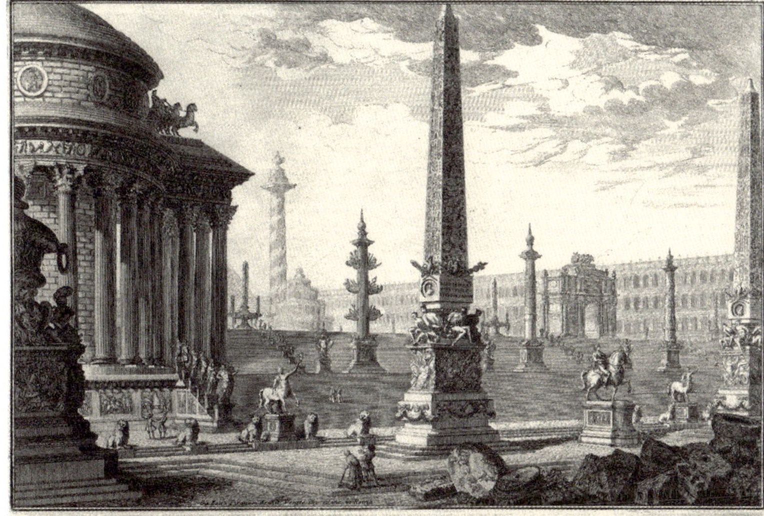

Fig. 22
Campidoglio antico
From the *Prima Parte di Architettura, e Prospettive*
c. 1743
Etching
237 × 361 mm (9⅜ × 14¼ in.)
Metropolitan Museum of Art, New York

25.

A classical forum with steps and a column

c. 1748–52

Pen and brown ink, grey-brown wash, over red chalk (some of the red chalk at upper right is over the wash), made up at left corner and at the centre of the right edge

153 × 212 mm (6⅛ × 8⅜ in.)

1908,0616.10

Provenance: Probably William Gott; and by descent to his son, John Gott, Bishop of Truro; his sale, Sotheby's, London, 20 March 1908, part of lot 172

Exhibitions: London 1968, part of no. 22; Rome, Dijon and Paris 1976, no. 146; London 1978, no. 42b; Cologne, Zurich and Vienna 1996–97, ex-catalogue; London and elsewhere 2002–4, no catalogue

Literature: Thomas 1954, no. 21

A Roman *capriccio* of a very similar type to cat. 24, this is again probably derived from the *Campidoglio antico* of the *Prima Parte* (see Fig. 22), but dates from around 1750. This space is perhaps more directly inspired by the Campidoglio, with its flights of steps, its two sculptures of horse-trainers on the terrace, and the palatial arcades and structures beyond. The technique is again entirely characteristic of this post-Venetian period, but its vigour places it around the time of the *Carceri* studies. Red chalk has been used for the underdrawing, for motifs such as the billowing smoke, and to reinforce the dense zigzag hatching in the sky.

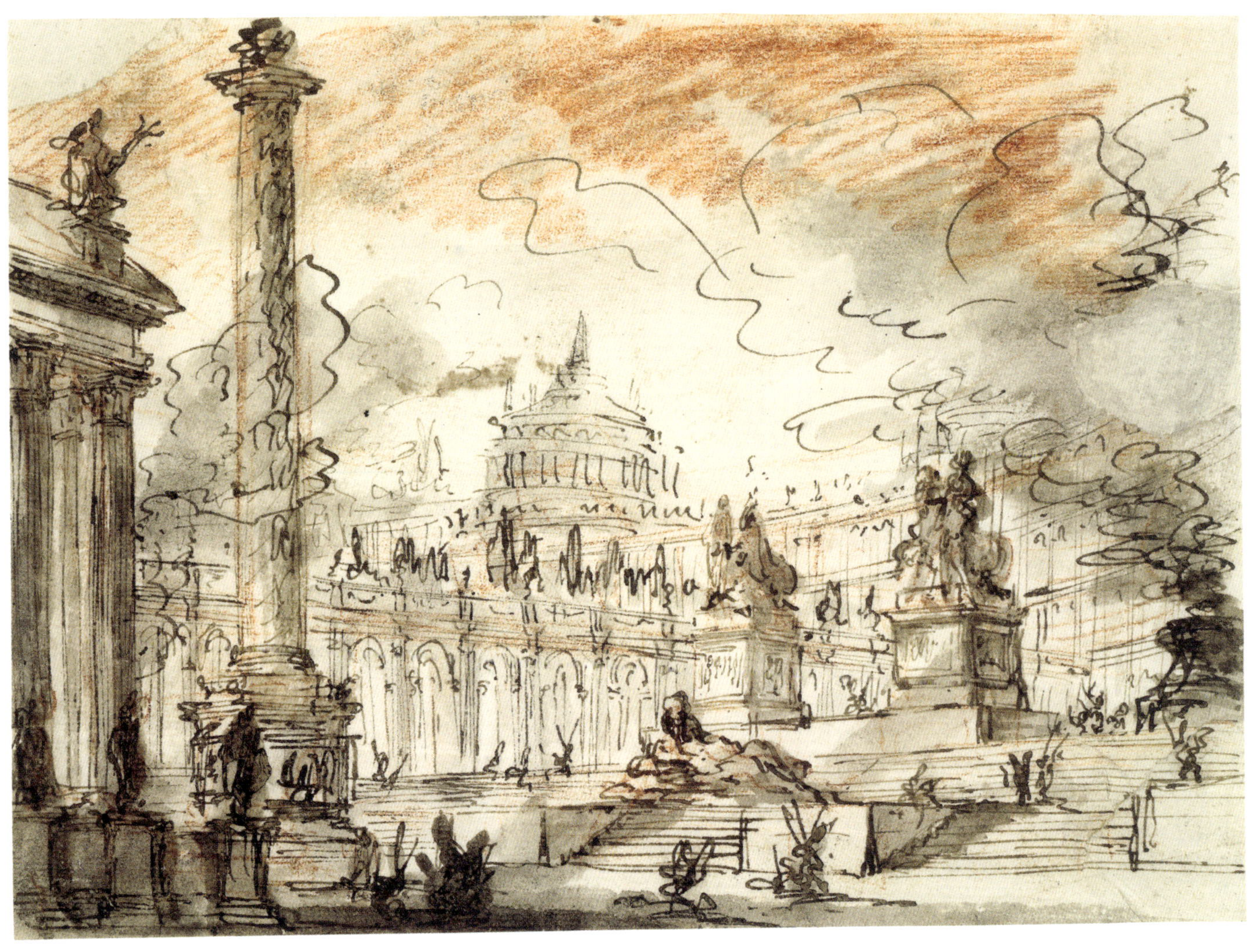

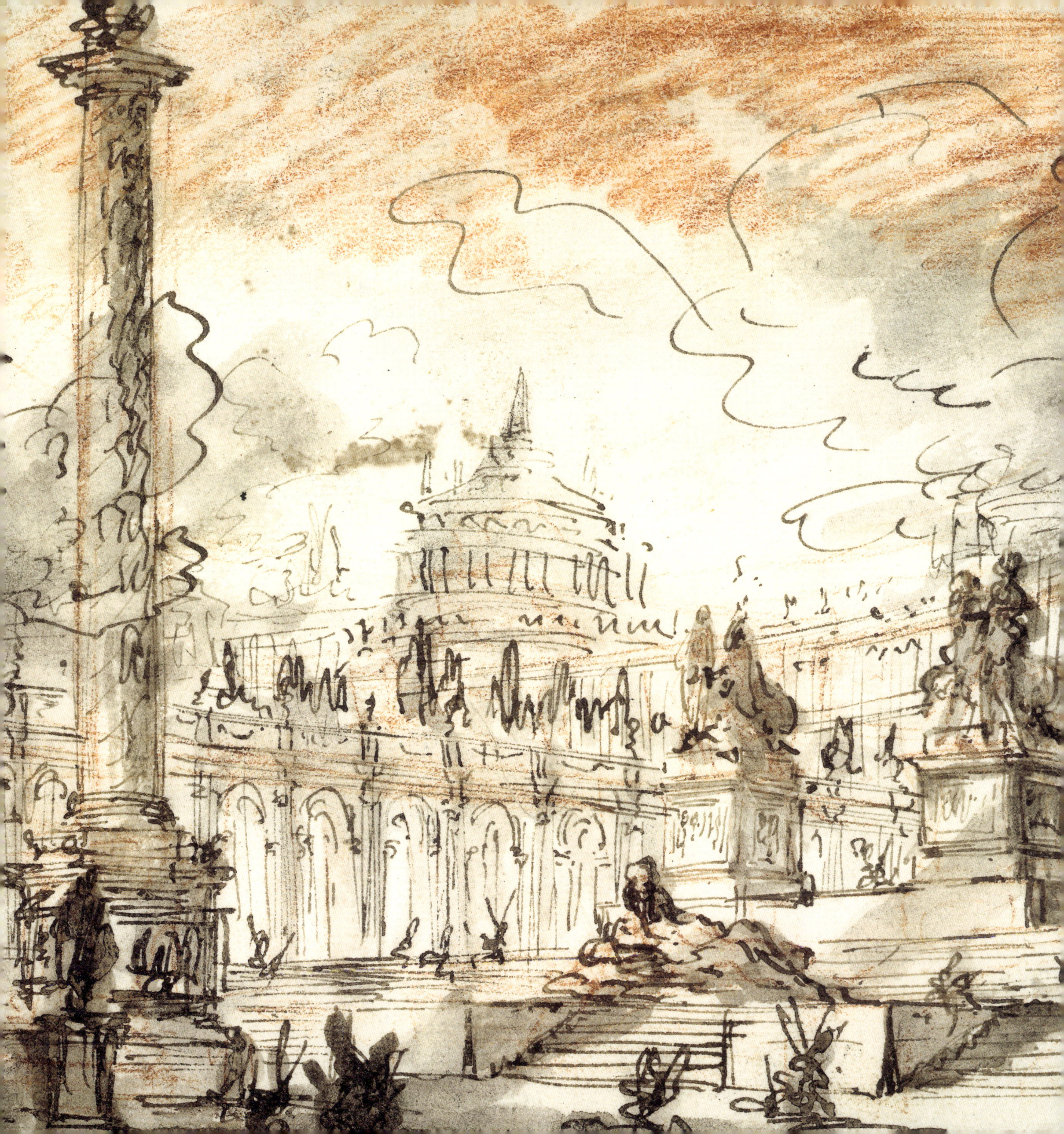

26.

An ornate triumphal arch with a grand staircase

c. 1747–50

Pen and brown ink, brown wash, over red chalk

147 × 211 mm (5⅞ × 8⅜ in.)

1908,0616.11

Provenance: Probably William Gott; and by descent to his son, John Gott, Bishop of Truro; his sale, Sotheby's, London, 20 March 1908, part of lot 172

Exhibitions: London 1968, part of no. 22; Rome, Dijon and Paris 1976, no. 147; London 1978, no. 42c; Cologne, Zurich and Vienna 1996–97, no. Z-20; London and elsewhere 2002–4, no catalogue

Literature: Thomas 1954, no. 19; Bacou 1974, p. 39

The grandeur of this drawing belies its small scale. Stylistically it is consistent with a date in the late 1740s, with red chalk underdrawing, fluid wash and the addition of darker, more abstract forms in the foreground and around the edges. It may well be distantly related to Piranesi's design for *Parte di ampio magnifico porto*, from the *Opere varie*, dating from *c.* 1749–50 (Fig. 23). The abstract forms in the foreground are probably supposed to be monuments or trophies, similar to those that appear in Piranesi's fantasy forums (cat. 25).

As in *Ampio magnifico porto*, a grand flight of stairs leads up to a splendid complex of buildings, here flanked by trophies and entered through a grandiose triumphal arch, which is richly encrusted with sculptures and, unusually, pierced by lateral arches to increase the play of light, shade, void and solidity.

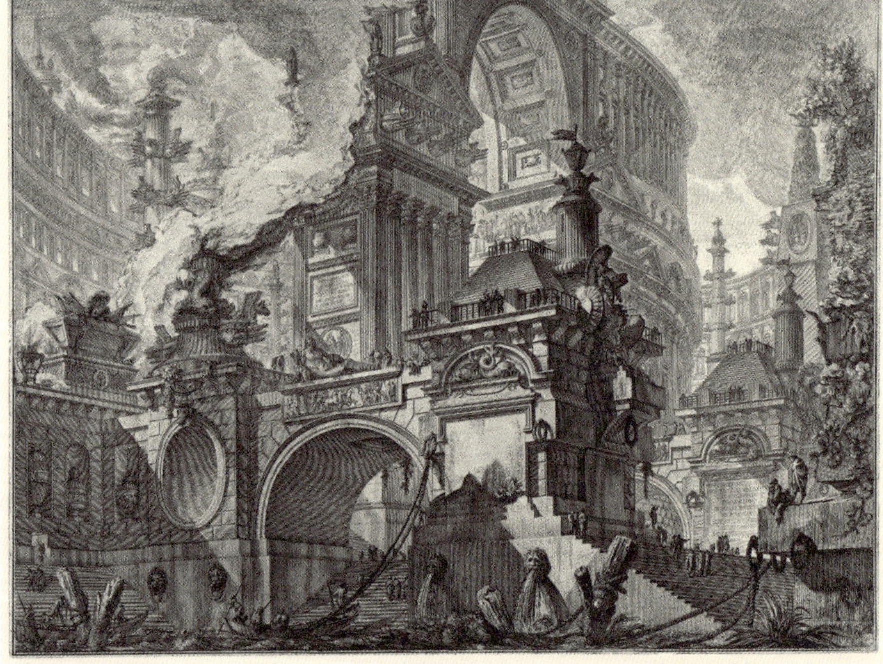

Fig. 23
Parte di ampio magnifico porto
From the *Opere varie di architettura, prospettive, grotteschi, antichità*
c. 1749–50
Etching, engraving, drypoint
400 × 545 mm (15¾ × 21½ in.)
Metropolitan Museum of Art, New York

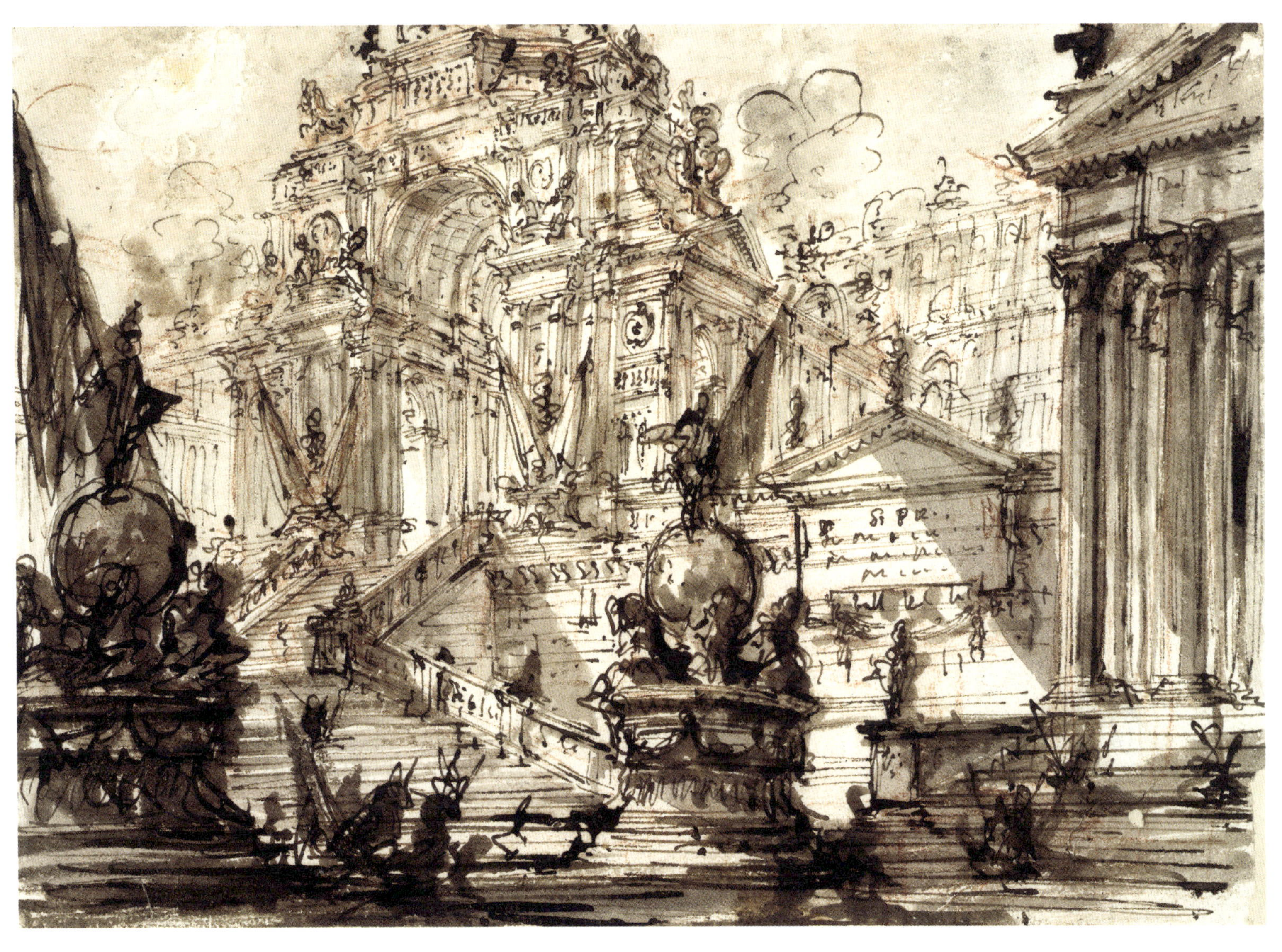

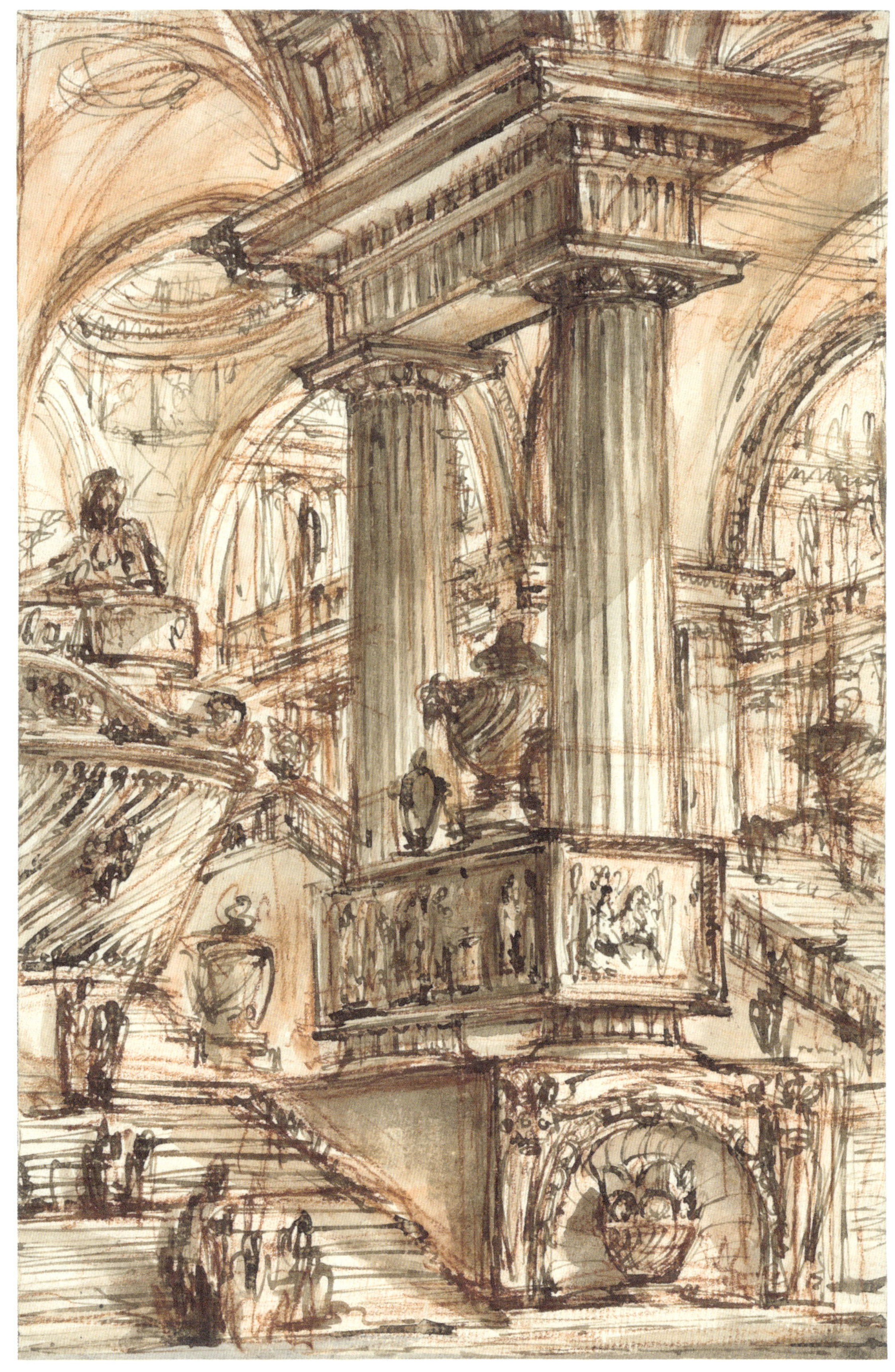

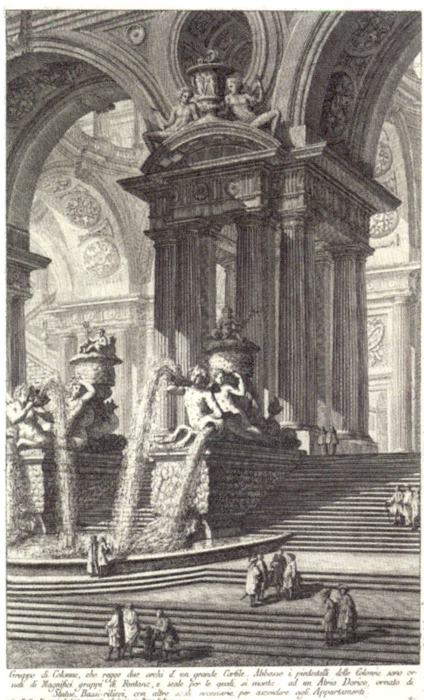

Fig. 24

*Group of columns which
support two arches of a
great courtyard*
From the *Prima Parte di
Architetture, e Prospettive*
c. 1743
Etching
401 × 247 mm (15⅞ × 9¾ in.)
Metropolitan Museum of Art,
New York

27.

A monumental staircase in a vaulted interior with columns

c. 1750–55

Pen and brown ink, brown and pink wash,
red chalk

381 × 254 mm (15 × 10 in.)

1840,0314.159

Provenance: William Kinnard, and by descent
to his daughter Miss Kinnard

Exhibitions: London 1968, part of no. 30;
London 1972, no. 301; Rome, Dijon and Paris
1976, no. 151; London 1978, no. 49; Venice
1978, no. 31; London and elsewhere 2002–4,
no catalogue

Literature: Samuel 1910, pl. XIX; Borenius 1926,
p. 642; Thomas 1954, no. 39; Vogt-Göknil 1958,
p. 21, fig. 5; Penny 1978, no. 43

One of the most impressive Piranesi drawings in the British Museum, this dates from the early 1750s and shows the artist transforming the spatial complexities of the *Carceri* into the classical language of his later Roman *capricci*. The composition may have its roots in *Group of columns*, plate 4 in the *Prima Parte* (Fig. 24), which presents a similarly monumental view of a grand staircase with tiny figures overshadowed by the vast relics of antiquity. Domes and staircases recede into the distance, which, typically with Piranesi, is shown as brighter than the foreground.

The most striking thing about this drawing is the technique, which combines red chalk with brown ink and wash in an aesthetic blend that appears nowhere else in the British Museum's Piranesi collection. It shows an artist at the height of his powers, able to articulate space and perspective with ease, and confident enough in his talents to add manifestly impossible features, such as the sarcophagus that 'floats' partway up the two central columns. It is closest stylistically to the grand preparatory drawing for *The meeting of the Via Appia and the Via Ardentina* (*c.* 1750–56; cat. 29), which supports the suggested dating for this drawing.

28.

Two semicircular buildings with coffered recesses connected by an arcade

c. 1750–55

Pen and brown ink, with brown wash,
over red chalk

159 × 262 mm (6⅜ × 10⅜ in.)

1908,0616.21

Provenance: Probably William Gott; and by descent to his son, John Gott, Bishop of Truro; his sale, Sotheby's, London, 20 March 1908, part of lot 172

Exhibitions: London 1968, part of no. 23; Rome, Dijon and Paris 1976, no. 149; London 1978, no. 193b; Sheffield 1988, no. 19; London and elsewhere 2002–4, no catalogue

This drawing is an early testament to Piranesi's interest in the burgeoning Greco-Roman controversy. The inscription, 'Idea Secondo L'abuso che i Romani han fatto delle maniere Greche' ('Example of the abuse the Romans have made of the Greek manner'), should be understood as entirely tongue-in-cheek. Piranesi emphasizes the most innovative features of Roman architecture, such as arches, coffered vaulting and curved walls, stressing its creativity and variety in the face of Greek functional purity.

Stylistically the drawing is similar to those Piranesi made shortly after his return from Venice, such as cats. 23 and 29, with its underlying red chalk and fluid wash. However, the dense ink additions in the foreground and the overall darker tonality of the drawing could well support a date in the 1750s, which would be consistent with the first flourishing of Piranesi's interest in the Greco-Roman debate, foreshadowing his much less light-hearted and more passionate involvement in the dispute in the late 1750s and early 1760s.

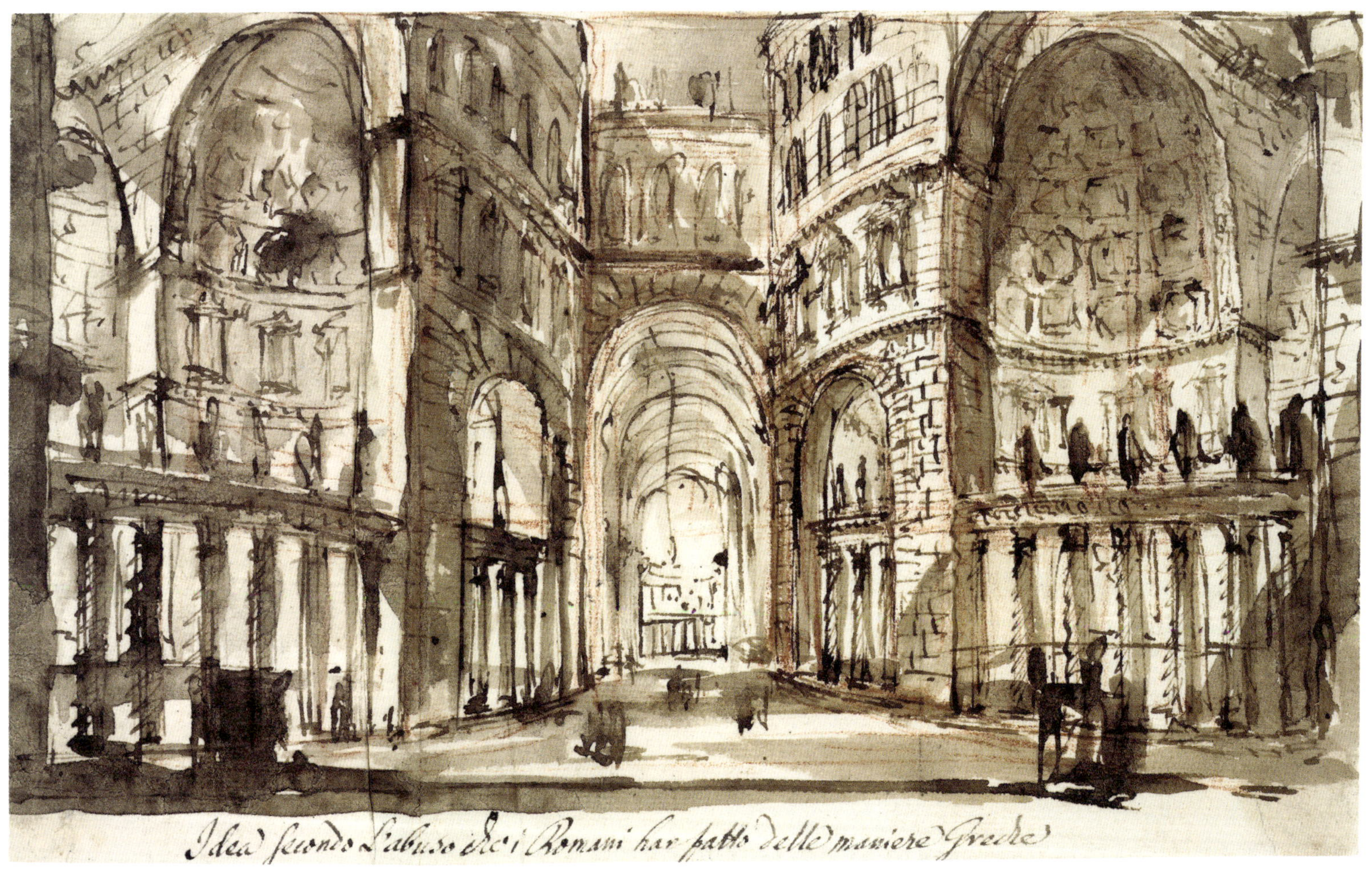

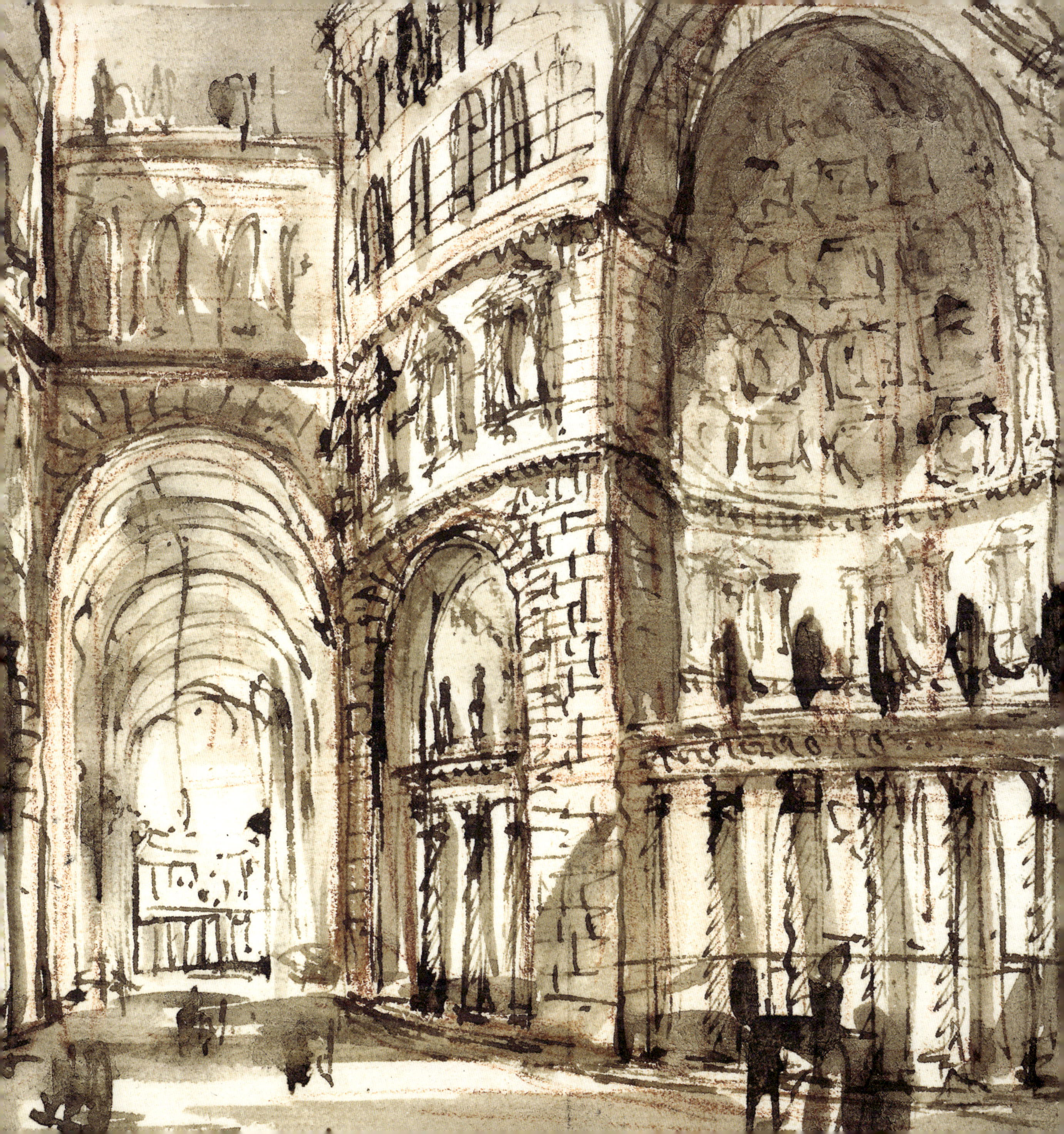

29.

The meeting of the Via Appia and the Via Ardentina, seen at the second milestone outside the Porta Capena

c. 1750–56

Pen and brown ink, brown and pink wash,
over black chalk (some lines drawn with a ruler)
and red chalk
399 × 635 mm (15¾ × 25 in.)
1908,0616.43

Provenance: Probably William Gott; and by
descent to his son, John Gott, Bishop of Truro;
his sale, Sotheby's, London, 20 March 1908,
part of lot 172
Exhibitions: London 1968, part of no. 29; Rome,
Dijon and Paris 1976, no. 150; London 1978,
no. 119; Venice 1978, no. 35; London 2003,
no catalogue
Literature: Focillon 1918, p. 24, under no. 225;
Hind 1922, p. 23; Corfiato 1951, p. 12, pl. 54;
Thomas 1954, no. 32; Murray 1971, fig. 59; Scott
1975, fig. 124, p. 109

This magnificent preparatory drawing is
for one of the secondary frontispieces of
the *Antichità Romane*, published in 1756,
and is entirely consistent stylistically with
what we know of Piranesi's work in the
early 1750s. The view shows the junction
of two great antique roads, the Via Appia
and Via Ardentina, outside Rome, but
Piranesi has sacrificed archaeological
exactitude for a dazzling *capriccio* of
Roman monuments and sculptures,
designed to show off the fecundity of
the classical architectural imagination.
The composition is made more imposing
by the choice of a theatrical *scena per
angolo* viewpoint, giving two vanishing
points, which lead the eye down each of
the roads, and allowing for the towering
crag covered with monuments and tombs
in the centre.

This is by far the most expressive
and lively of the known drawings for
the *Antichità Romane* frontispieces. Those
for *Circus Maximus*, from the second title
page of the third volume,[44] and *Architectural
fantasy* (Fig. 10) are much more precise
and highly finished, and it is likely that
a similarly polished final drawing was
made for *The meeting of the Via Appia and
the Via Ardentina*. If so, it does not survive.

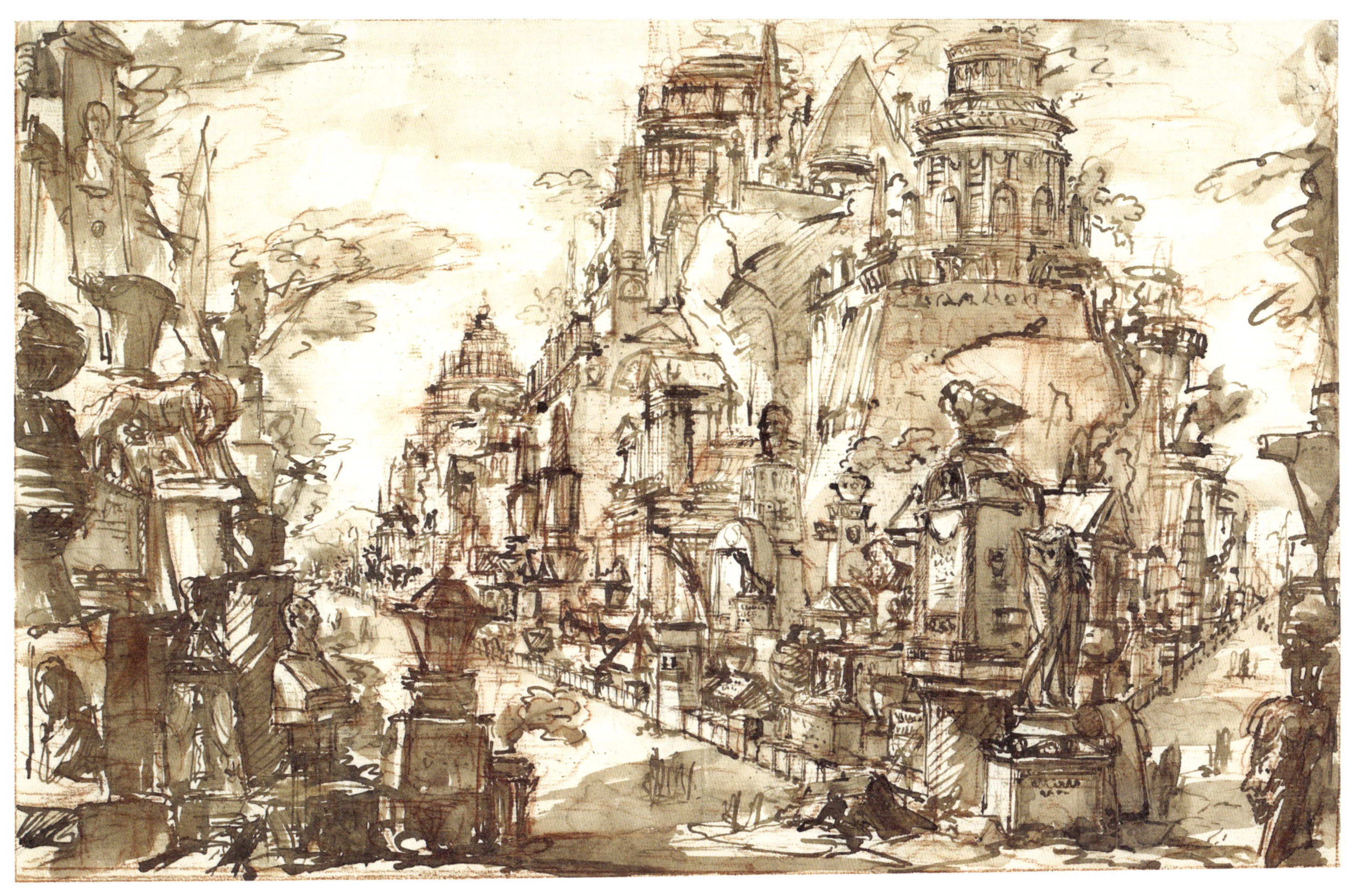

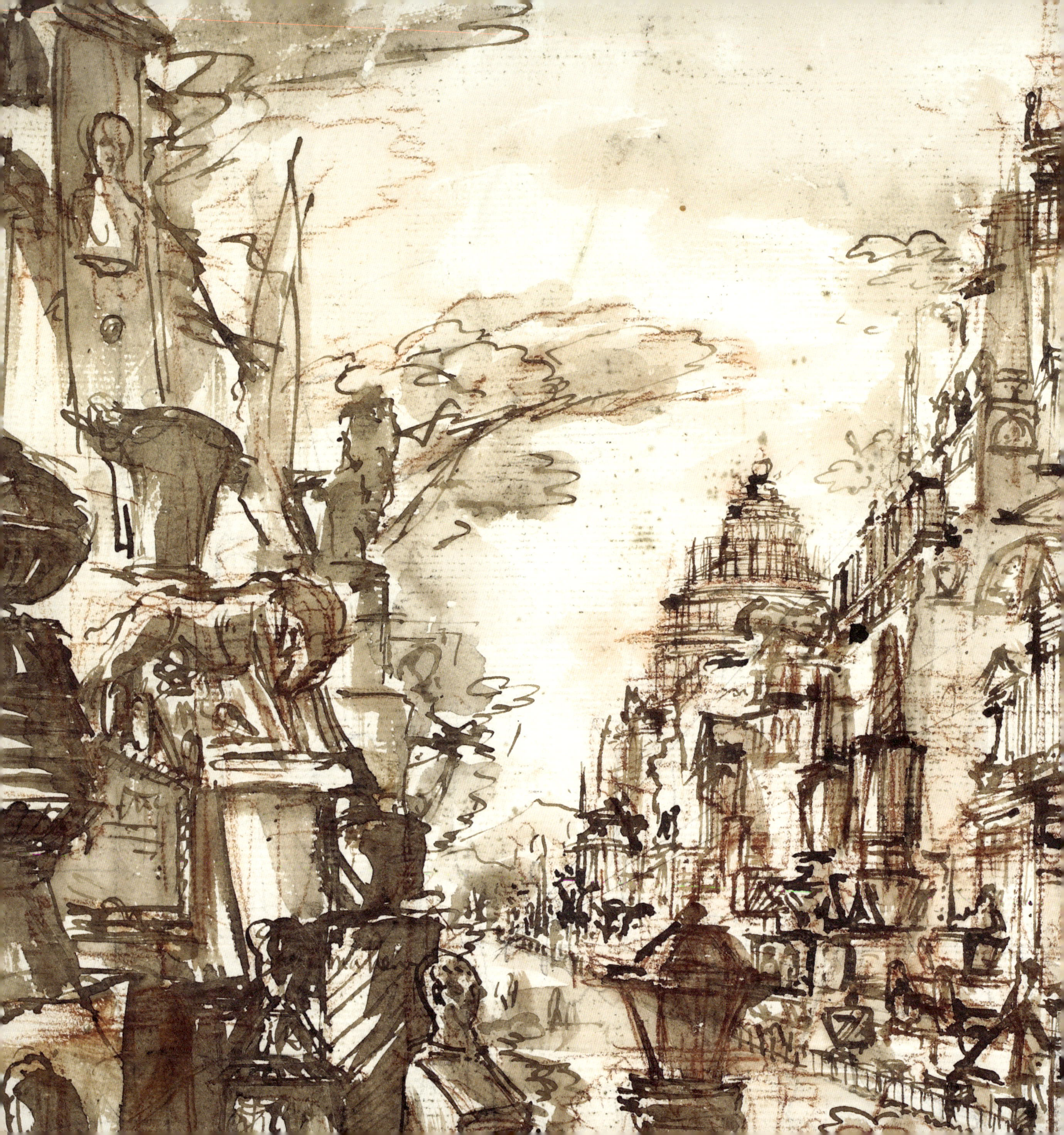

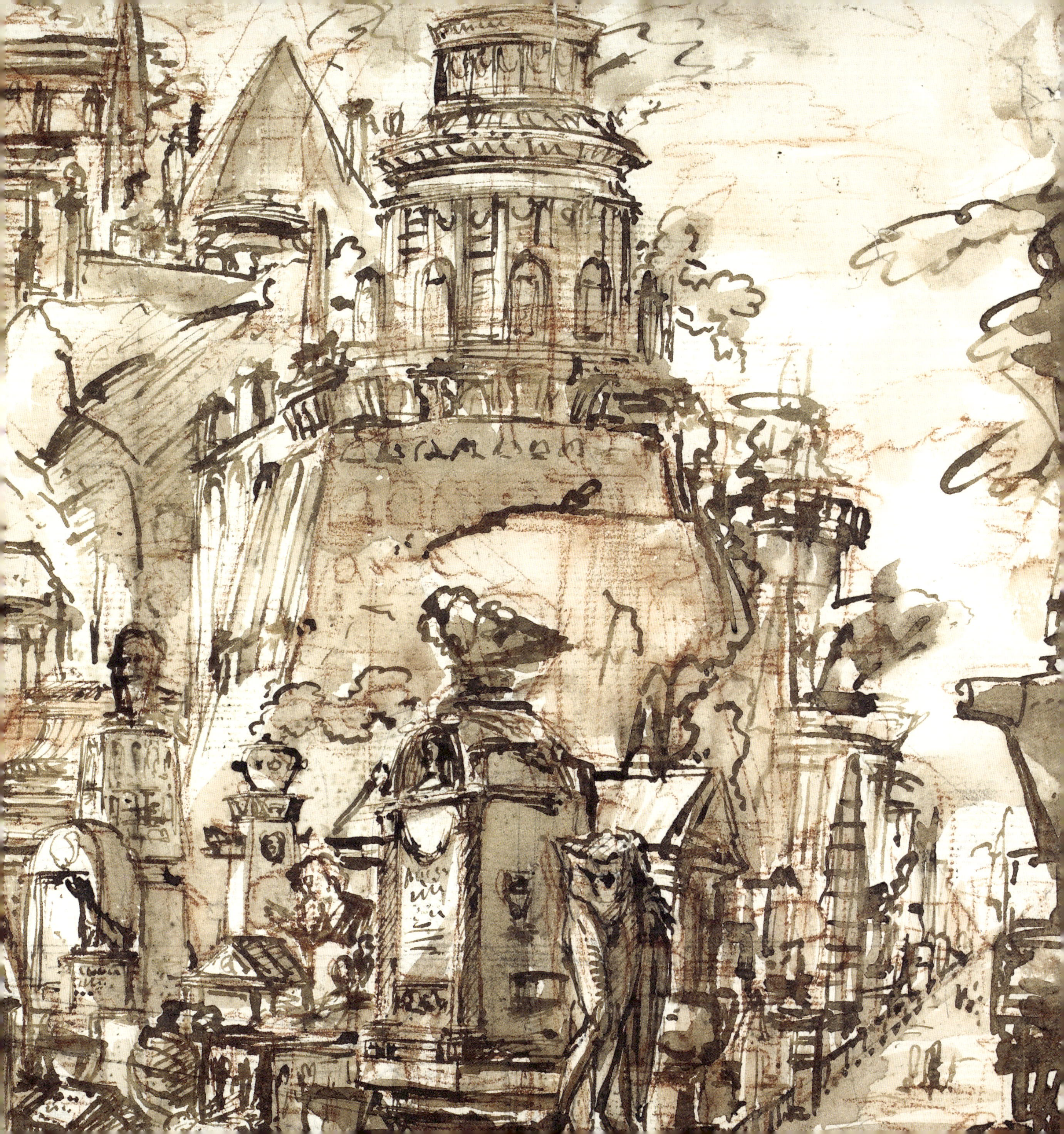

30.

A piazza before a palace with a semicircular colonnade and arches

c. 1755–62

Pen and brown ink, over black chalk

123 × 176 mm (4⅞ × 7 in.)

1908,0616.5

Provenance: Probably William Gott; and by descent to his son, John Gott, Bishop of Truro; his sale, Sotheby's, London, 20 March 1908, part of lot 172

Exhibitions: London 1968, part of no. 27; London 1978, no. 102a; Venice 1978, no. 26

Probably dating from the late 1750s, this is a natural development from the sketchy exploratory drawings on the back of Piranesi's early scenographic drawings (cats. 1 and 2), but the exploration is increasingly becoming an end in itself. Figures drawn with thick lines and blobs populate the scene, although not on the miniature scale that Piranesi had adopted in his scenes of antique magnificence (see for example cat. 14).

The curious feature of this drawing is a circular building set into the corner of the palatial structure. Similar round buildings feature in the corners of the extravagant *Architectural fantasy* in the Morgan Library (Fig. 25), dated there to *c.* 1765, and it is possible that this drawing represents an early essay on a similar theme.

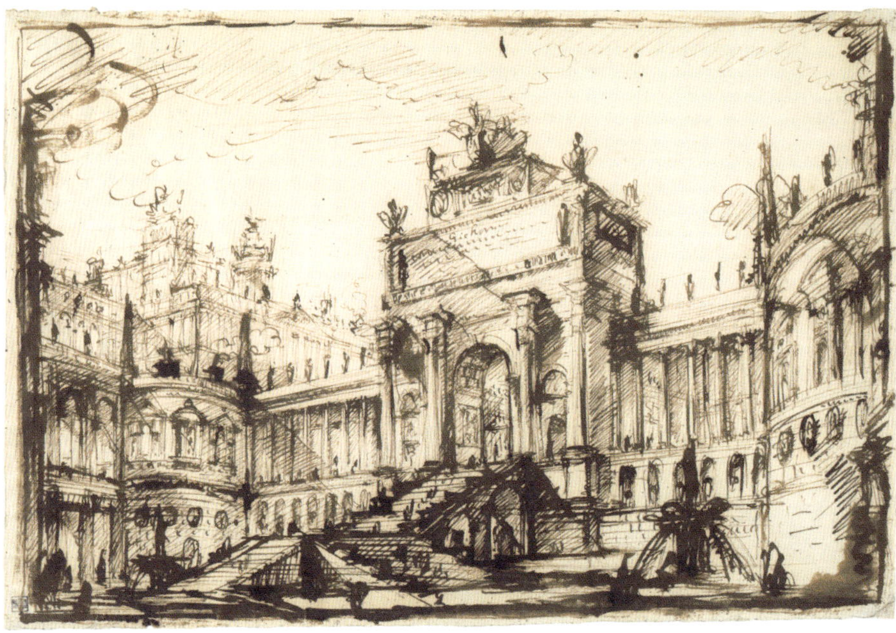

Fig. 25
Architectural fantasy
c. 1765
Pen and brown ink, with
brown wash
329 × 491 mm (13 × 19⅜ in.)
The Morgan Library and
Museum, New York

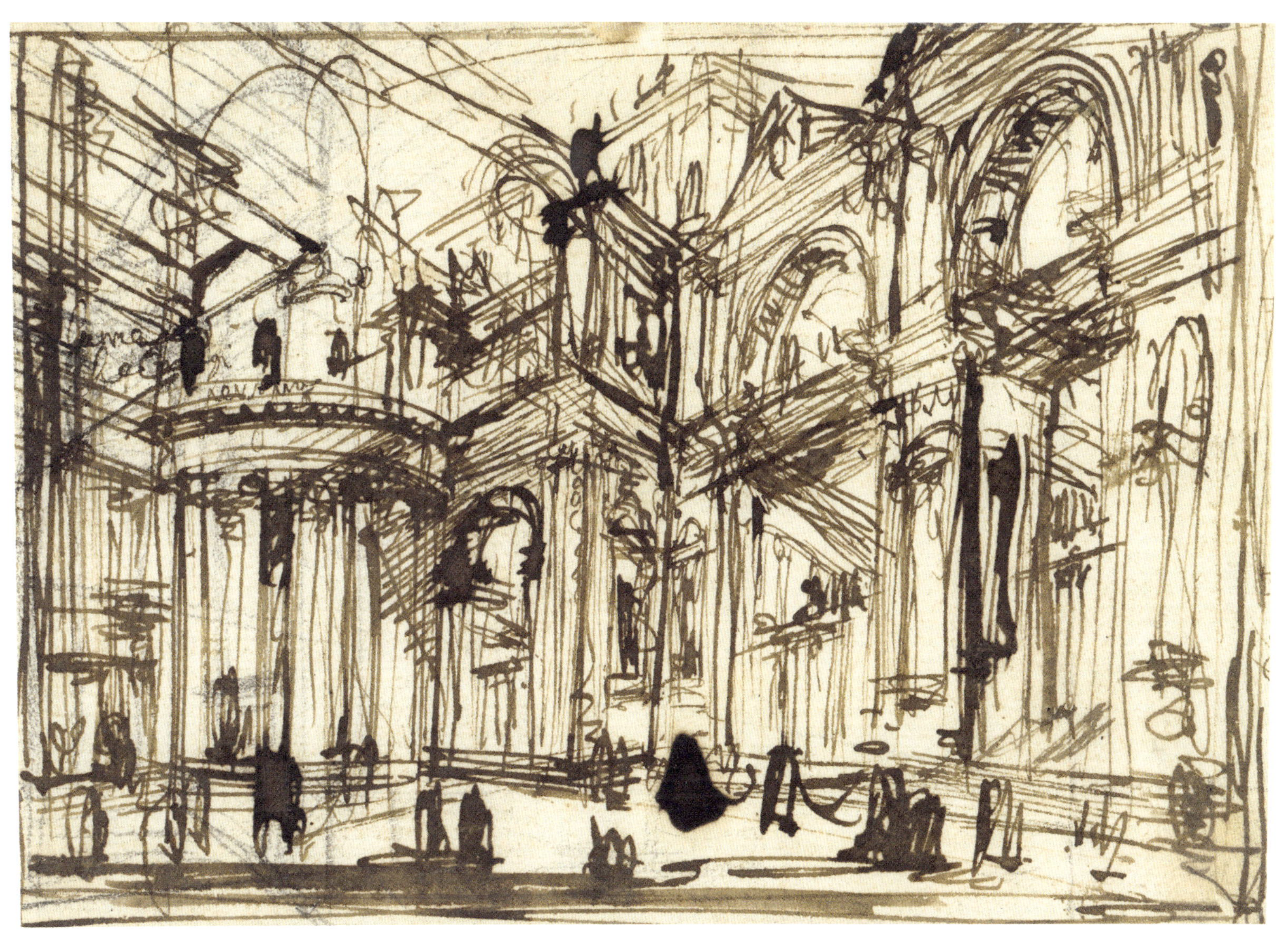

31.

A monument flanked by sphinxes in a vaulted interior

c. 1748–55
Pen and brown ink and brown wash,
over black chalk
89 × 66 mm (3⅝ × 2⅝ in.)
1908,0616.31
Provenance: Probably William Gott; and by
descent to his son, John Gott, Bishop of Truro;
his sale, Sotheby's, London, 20 March 1908,
part of lot 172
Exhibitions: British Museum 1968, part of no. 24
Literature: Thomas 1954, under no. 18

The loose yet fine pen lines, combined
with dark layers of wash, place this
drawing at the end of the 1740s or the
beginning of the 1750s; its more expressive
nature probably places it slightly later
than cat. 16, with which it nevertheless
shares underlying scratchy penwork. As
in cat. 21, Piranesi has added an Egyptian
motif to his aesthetic vocabulary, this
time in the form of a sphinx. The interior
appears to be a mausoleum, with a grand
tomb in the centre and another funerary
monument on the left, worked over
in dark wash so that it forms a more
dramatic framing device.

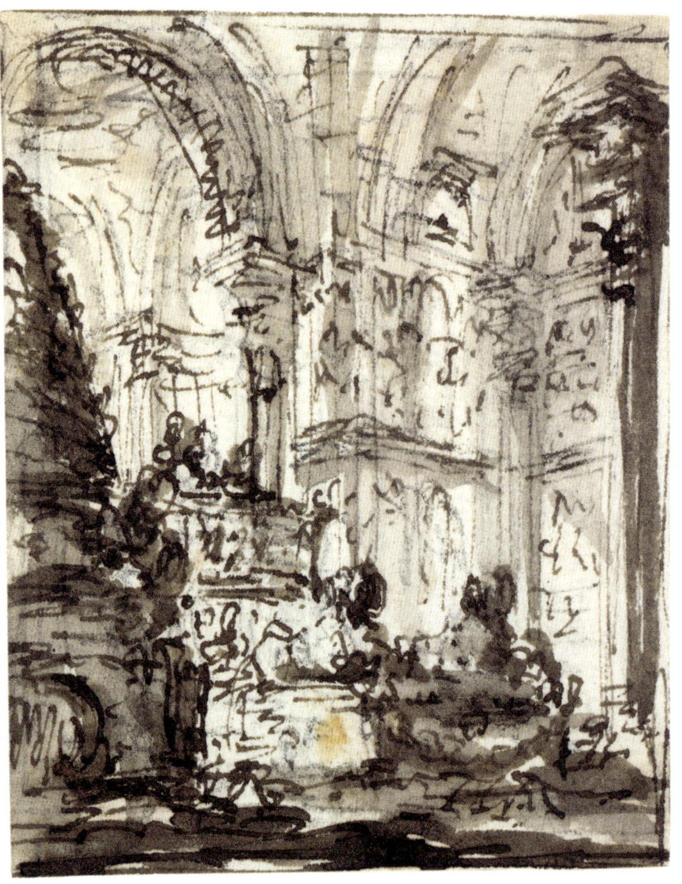

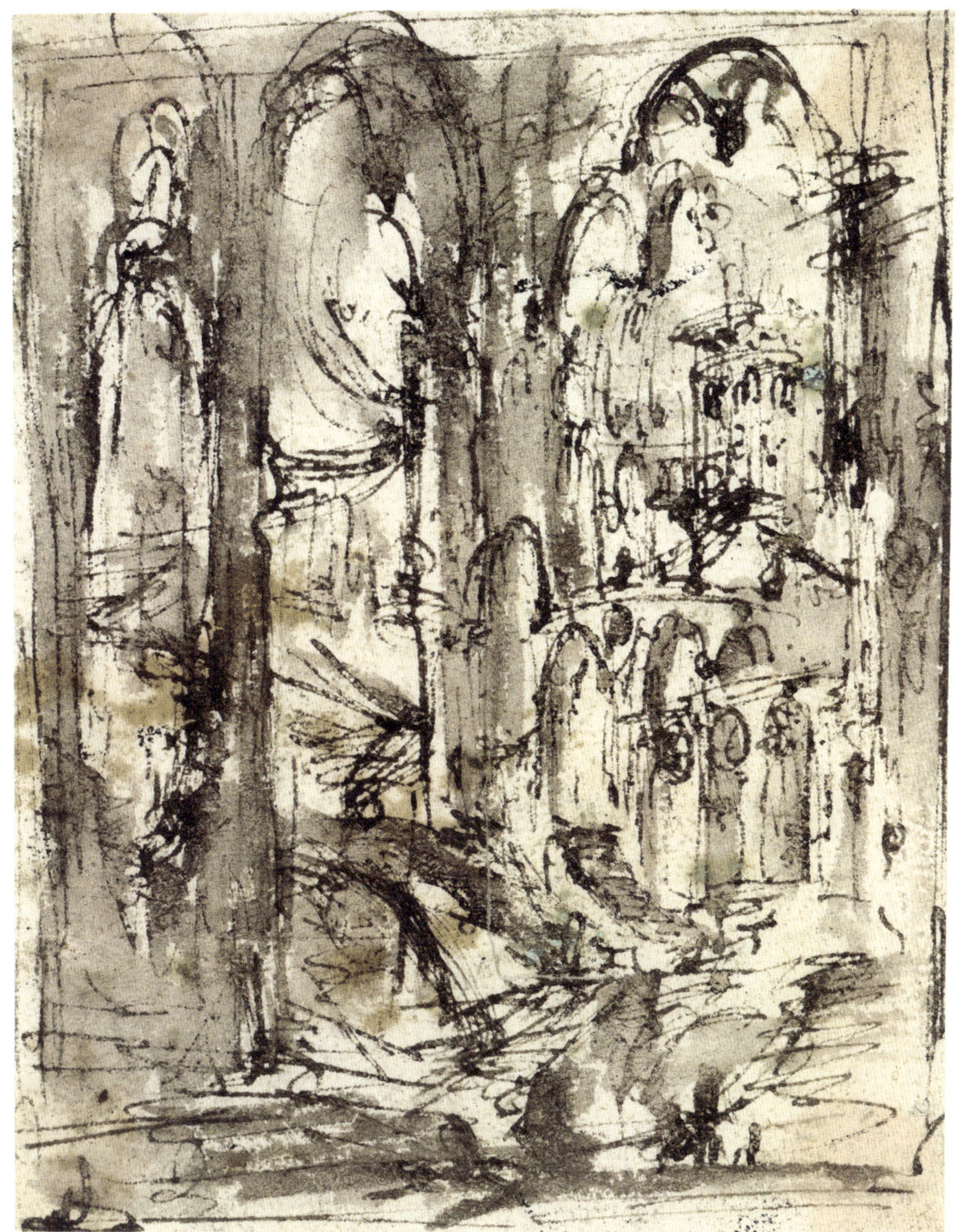

Architectural fantasy with arches and flights of steps

c. 1755–60
Pen and brown ink, with brown wash
155 × 122 mm (6⅛ × 4⅞ in.)
1908,0616.32
Provenance: Probably William Gott; and by descent to his son, John Gott, Bishop of Truro; his sale, Sotheby's, London, 20 March 1908, part of lot 172
Exhibitions: London 1968, part of no. 24

With its overlapping arches leading the eye back into the composition, and its flights of steps, this drawing is close in spirit to the designs for the *Carceri*, although its style places it later, in the late 1750s. It may be connected to Piranesi's ideas for the revision and second edition of the *Carceri*, although it is not directly related to any of the compositions in the series. It is a particularly rough and spontaneous drawing, emphasizing the idea of the soaring steps and vast space rather than articulating them clearly.

33.

**Interior with a well and a crane,
a staircase beyond**

c. 1755–61

Pen and brown ink, and brown wash,
over black and red chalk
153 × 218 mm (6⅛ × 8⅝ in.)
1929,0516.2
Provenance: Prince Wladimir Argoutinsky-
Dolgoroukoff
Exhibitions: London 1968, part of no. 25;
Washington 1978, section on the *Carceri*, no. 23;
London and elsewhere 2002–4, no catalogue
Literature: Robison 1977, p. 398, fig. 12; Robison
1986a, p. 40, fig. 48, and p. 189, under no. 39

This drawing relates directly to *The well*, plate 13 of the *Carceri*. It has been seen as a preparatory drawing for the plate,[45] but the style of the drawing does not fit well with Piranesi's works of *c.* 1750. The looseness of the penwork, the strong tonal contrasts and the near-abstraction of forms and figures correspond far better with his work of the later 1750s.

It is possible that this drawing in fact forms a record of the first edition of the print, made with a view to the preparation of the second edition of the *Carceri* in 1761. This would explain the almost identical compositions of print and drawing, where figures and even details such as the chains on the walls are faithfully replicated. At this period in his career, Piranesi worked up the final details for compositions directly onto the plate, and it would be most uncharacteristic for him slavishly to follow a preparatory drawing to such a degree. The speed of the drawing also suggests that it was made quickly after the print as a basis for further experimentation. It would also explain the striking disparity in size between drawing and print – *The well* is more than twice as big as this sheet.[46]

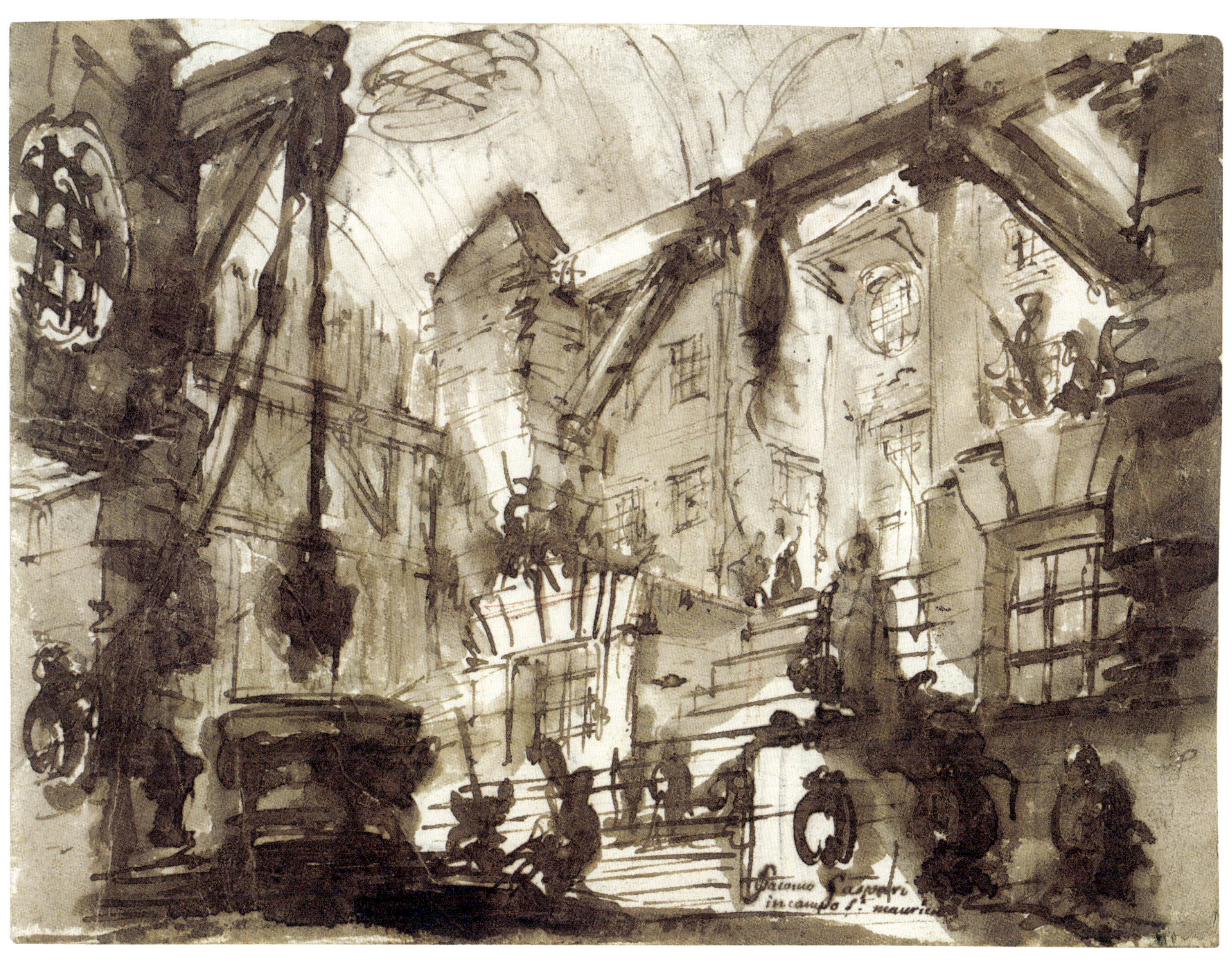

Giovanni Gasparri
in campo S.ᵗᵒ maurizio

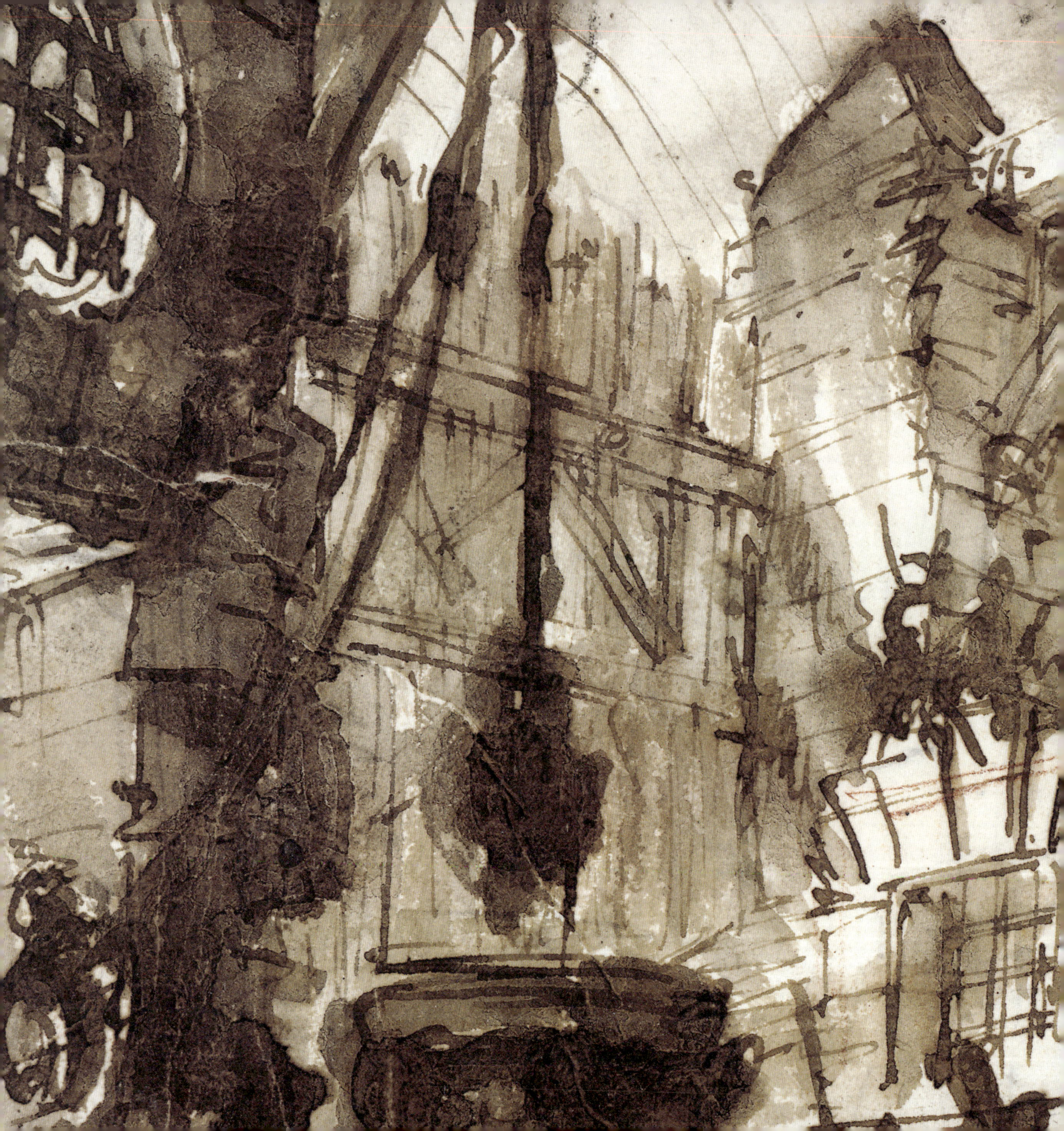

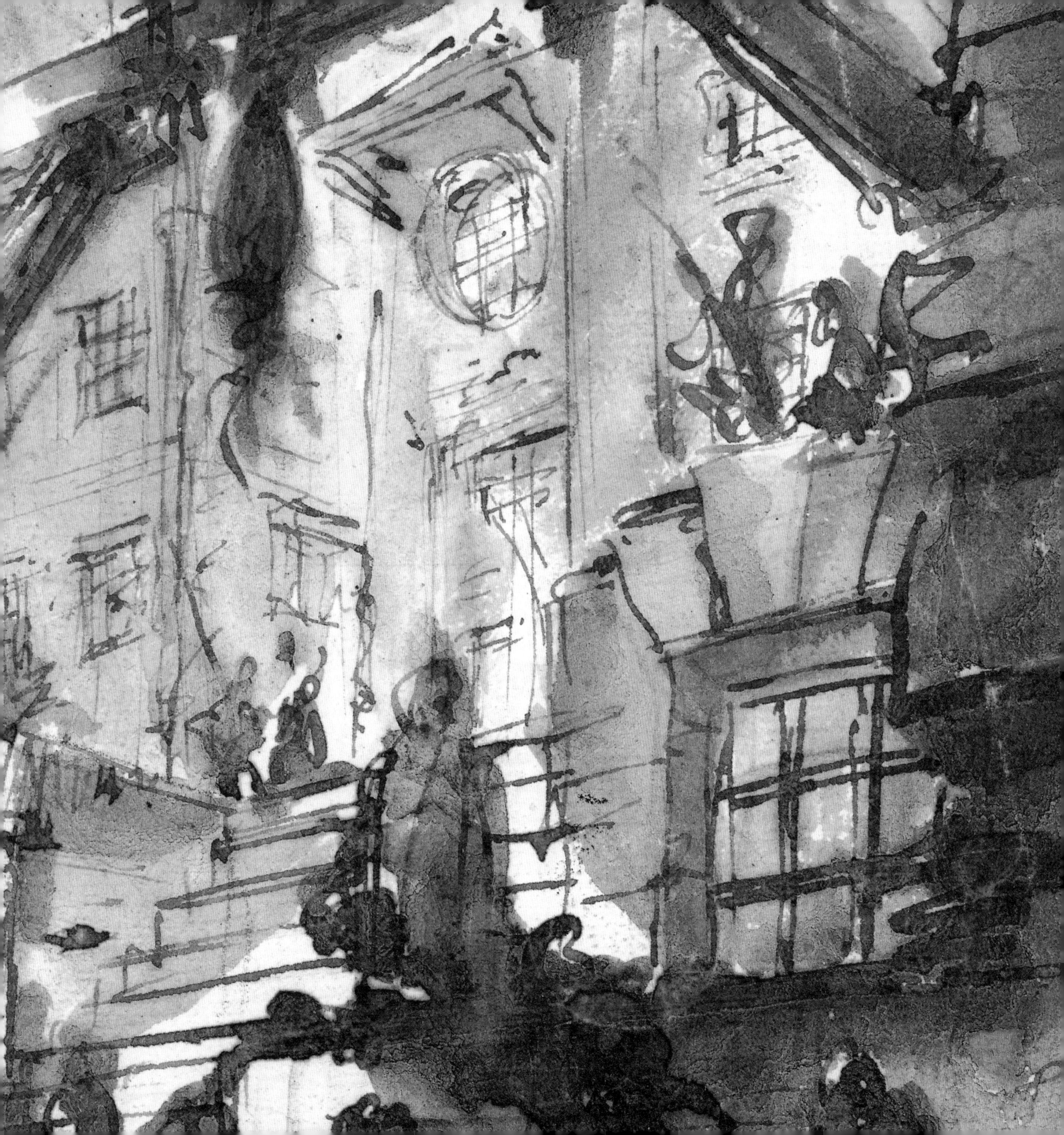

34.

Interior with arches, bridges and flights of steps

c. 1755–61
Pen and brown ink, brown wash, over red chalk
(some of the red chalk added over the wash),
with an accidental splash of green paint in the
upper right corner
178 × 242 mm (7⅛ × 9⅝ in.)
1908,0616.8
Provenance: Probably William Gott; and by
descent to his son, John Gott, Bishop of Truro;
his sale, Sotheby's, London, 20 March 1908,
part of lot 172
Exhibitions: London 1968, part of no. 23; London
1978, no. 196; Sheffield 1988, no. 18; London
and elsewhere 2002–4, no catalogue
Literature: Thomas 1954, no. 9; Seckler 1962,
fig. 19; Scott 1975, p. 53, fig. 61; Robison 1986a,
p. 41, fig. 49 and under no. 40; Gavuzzo-Stewart
1999, p. 84, fig. 43

This is undoubtedly connected to the
Carceri, particularly to plate 14, *The Gothic
arch*. Stylistically, however, it is much
broader and more expressive than
Piranesi's works of the late 1740s, and the
use of red chalk is much more forceful.
It is closer in technique to works of the
late 1750s, and it is likely that it relates to
Piranesi's reworking of the *Carceri* ready
for their reissue in considerably reworked
form in 1761. A comparable drawing, also
linked to a prison interior with stairs and
Gothic arches, and probably dating from
the same later period, is in the National
Gallery of Scotland (Fig. 26).

Fig. 26
An imaginary prison
c. 1755–61
Pen, brown ink and wash over
black chalk
217 × 252 mm (8⅝ × 10 in.)
National Galleries of Scotland

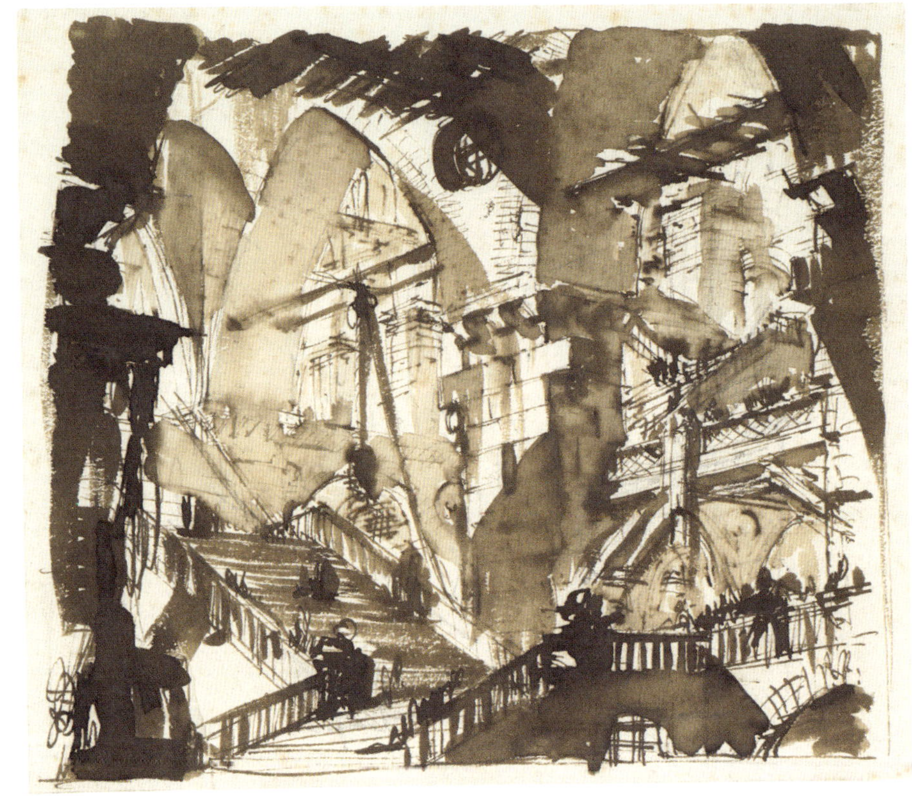

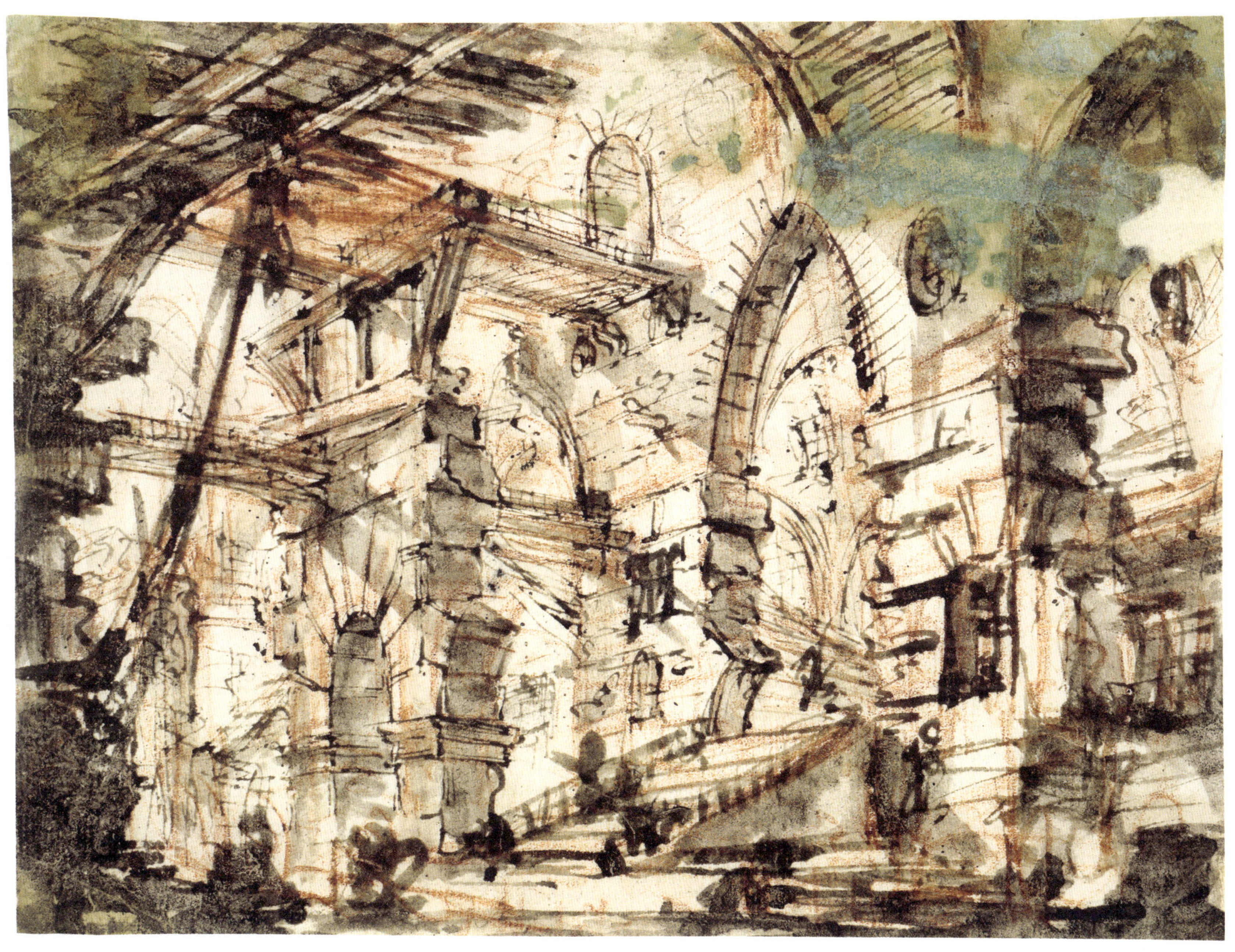

35.

A piazza seen through a curving colonnade

c. 1755–62

Pen and brown ink, brown wash
(some ink gall losses)
265 × 410 mm (10½ × 16¼ in.)
1908,0616.46

Provenance: Probably William Gott; and by descent to his son, John Gott, Bishop of Truro; his sale, Sotheby's, London, 20 March 1908, part of lot 172

Exhibitions: London 1968, part of no. 27; Venice 1978, no. 27; London 1978, no. 21, pp. 17–18; Southampton and Manchester 1995, no. 162

Literature: Thomas 1954, no. 25; Thomas 1957, p. 11; Vogt-Göknil 1958, p. 25, fig. 11; Murray 1971, p. 21, fig. 19; Scott 1975, fig. 51

Like cat. 37, this has been connected to Filippo Juvarra's stage designs for Filippo Amadei's opera *Teodosio il Giovane* (published in 1711), and linked to Scene 4.[47] There does appear to be a connection, especially in the articulation of the curving arcade on the left, although Piranesi seems to use Juvarra's design as a starting point for a *capriccio*, in which the figures are, as usual, miniaturized to emphasize the scale of the architecture.

The British Museum drawing certainly does not seem to have been made with the aim of creating a scene set. Stylistically it is close not only to cat. 37 but also to cat. 36, which is not connected to *Teodosio* but shows Piranesi exploring similar motifs and architectural constructions inspired by a real place, the crossing of St Peter's. It is possible that Piranesi may have come into contact with a cache of drawings by Juvarra in Rome at this period: this would explain the sudden inspiration drawn from his stage sets, and perhaps the adoption of a more forceful drawing style, which appears to be influenced by that of the earlier artist.

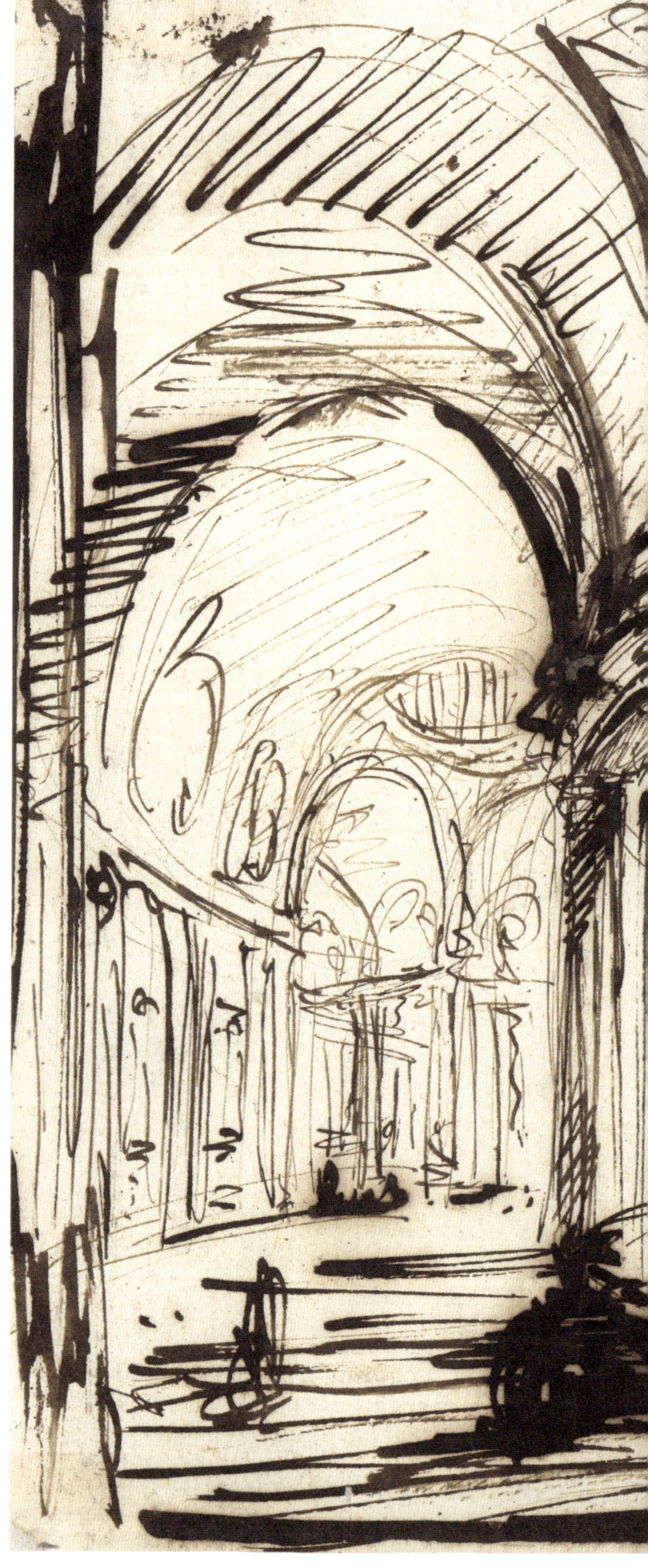

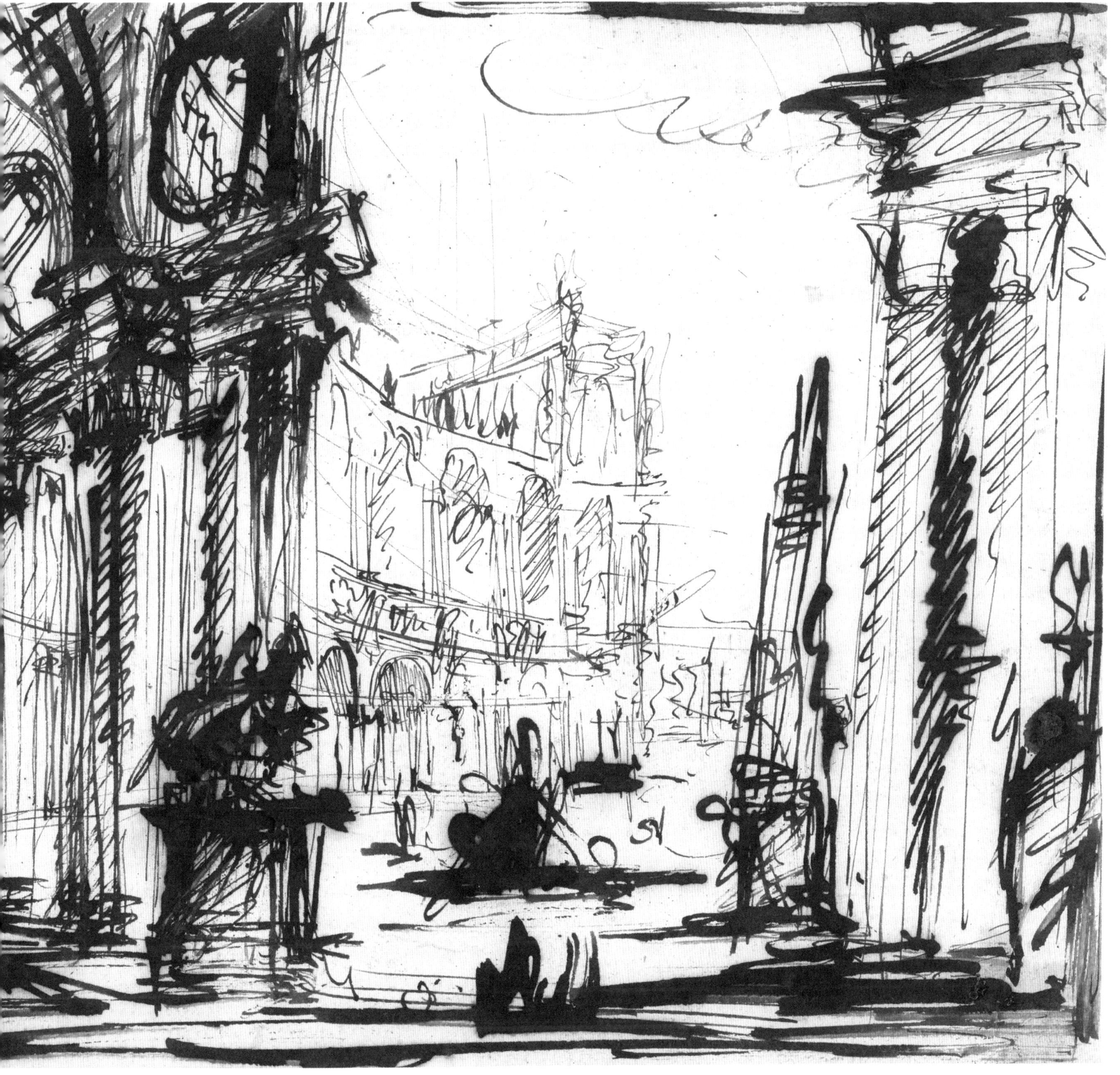

36.

Architectural interior with a crossing beneath a dome

c. 1755–62

Pen and brown ink (some ink gall losses)

199 × 275 mm (7⅞ × 10⅞ in.)

1908,0616.6

Provenance: Probably William Gott; and by descent to his son, John Gott, Bishop of Truro; his sale, Sotheby's, London, 20 March 1908, part of lot 172

Exhibitions: London 1968, part of no. 27; London 1978, no. 102b; Venice 1978, no. 29

Literature: Hind 1911–12, no. 15; Leporini 1925, p. 74, pl. 271; Corfiato 1951, p. 12, no. 53; Thomas 1954, under no. 25; Thomas 1957, p. 11

This drawing has been linked to Piranesi's print *The crossing of St Peter's* from the *Vedute di Roma* (Fig. 27), a series on which he worked from 1747 until his death. However, there are too many differences for it to be directly related: the high altar and baldacchino are omitted, while arched openings pierce the walls above the cornices and Piranesi uses a theatrical *scena per angolo* viewpoint to add drama. It is more likely to be a parallel experiment on the same theme.

The basic composition must have been inspired by St Peter's, but the drawing is proof of Piranesi's gift for using existing buildings as starting points for grandiose, magnificent fantasy structures, emphasizing their vast scale and the flow of space. Stylistically it belongs to the late 1750s or early 1760s, with thick lines drawn with the side of the nib and scribbled hatching. The human figures in the scene are drawn with a remarkable level of abstraction and are shown on a miniature scale, to emphasize the monumentality of the interior. A similar combination of receding barrel-vaulted corridors, arches and oval niches appears in cat. 37.

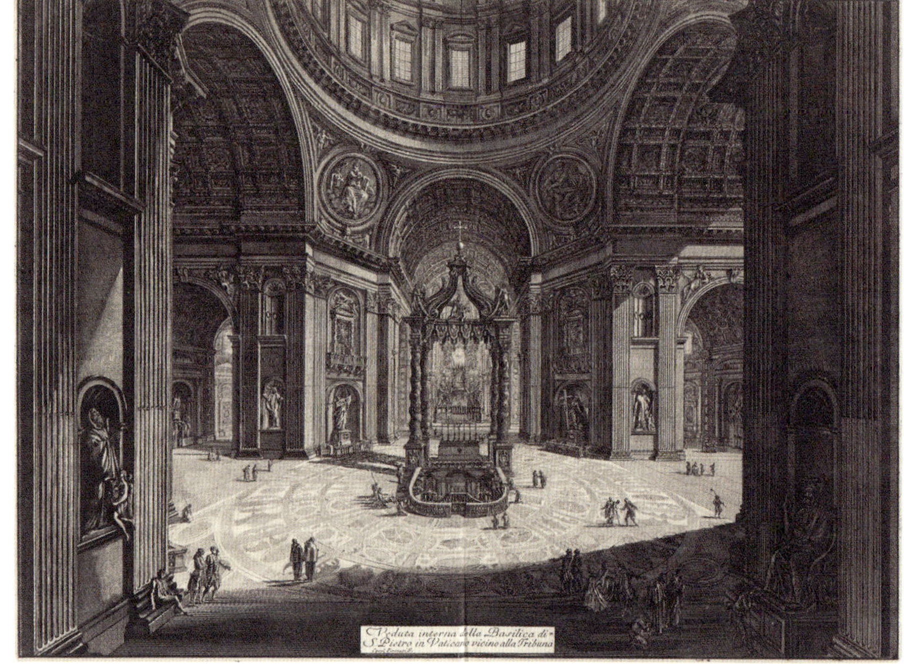

Fig. 27
The crossing of St Peter's
From the *Vedute di Roma*
1773
Etching
485 × 675 mm (19⅛ × 26⅝ in.)
Yale University Art Gallery

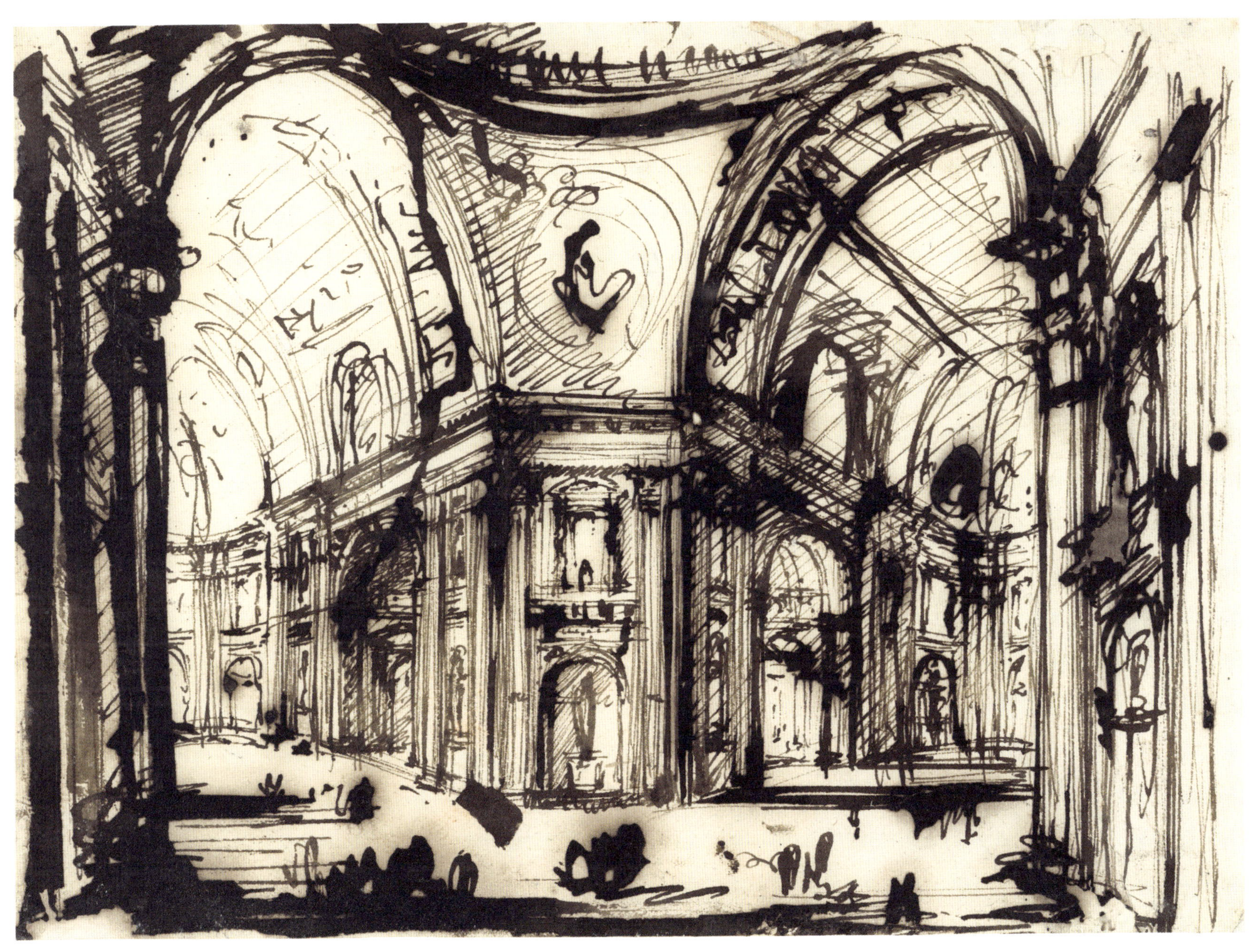

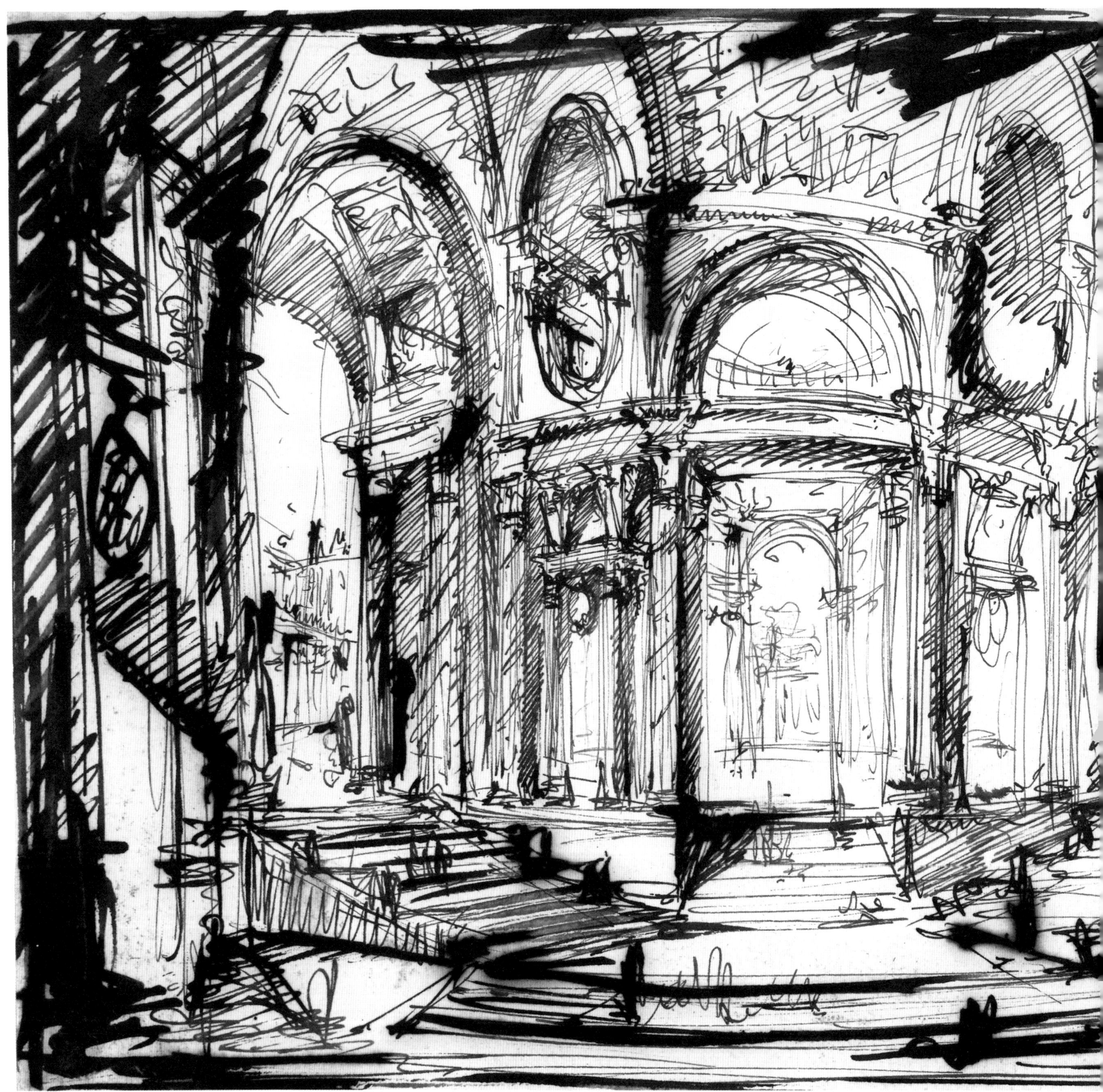

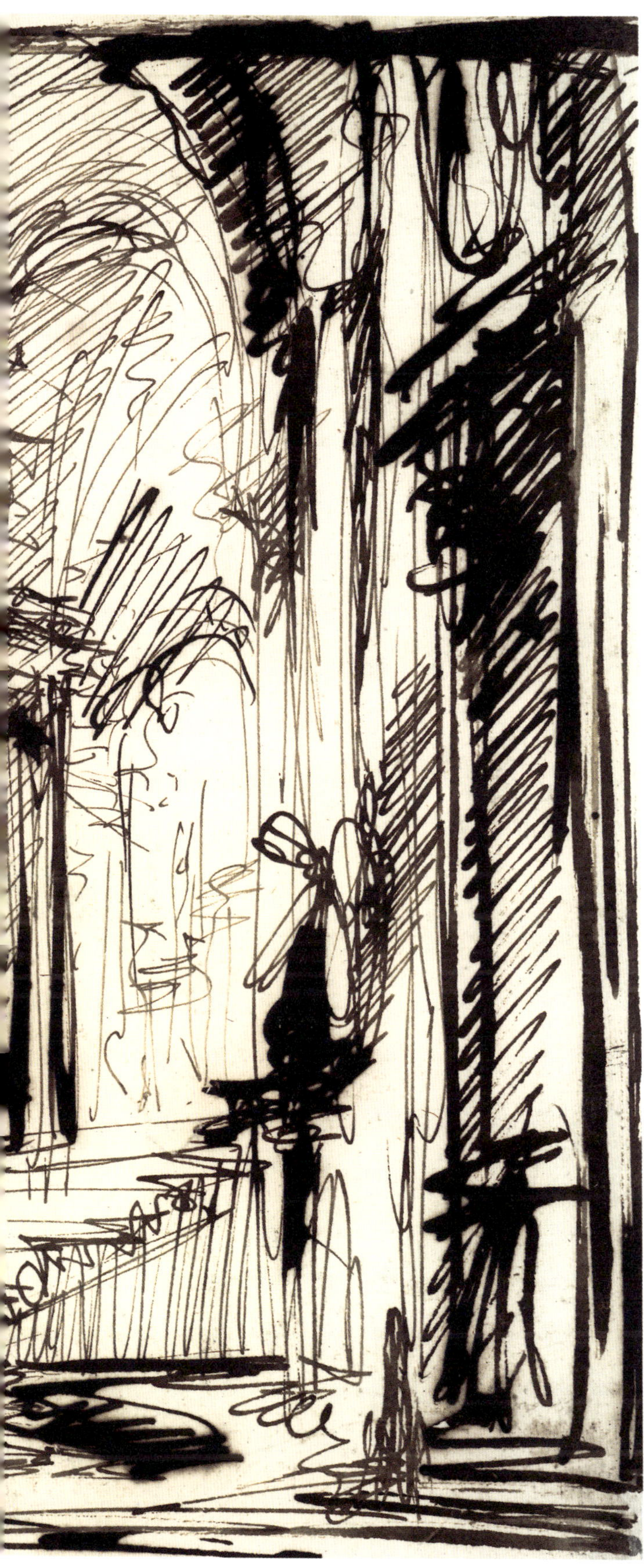

37.

Interior of a circular building with arches and flights of steps

c. 1755–62

Pen and brown ink

270 × 410 mm (10¾ × 16¼ in.)

1908,0616.39

Provenance: Probably William Gott; and by descent to his son, John Gott, Bishop of Truro; his sale, Sotheby's, London, 20 March 1908, part of lot 172

Exhibitions: London 1968, part of no. 27; Venice 1978, no. 28; Hull and London 1995, no. 163; Poole and elsewhere 2016–18, no. 53

Literature: Thomas 1954, under no. 25

Although similar in spirit and motifs to cat. 36 and thus probably dating from the same period, this drawing cannot be related to *The crossing of St Peter's* from the *Vedute di Roma*. It has usually been described as a free adaptation of a design by Filippo Juvarra for Scene 10 of Filippo Amadei's opera *Teodosio il Giovane* (1711), but the connection is loose at best. The style of the drawing, with its scribbled hatching and powerful ink lines, makes it clear that it must date from the 1750s or 1760s. Although the residual influence of Juvarra cannot be discounted (see also cat. 35), it seems more likely that Piranesi conceived this composition as an independent fantasy, based around the play of curved forms.

38.

View of the Portico of Gaius and Lucius, at the intersection of the Vicus Jugurius with the Via del Teatro di Marcello, Rome

c. 1760–65

Black chalk, squared for transfer in black chalk

500 × 700 mm (19¾ × 27⅝ in.)

1905,1110.65

Provenance: Ludwig Hermann Philippi (L. 1335)

Exhibitions: London 1968, part of no. 35; London 1978, no. 156

An unusually highly finished drawing from Piranesi's late period, this is not connected to any known print, despite the squaring, which suggests that the composition may have been transferred. The viewpoint chosen for the composition, with its oblique setting similar to that used in Piranesi's *Campo Marzio dell'Antica Roma* from the *Vedute di Roma* (1762),[48] in which the portico appears, but the correspondence is not exact. It is most uncharacteristic in technique, as at this period Piranesi tended to use red chalk for his large-scale drawings. However, the handling does appear to be authentic, as do the tiny gesticulating figures who populate the scene. Piranesi's unusual care suggests that this may have been a model drawing intended for one of his assistants or children, who would have needed crisp, clear guidance rather than the more expressive drawings he made for his own use.

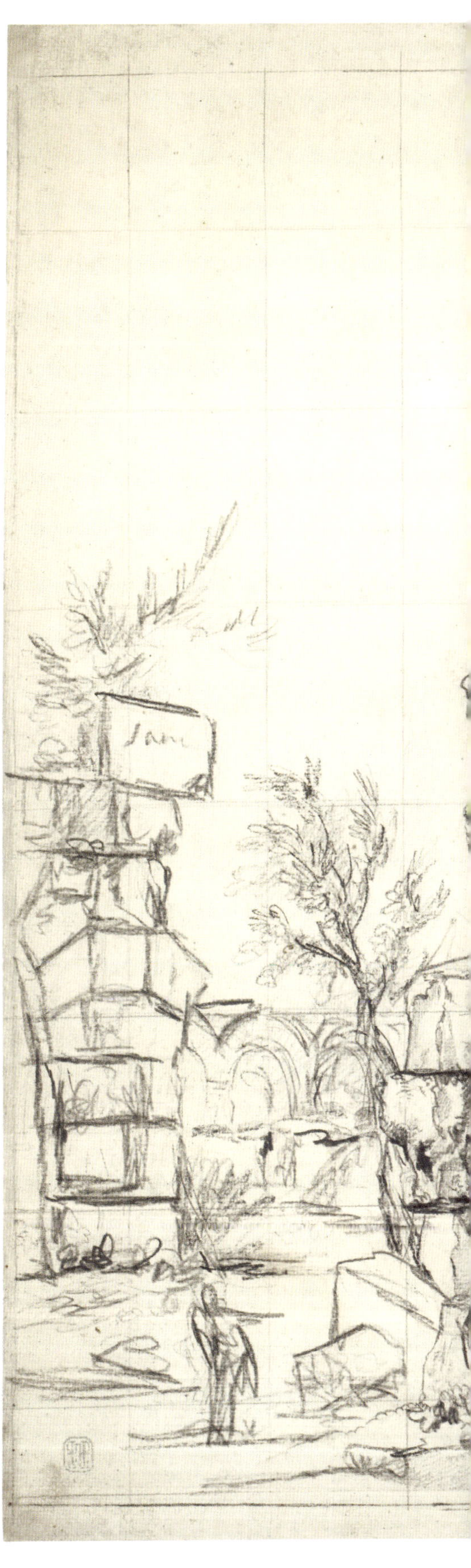

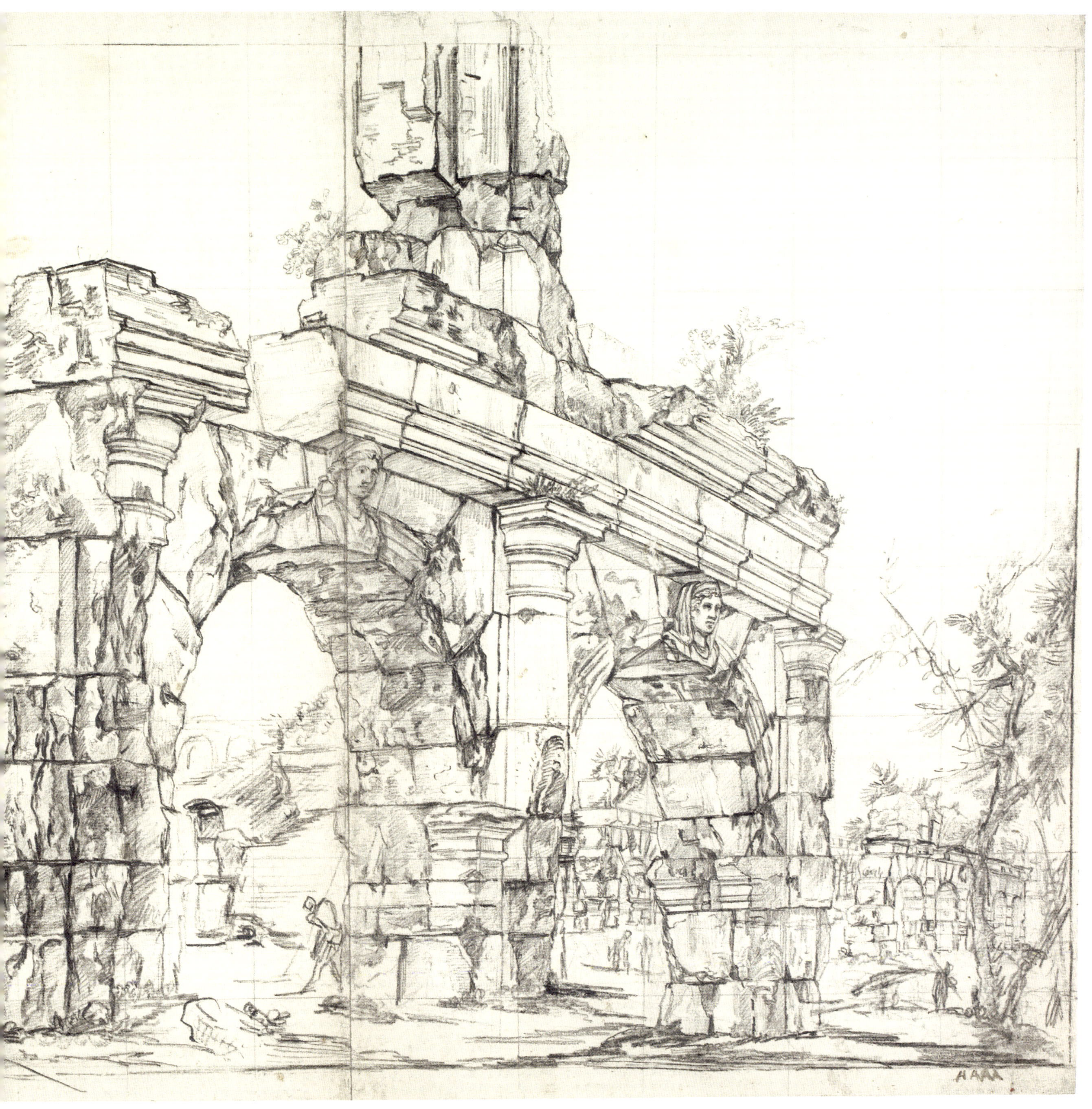

39.

A forum with triumphal arches (recto); Fragment of a print price list (verso)

c. 1760–65

Pen and brown ink

100 × 151 mm (4 × 6 in.)

1908,0616.24

Provenance: Probably William Gott; and by descent to his son, John Gott, Bishop of Truro; his sale, Sotheby's, London, 20 March 1908, part of lot 172

Exhibitions: London 1968, part of no. 27; London 1978, no. 44a

Literature: Corfiato 1951, p. 3; Thomas 1954, under no. 24

These three drawings (cats. 39–41) show Piranesi exploring variations on the same theme: a triumphal arch seen at an oblique angle and from a low viewpoint. A similar structure, with the arch fully integrated into surrounding architecture, also appears in Piranesi's *Architectural fantasy* in the Morgan Library (Fig. 25), in which the design is brought to a higher level of finish. Cats. 40 and 41 have additional layers of iron-gall ink, which have now darkened and lost their tonal subtlety, making the draughtsmanship look broader than it would have originally. The verso shows a fragment of a price list for volumes of prints.

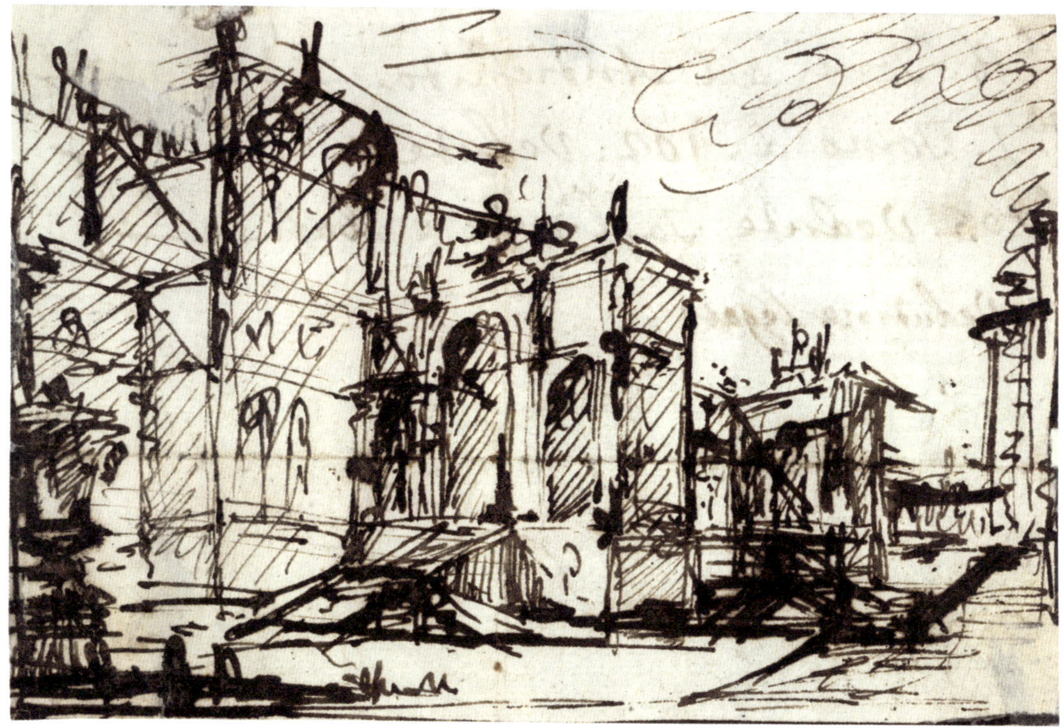

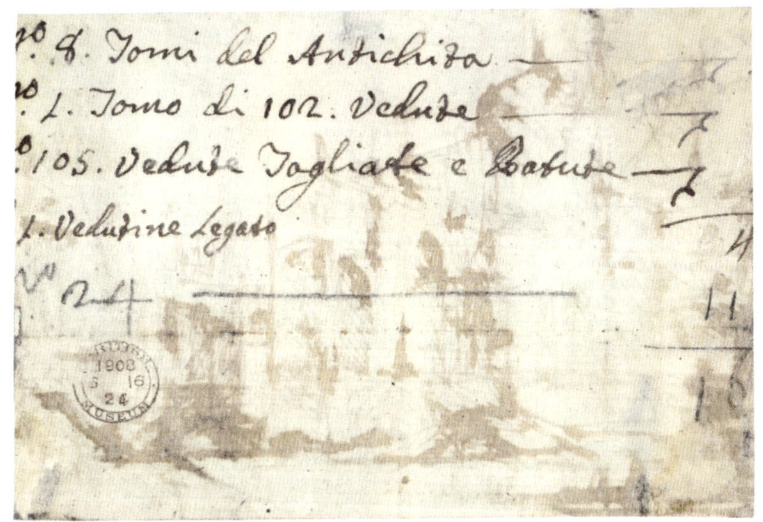

40.

A triumphal arch with flights of steps leading up to it

c. 1760–65

Pen and brown ink (iron gall damage)

123 × 178 mm (4⅞ × 7⅛ in.)

1908,0616.25

Provenance: Probably William Gott; and by descent to his son, John Gott, Bishop of Truro; his sale, Sotheby's, London, 20 March 1908, part of lot 172

Exhibitions: London 1968, part of no. 27; London 1978, no. 44b

Literature: Corfiato 1951, p. 9; Thomas 1954, under no. 24

See cat. 39 for caption

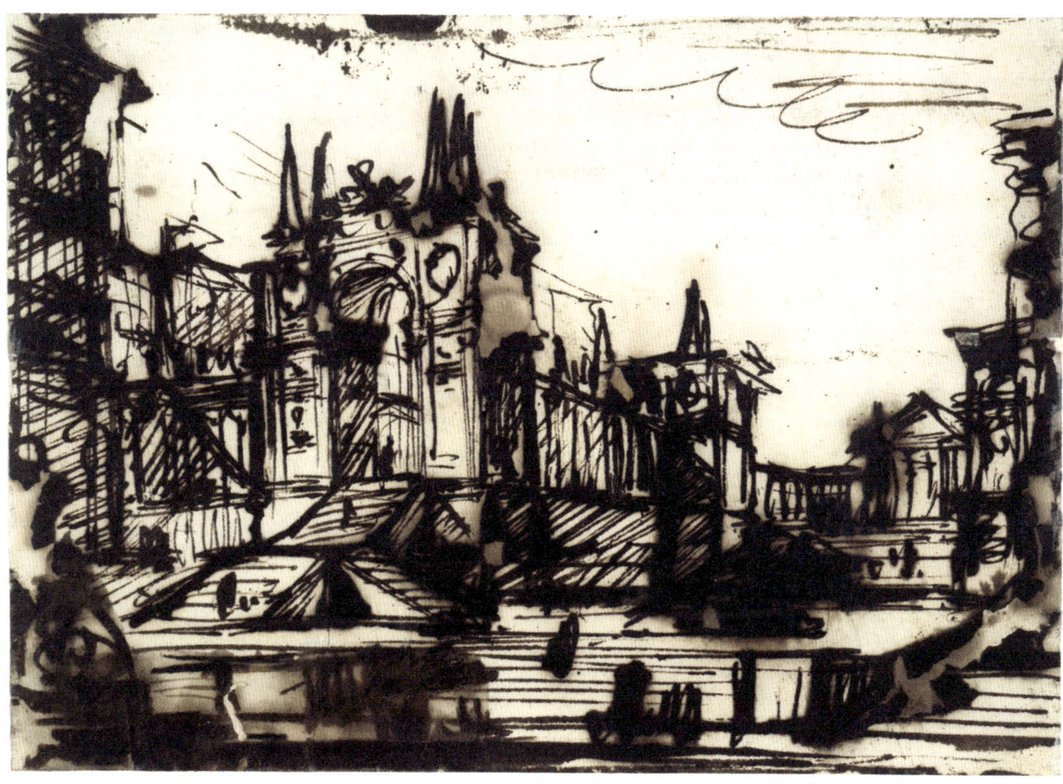

41.

A triumphal arch flanked by two obelisks

c. 1760–65

Pen and brown ink (iron gall damage)

123 × 191 mm (4⅞ × 7⅝ in.)

1908,0616.26

Provenance: Probably William Gott; and by descent to his son, John Gott, Bishop of Truro; his sale, Sotheby's, London, 20 March 1908, part of lot 172

Exhibitions: London 1968, part of no. 27; London 1978, no. 44c

Literature: Corfiato 1951, p. 12; Thomas 1954, no. 24

See cat. 39 for caption

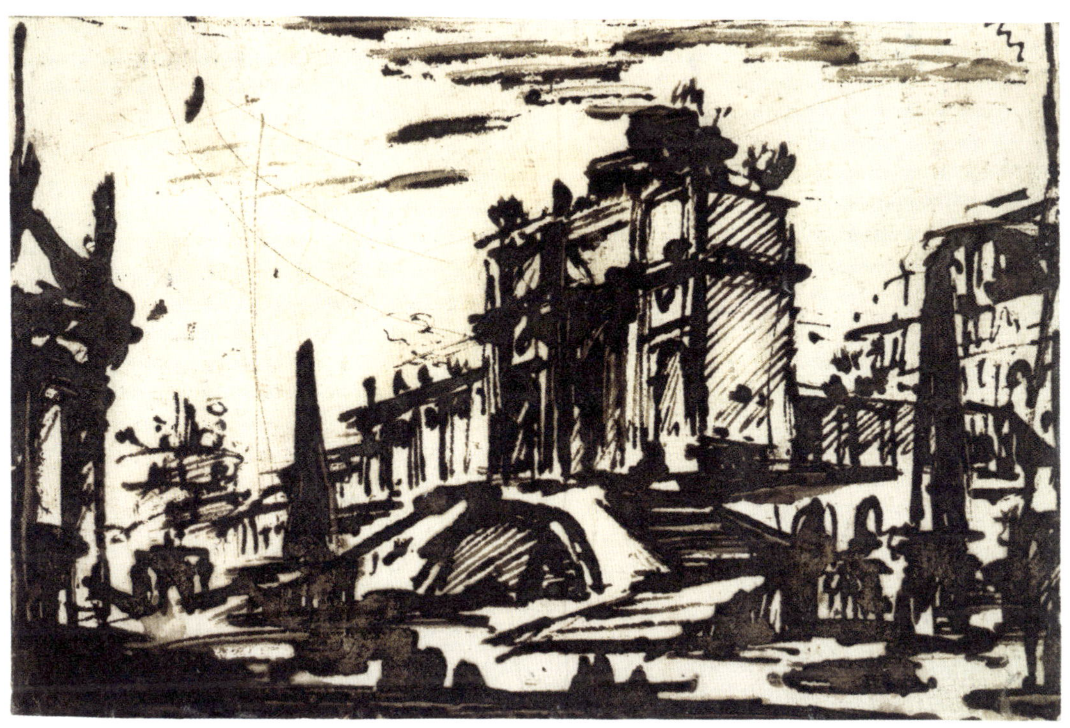

The Campidoglio, Rome (recto; overleaf); Interior of the Pantheon, Rome (verso; opposite)

c. 1760–61

Red chalk, over black chalk and stylus indications, touched with pen and ink (recto); red and black chalk (verso)

404 × 701 mm (16 × 27⅝ in.)

1908,0616.45

Provenance: Probably William Gott; and by descent to his son, John Gott, Bishop of Truro; his sale, Sotheby's, London, 20 March 1908, part of lot 172

Exhibitions: London 1968, part of no. 31; London 1978, no. 88; London 1984, no. 40; Hull and London 1995, no. 164; London and elsewhere 2002–4, no catalogue; Bonn 2012–13

Literature: Hind 1922, under no. 39; Scott 1975, fig. 311

The only Piranesi drawing in the British Museum in red chalk, this is a characteristic example of the late drawings for the large-scale *Vedute di Roma* series, on which Piranesi worked from 1747 until the very end of his life. The recto (illustrated overleaf) is a preparatory study for a print of the Campidoglio,[49] which is on the same scale and viewed from the same direction as the finished etching. Touches of brown ink pick out the classical sculptures arranged along the balustrade. The print has been dated to 1761,[50] which suggests that the drawing must have been executed around 1760–61. Although drawn in chalk, the essence of Piranesi's style is still clearly visible in elements such as the forceful hatching in the sky, and the addition of darker elements in the foreground and on the right-hand side to act as framing devices.

The verso (opposite) shows an upright view of the Pantheon, which emphasizes the vastness of the space far more effectively than Piranesi's roughly contemporary studies of the same subject (cat. 46). This drawing does not relate to any of Piranesi's etchings of the temple. The concept of showing the Pantheon in an upright format, from the edge, seen through a doorway or a screen of columns, was not original to Piranesi. It appears in paintings by Giovanni Paolo Panini, such as a view of 1732.[51]

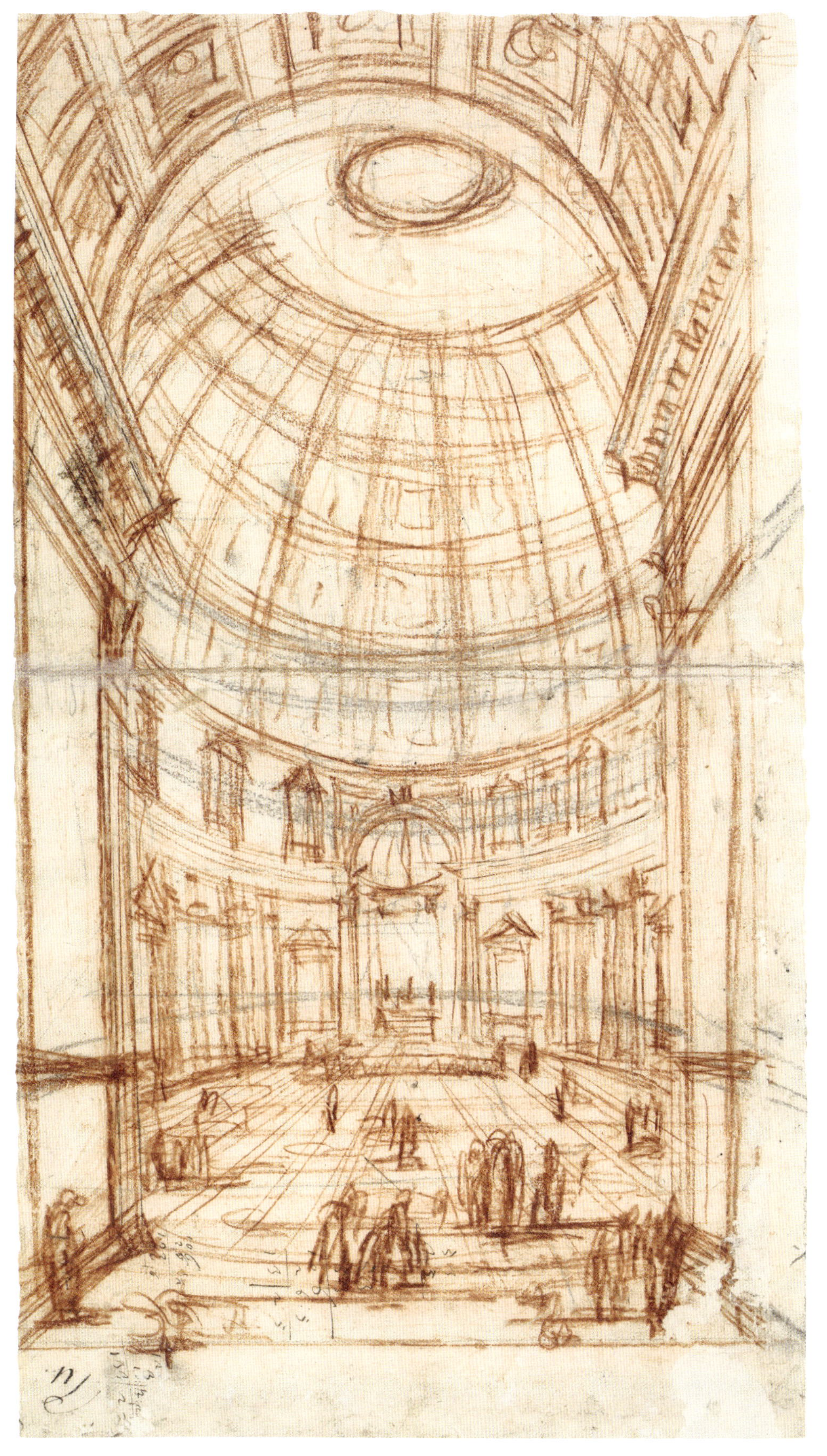

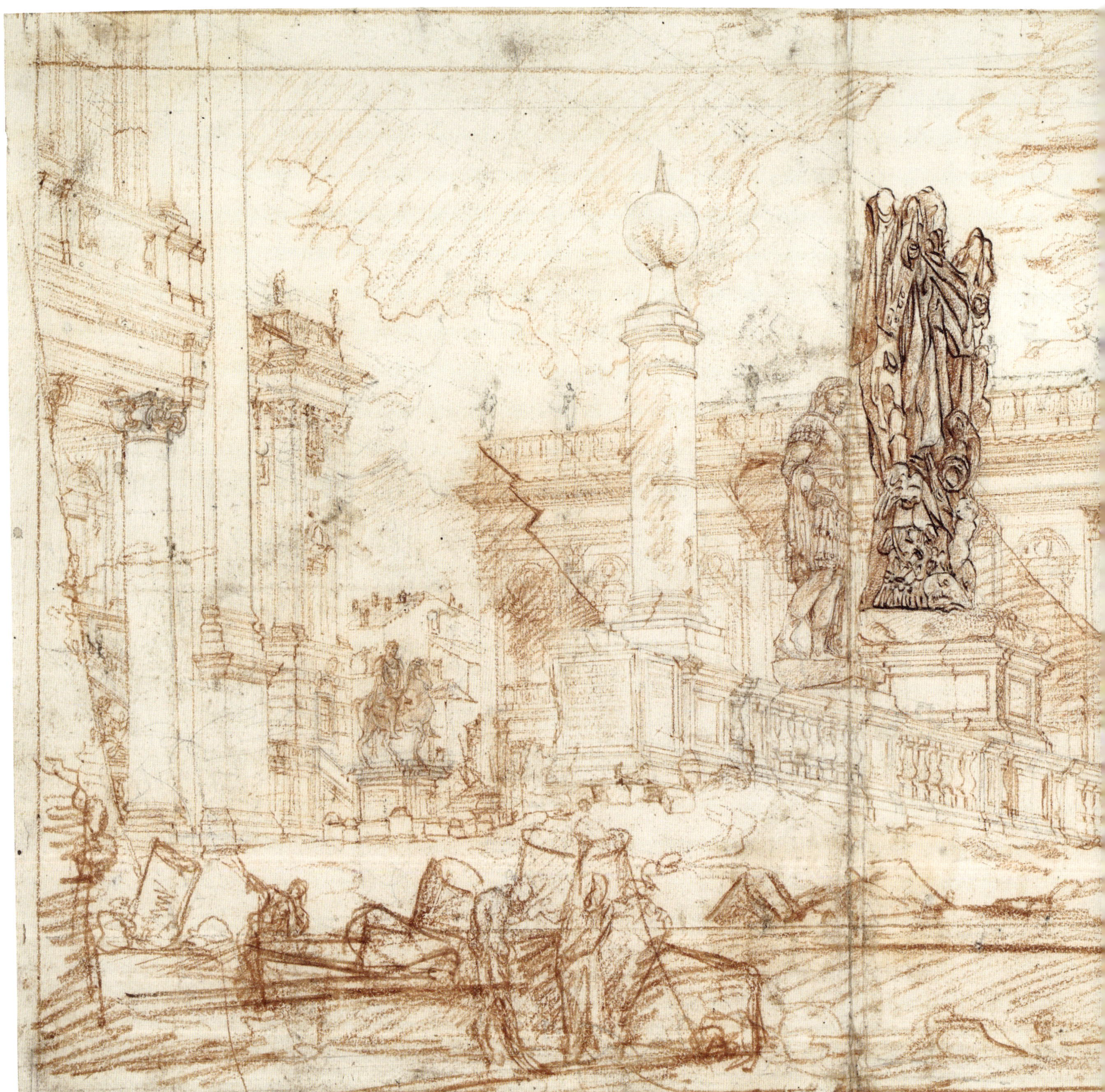

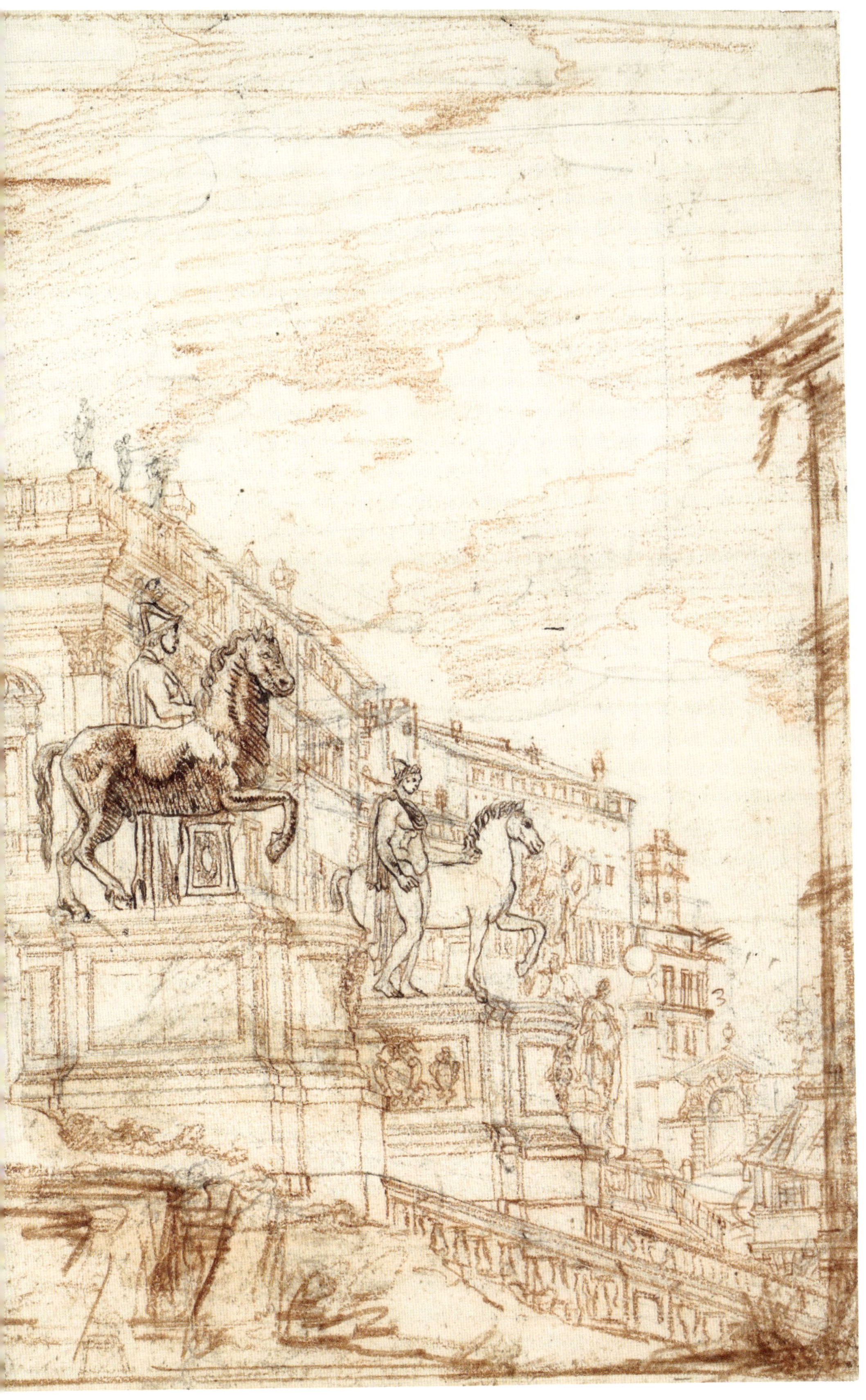

See cat. 42 for caption

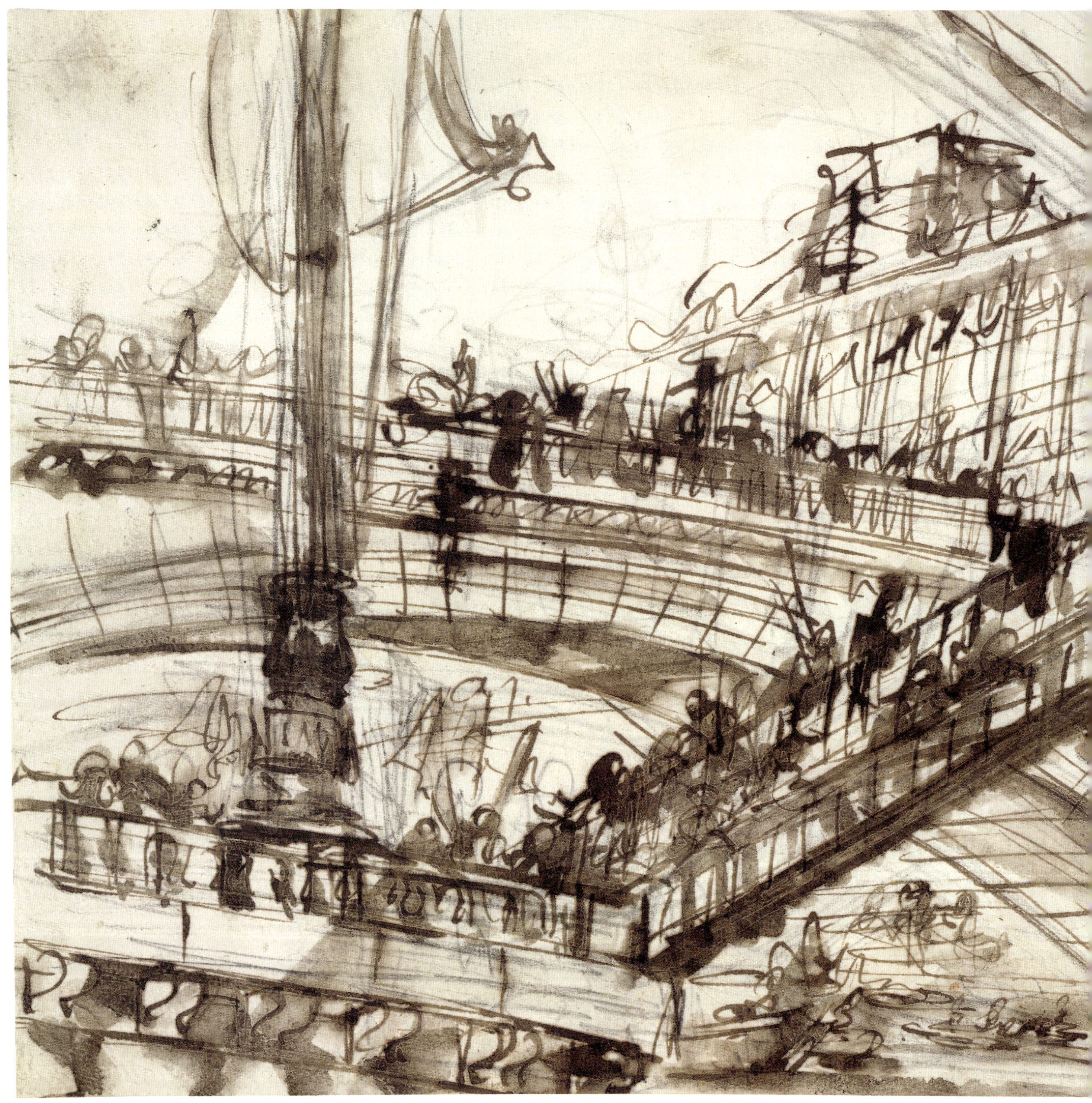

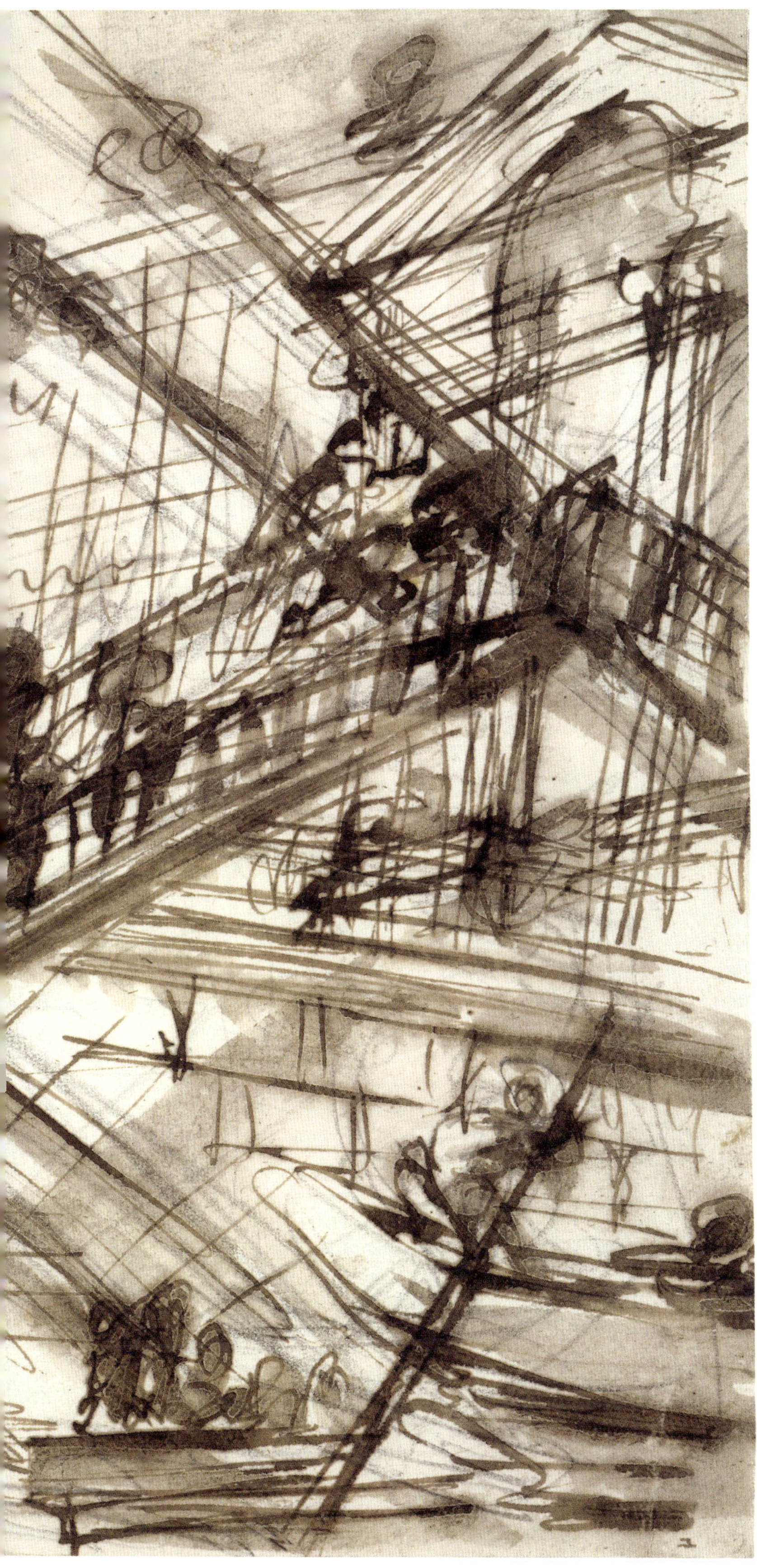

Architectural fantasy with boats beneath intersecting bridges

c. 1760–65

Pen and brown ink, with brown wash,
over black chalk

268 × 424 mm (10⅝ × 16¾ in.)

1908,0616.42

Provenance: Probably William Gott; and by
descent to his son, John Gott, Bishop of Truro;
his sale, Sotheby's, London, 20 March 1908,
part of lot 172

Exhibitions: London 1968, part of no. 32; London
1972, no. 300; Venice 1978, no. 19; London and
elsewhere 2002–4, no catalogue

Literature: Seckler 1962, p. 346, fig. 23;
Gavuzzo-Stewart 1999, pp. 86–87, fig. 46

In this loose and highly expressive drawing, bridges and walkways criss-cross in front of a palatial structure. The large arched bridge in the background is a motif that goes back to Piranesi's *Ponte magnifico* (Fig. 20) in the *Prima Parte*, but it is here dominated by the eccentric arrangement of walkways in the foreground. The staircase at the centre, in particular, does not seem to be satisfactorily anchored at either end, and Piranesi seems to have considered extending it back on itself at the top of the sheet, only to abandon the idea.

While this drawing repeats motifs from the *Carceri*,[52] its outdoor setting and the grandeur of the surrounding buildings set it apart from the claustrophobic interiors of either the first edition of 1749–50 or the second edition of 1761. However, stylistically it may well belong to the years around the reissue. No related print is known.

44.

**A standing man in profile (recto);
Fragment of a letter in the artist's
hand (verso)**

c. 1763–67
Pen and brown ink and brown wash
171 × 75 mm (6¾ × 3 in.)
2019,7047.2
Presented by Jean-Luc Baroni, in honour
of Hugo Chapman
Provenance: Henri Mayeux; Étienne Deyer;
J.M. Lannegrand d'Augimont (his collector's
mark, not in Lugt); Tajan, Paris, 3 May 2012,
lot 18; Galerie Terrades, Paris; Sotheby's,
28 March 2019, lot 118, where purchased
by Jean-Luc Baroni for the British Museum
Exhibitions: Paris 1971, no. 152

A new acquisition, presented to the
British Museum especially for this
exhibition, this is the first figure drawing
by Piranesi to enter the collection.
Piranesi made numerous such studies,
which he used as models for the
tiny figures that populate his prints,
emphasizing the exaggerated scale of
the architecture. The catalogue note for
the drawing in the 2019 auction catalogue
suggests a date in the mid-1760s, on
the basis of stylistic comparison to two
similar drawings of standing men.[53]

The sheet demonstrates Piranesi's
characteristic habit of reusing pieces
of paper in his studio: the versos of
his drawings show fragments of other
drawings, prints or proofs. In this case,
he has sketched the figure on the back
of a draft letter, trimming it to size
around the standing man.

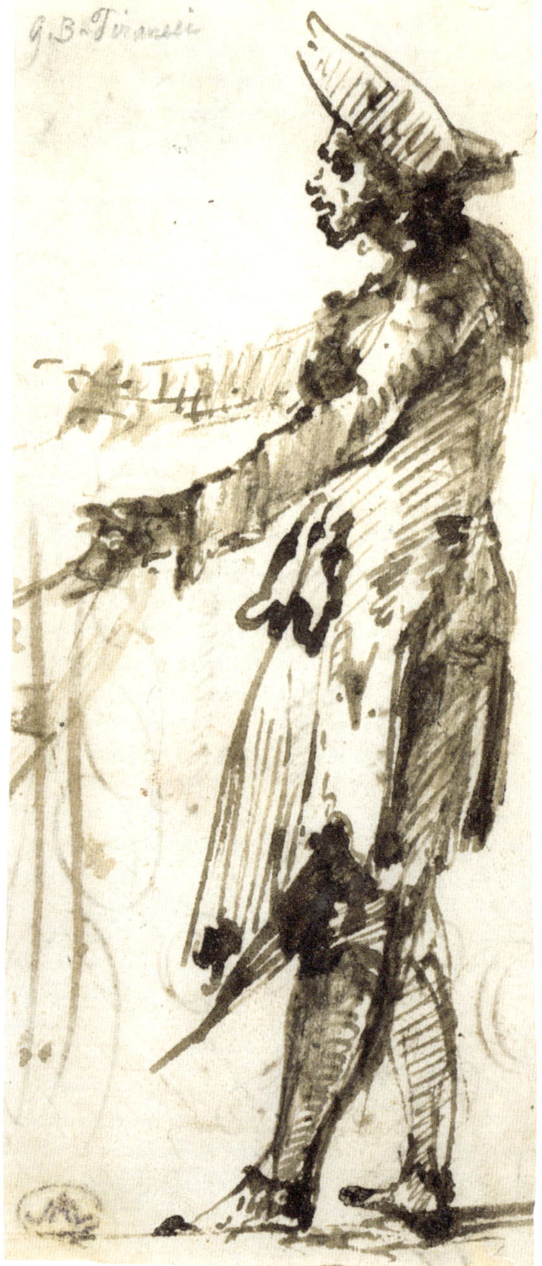

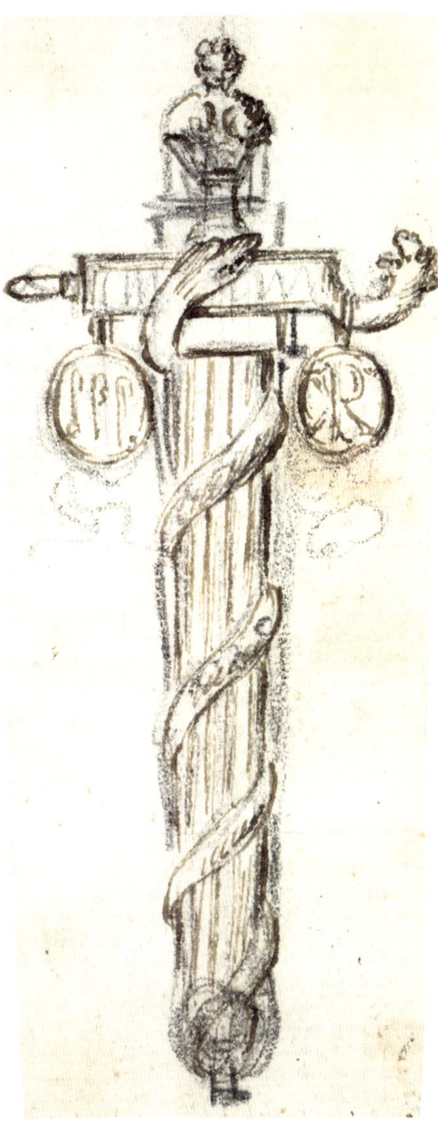

45.

Study of an ornamental sword for the decorative pilasters on the façade of Santa Maria del Priorato in Rome

c. 1764–65

Pen and brown ink, with revisions to the design in black chalk

147 × 55 mm (5⅞ × 2¼ in.)

1908,0616.34

Provenance: Probably William Gott; and by descent to his son, John Gott, Bishop of Truro; his sale, Sotheby's, London, 20 March 1908, part of lot 172

Exhibitions: London 1968, part of no. 37; London 1978, no. 310b; Venice 1978, no. 42; Rome 1998, no. 40; New York and Haarlem 2007–8, unnumbered

Literature: Thomas 1954, under no. 46; Wilton-Ely 1976, p. 220, fig. 14; Stampfle 1978, under no. 52

In 1764–65 Piranesi was commissioned to restore the church of the priory of the Order of Malta on the Aventine Hill. This is an unused design for the façade. The sword alludes to the order's military function, but the scabbard is encircled by a serpent, a reference to the order's responsibilities to heal and care for travellers. The serpent has further significance because the priory was said to have been built on the site of an ancient temple to Bona Dea, the goddess of healing, whose attribute was a snake; similarly, this area of the Aventine was once the site of the temple of Juno Regina, to whom snakes were sacred. A first, very brisk drawing in black chalk is succeeded by the precision of the design in brown ink.

The drawing was a first idea for the relief of a sword and scabbard on the right-hand side of the church's façade, which seems to have changed at a late stage: a copy of a plan for the full façade[54] shows the sword corresponding to this design. Only one other drawing for the façade is known (Fig. 28).

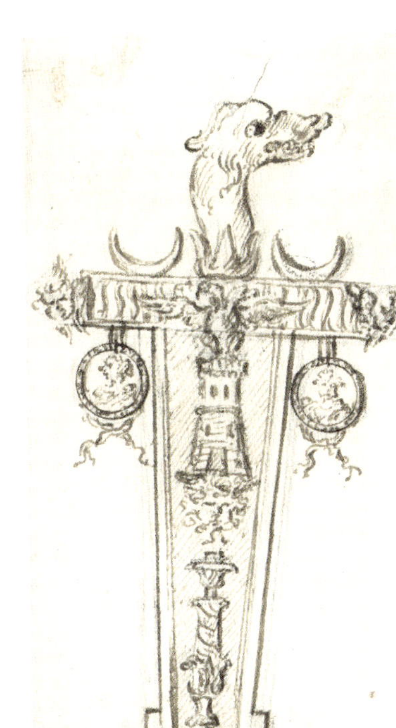

Sketch for ornamental scabbard for the façade of Santa Maria del Priorato

c. 1764–65

Pen and brown ink, over black chalk

159 × 72 mm (6⅜ × 2⅞ in.)

The Morgan Library and Museum, New York

46.

Three studies of the interior of the Pantheon

c. 1764–70

Pen and brown ink, on the reverse of a
fragment of a print by Giovanni Ottaviani
151 × 299 mm (6 × 11⅞ in.)
1908,0616.4

Provenance: Probably William Gott; and by
descent to his son, John Gott, Bishop of Truro;
his sale, Sotheby's, London, 20 March 1908,
part of lot 172
Exhibition: London 1968, part of no. 27

This drawing was lifted from its old
mount during conservation for this
exhibition, revealing that it had been
drawn on the reverse of a print fragment.
The print is identifiable as *Angelica and
Medoro* by Giovanni Ottaviani (1735–1808),
plate 26 in the *Raccolta di alcuni disegni
del Barberi da Cento detto il Guercino* (1764),
a series of etchings after drawings by
Giovanni Francesco Barbieri (1591–1666)
and other masters. Piranesi himself
published the series, which was largely
made by other printmakers under his
direction: he etched only two plates and
the frontispiece.[55] The connection to the
print means that the drawing must postdate
1764, although it was previously dated to
an earlier period on stylistic grounds.

Probably made on the spot, these small
studies show the interior of the Pantheon
from subtly different angles, as Piranesi
progressively refined his concept. The
largest drawing, on the left, was made
first. Piranesi then added another view on
the right, boxing it in with framing lines,
before finally adding the densely worked
drawing at upper centre. The sheet has
been trimmed, as a fragment of a fourth
view at upper right makes clear. The
drawing cannot be related directly to
any of Piranesi's prints, although it dates
from the period when he was working
closely on his large-scale *Vedute di Roma*.
For another view of the Pantheon, in
which Piranesi adopts a vertical rather
than horizontal viewpoint, see cat. 42.

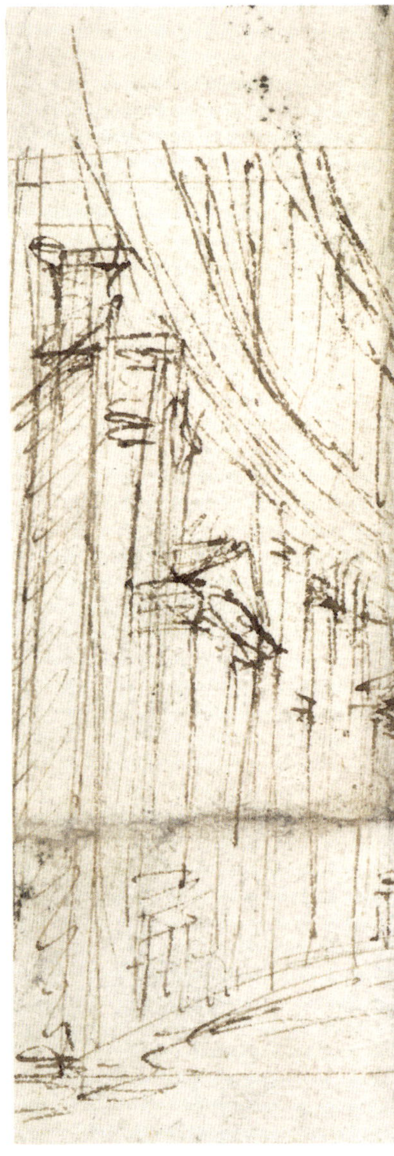

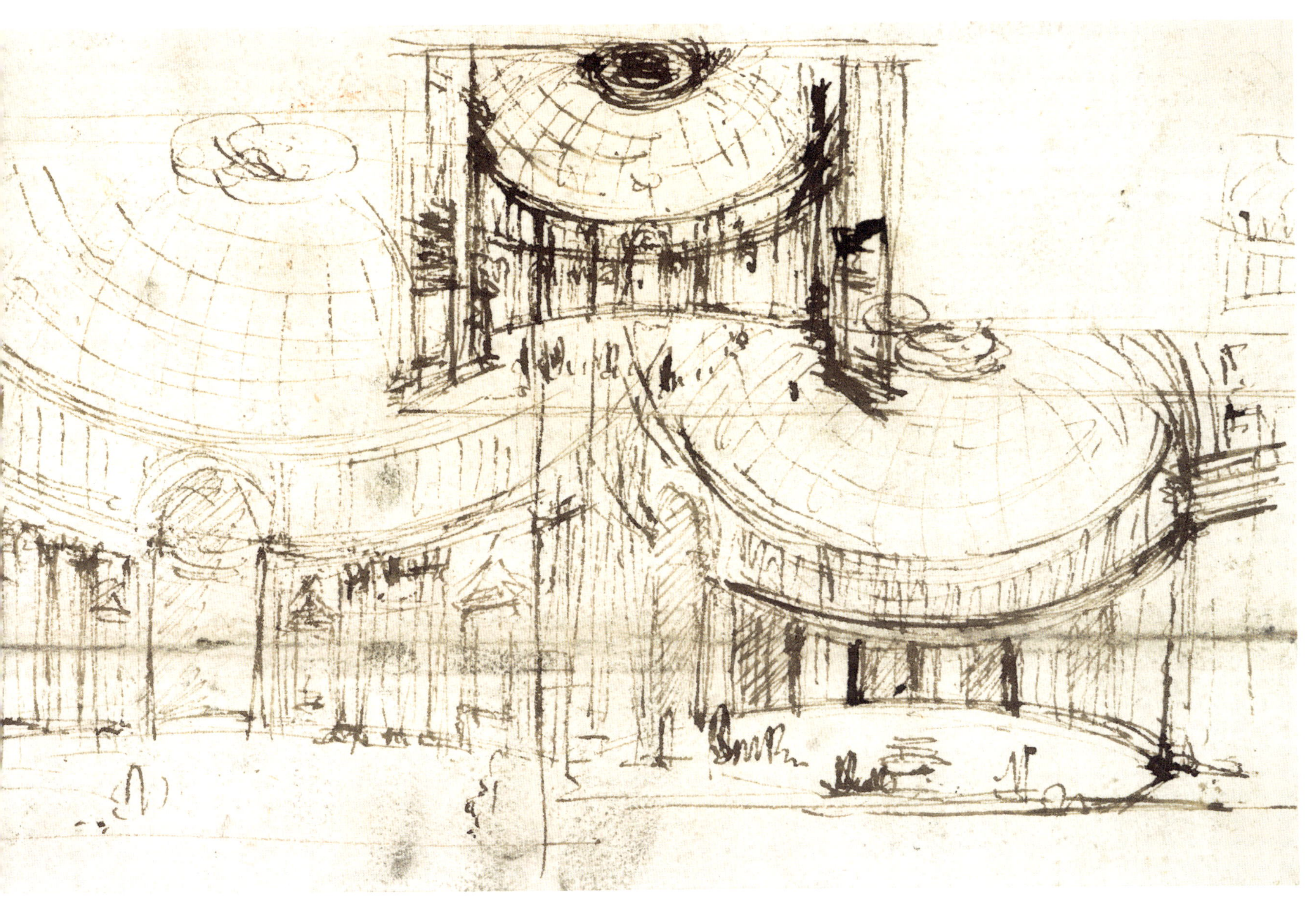

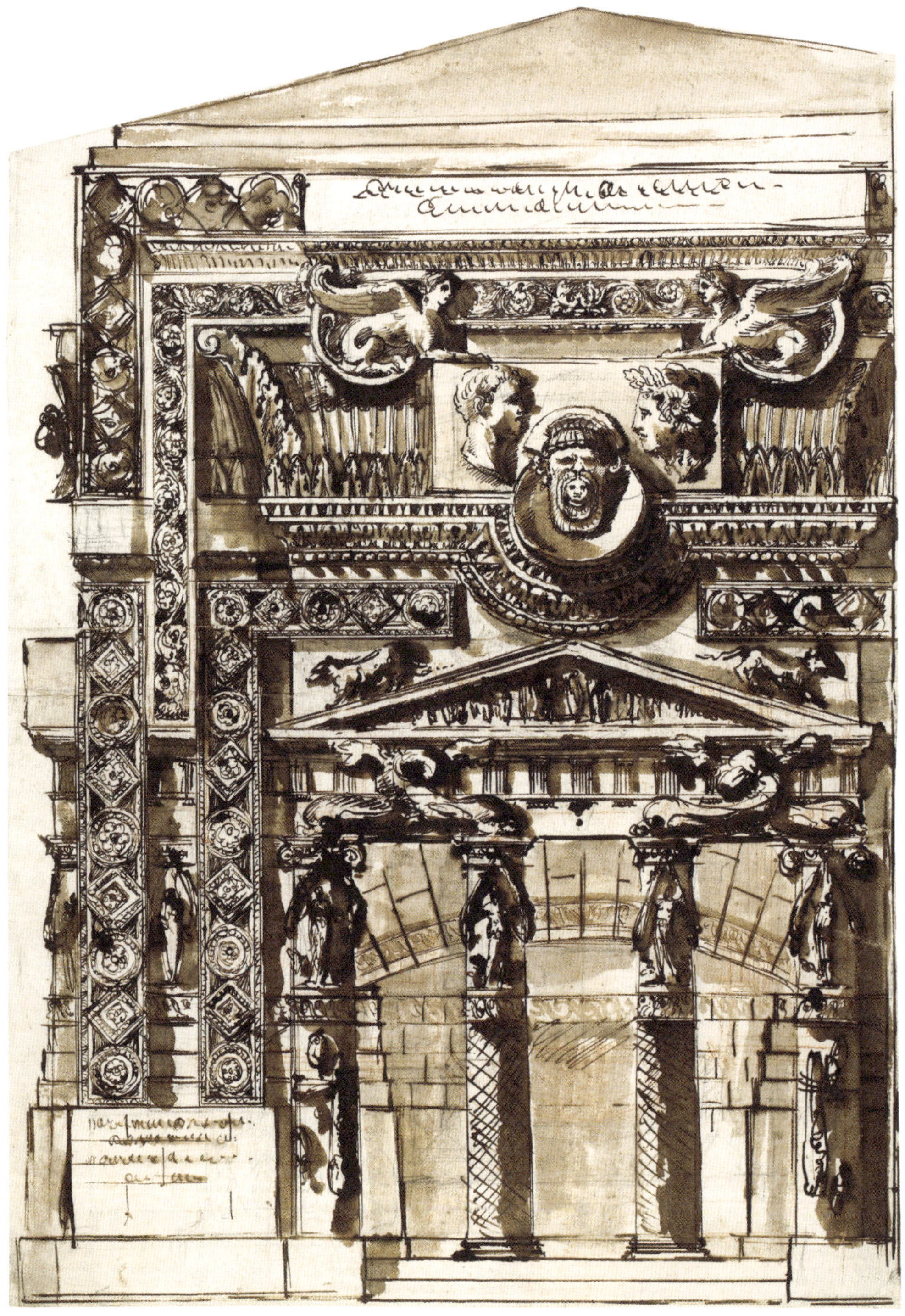

47.

Fantastical façade of an antique building (recto; left); Arcaded colonnades (verso; opposite)

c. 1765–69

Pen and brown ink, brown wash, over red and
black chalk (recto); pen and brown ink (verso)

666 × 473 mm (26¼ × 18⅝ in.)

1908,0616.44

Provenance: Probably William Gott; and by
descent to his son, John Gott, Bishop of Truro;
his sale, Sotheby's, London, 20 March 1908,
part of lot 172

Exhibitions: London 1968, part of no. 30; London
1972, no. 302; Rome, Dijon and Paris 1976,
no. 152; London 1978, no. 172; Venice 1978,
no. 37; London 1990, no catalogue; London
and elsewhere 2002–4, no catalogue

Literature: Scott 1975, fig. 184; Robison 1996,
p. 305, note 2, under no. 84

Though not related to a finished print, this drawing is certainly connected to Piranesi's addition of six new plates to his *Parere sul'Architettura* for its reissue in 1769. For unknown reasons, it was not turned into an etching for this series. One of the most impressive drawings by Piranesi in the British Museum, it uses dense contrasts of heavy brown ink to create an imposing melange of architectural elements from Roman, Egyptian and Etruscan cultures, designed to support Piranesi's belief in combining motifs into new and visionary creations. In his *Ragionamento Apologetico in difesa dell'Architettura Egizia e Toscana*, which accompanied the publication of the *Diverse maniere* (1769), he specifically argued that ornament was not disturbing in itself, but only when it lacked an overriding order. Here, symmetry dominates, keeping the various unrelated motifs in check, and giving the composition a sense of integrity. A drawing in the Morgan Library (Fig. 29) shows very similar sphinxes in volutes, at almost the same scale as they are drawn here.[56]

A very similar drawing in Washington (Fig. 3) was used for the additional plate V in the 1769 *Parere*. There are preparatory drawings for additional plates VI and VIII in the Kunstbibliothek, Berlin,[57] while a third drawing in Berlin appears, like the British Museum drawing, to be an unused design.[58]

The verso of the sheet shows a typically vigorous late architectural study of arched colonnades, which has not been connected to any finished work.

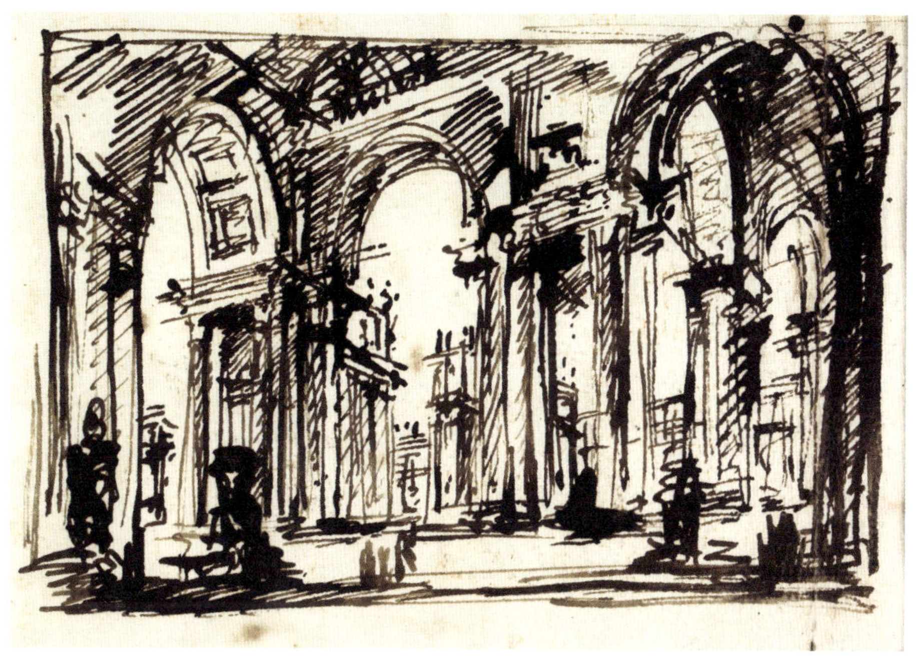

Fig. 29
Capital with confronted sphinxes
c. 1760–61
Red chalk, over black chalk
90 × 139 mm (3⅝ × 5½ in.)
The Morgan Library and Museum, New York

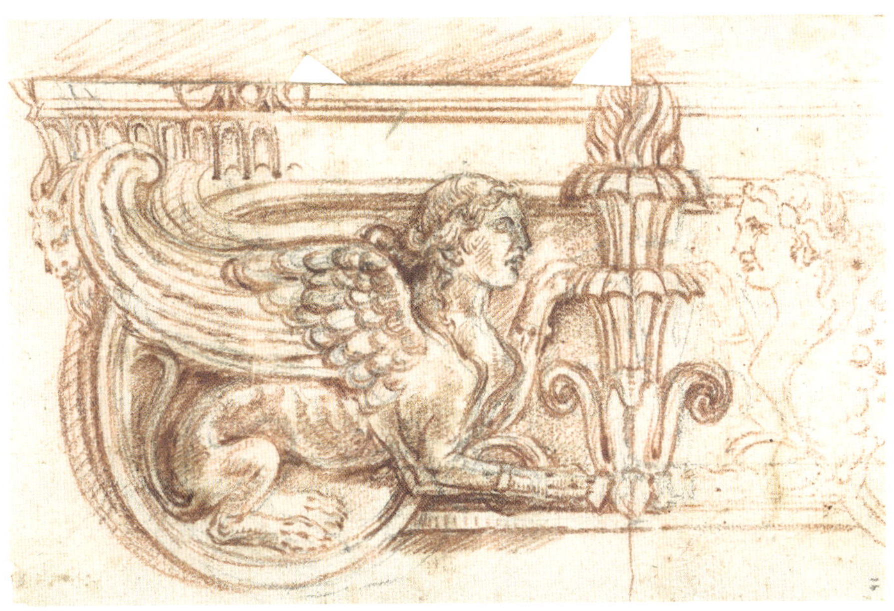

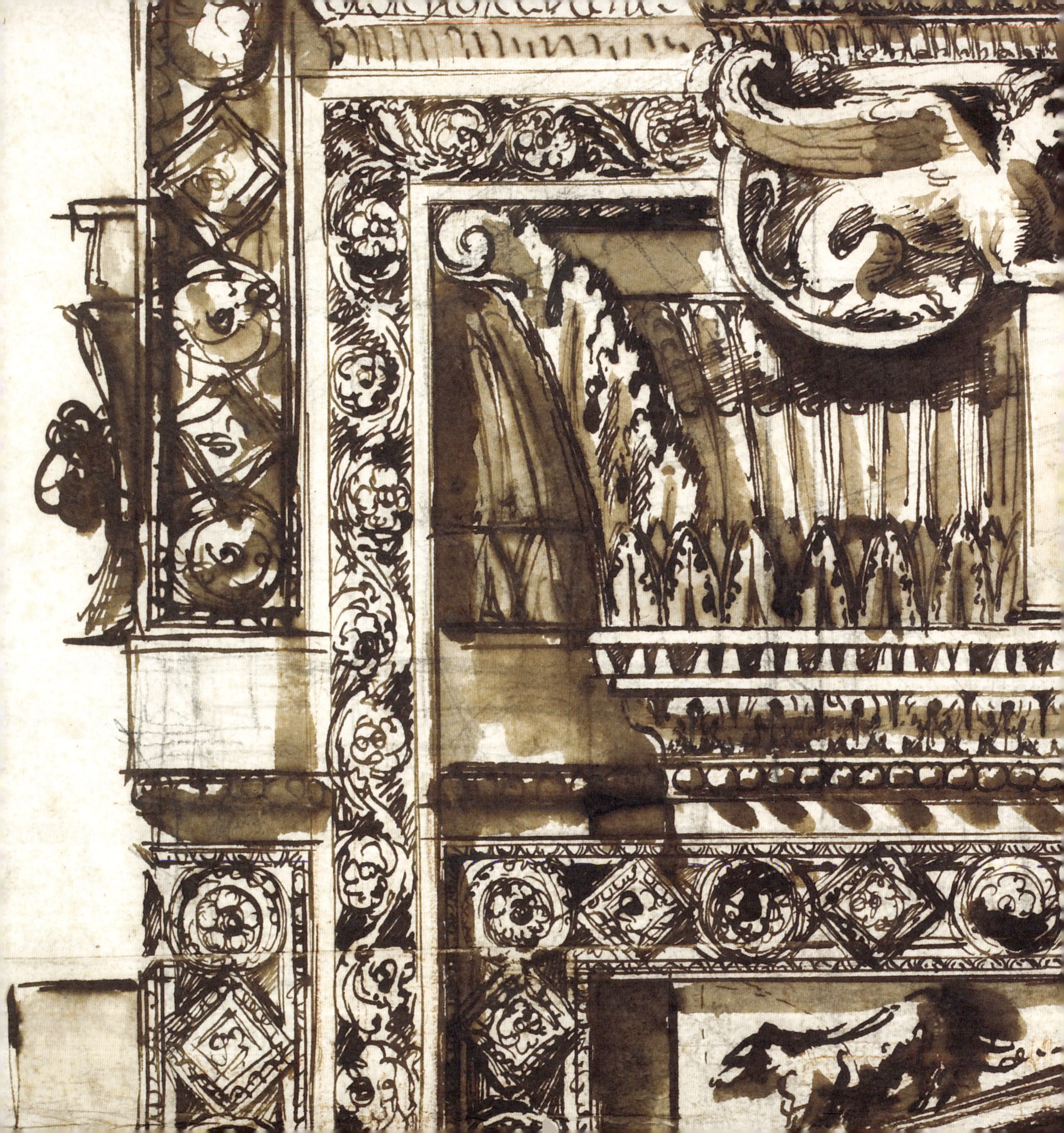

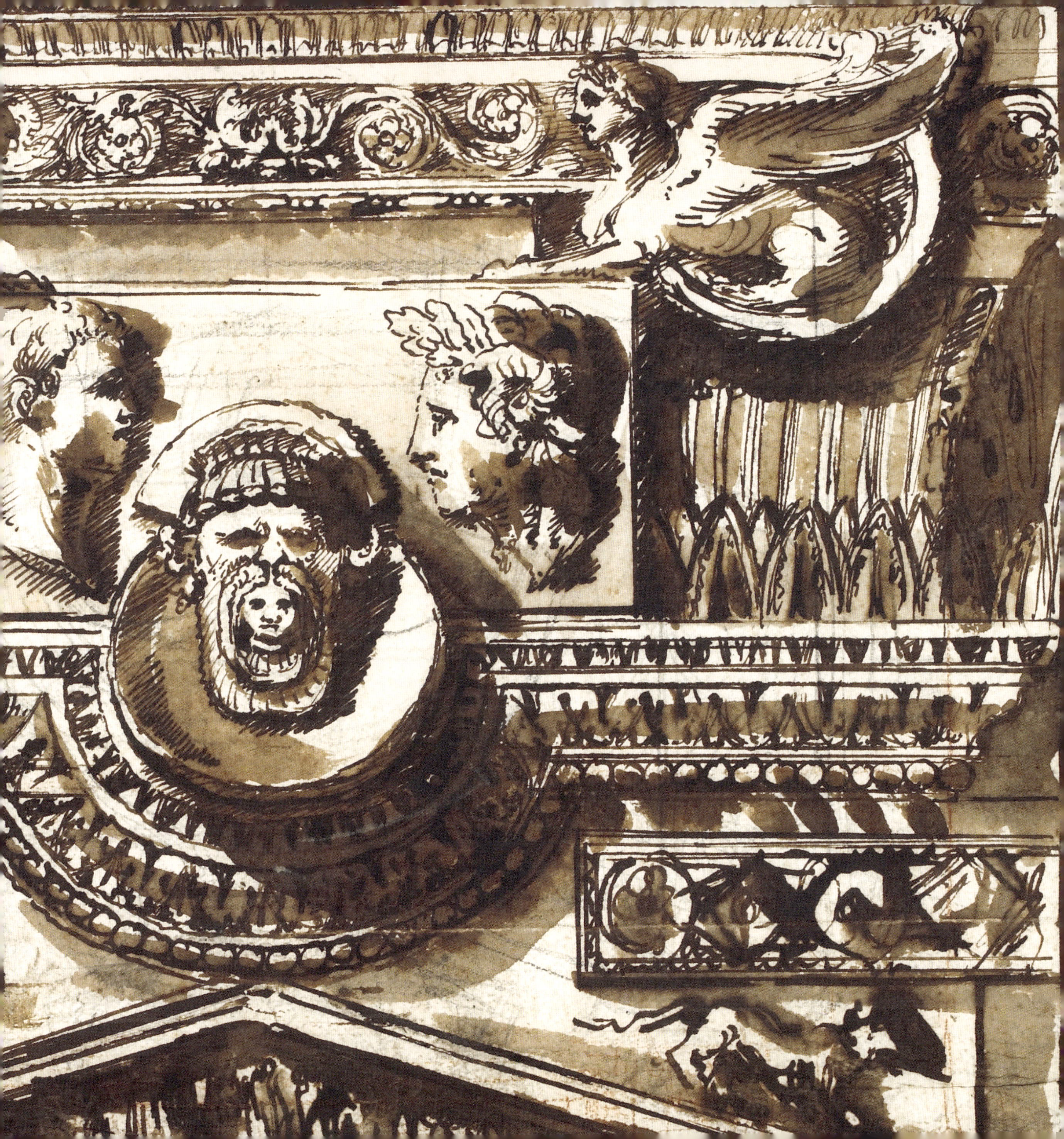

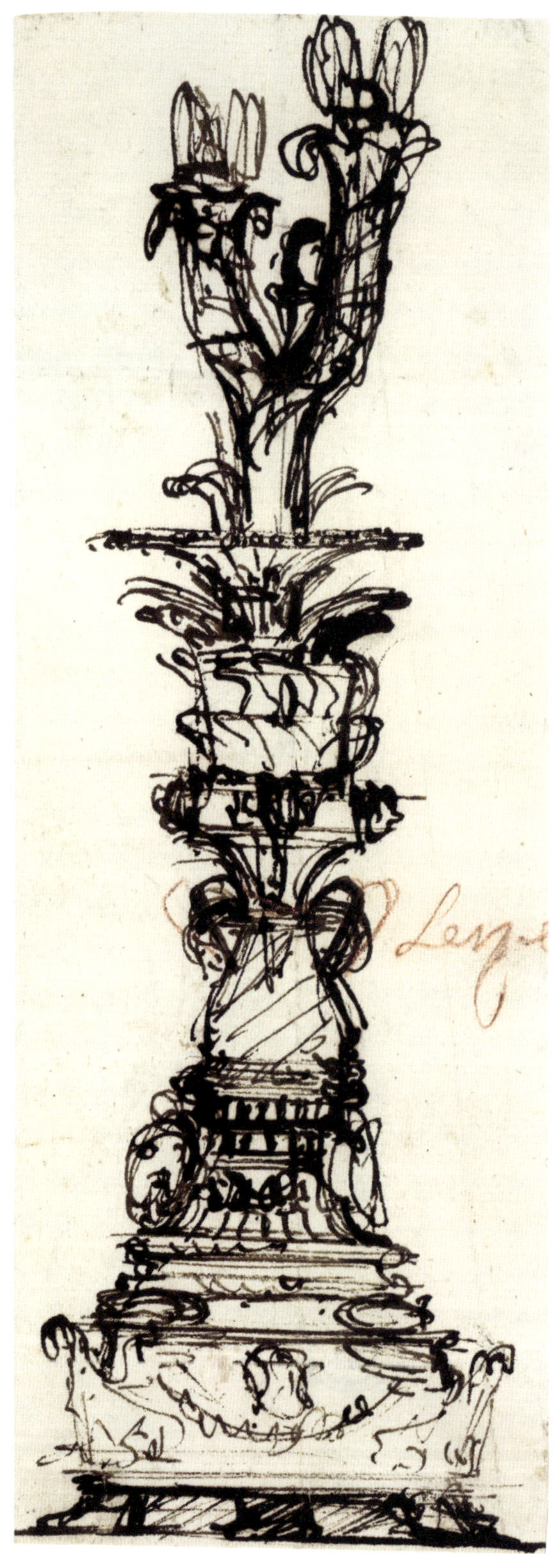

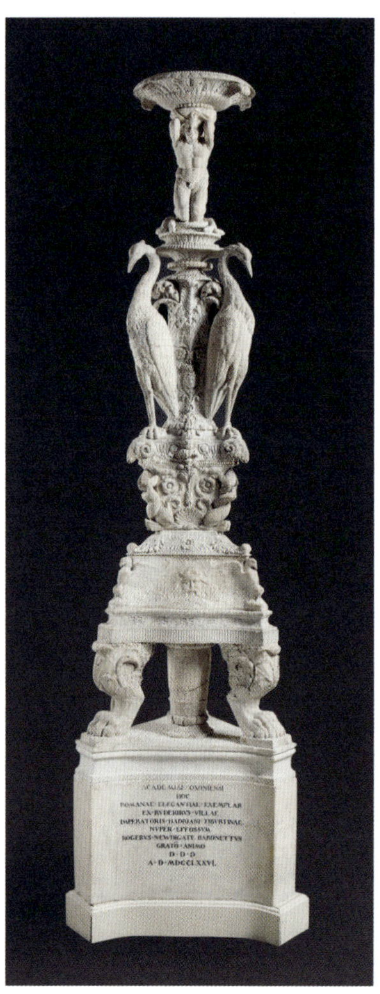

Fig. 30
The Newdigate Candelabrum
Roman, extensively restored
by Piranesi between 1769
and 1775
Carved marble
230 × 69 × 80.5 cm
(90⅝ × 27¼ × 31¾ in.)
The Ashmolean Museum of Art
and Archaeology, Oxford

48.

Design for an ornate candelabrum

c. 1772–77
Pen and brown ink, with a correction
in red chalk
247 × 89 mm (9¾ × 3⅝ in.)
1908,0616.33
Provenance: Probably William Gott; and by
descent to his son, John Gott, Bishop of Truro;
his sale, Sotheby's, London, 20 March 1908,
part of lot 172
Exhibitions: London 1968, part of no. 37; London
1978, no. 310a; Venice 1978, no. 44; Rome 1998,
no. 45; New York and Haarlem 2007–8,
unnumbered
Literature: Corfiato 1951, no. 49a; Wilton-Ely
1978, p. 113; Wilton-Ely 1994b, p. 139

This is a design for a reconstructed
antique candelabrum, probably including
various original fragments combined in a
new form, of the type that Piranesi dealt
in during the 1770s. The design cannot
be linked to any of his published ideas for
candelabra, but its elaborate ornamentation
is comparable to finished works such
as the Newdigate Candelabrum in the
Ashmolean Museum (Fig. 30). The design
was initially drawn in lighter brown ink,
with a thin, rather dry nib, and has been
gone over and developed using the thick
reed pen and dark iron-gall ink that
Piranesi favoured towards the end of his
life. Traces of red chalk suggest a revision
to the trunk of the candelabrum, but for
the most part the drawing demonstrates
the vibrant force of Piranesi's creativity
at this late stage of his career.

49.

Design for a tripod

c. 1772–77

Pen and brown ink, some marks
and calculations in red chalk

163 × 75 mm (6½ × 3 in.)

1908,0616.35

Provenance: Probably William Gott; and by
descent to his son, John Gott, Bishop of Truro;
his sale, Sotheby's, London, 20 March 1908,
part of lot 172
Exhibitions: London 1968, part of no. 37; London
1978, no. 310c; Venice 1978, no. 45; Rome 1998,
no catalogue; New York and Haarlem 2007–8,
unnumbered
Literature: Corfiato 1951, no. 49b

This is a characteristic drawing showing
Piranesi's plans for reconstructing or
restoring an antiquity. The design has
first been drawn in light-brown ink, and
then gone over with dark-brown iron-gall
ink, with accents and measurements
added in red chalk. The shape of the
tripod and its feet, in the form of lions'
paws, were inspired by an ancient altar
in S. Maria della Stella in Albano, which
Piranesi had etched for his publication
Antichità di Albano e di Castel Gandolfo
(1764).[59] This drawing would have
been intended purely for use within the
workshop and has much in common
with similar studies of antiquities included
in the albums of drawings from Piranesi's
workshop recently discovered in the
Karlsruhe Kunsthalle.[60]

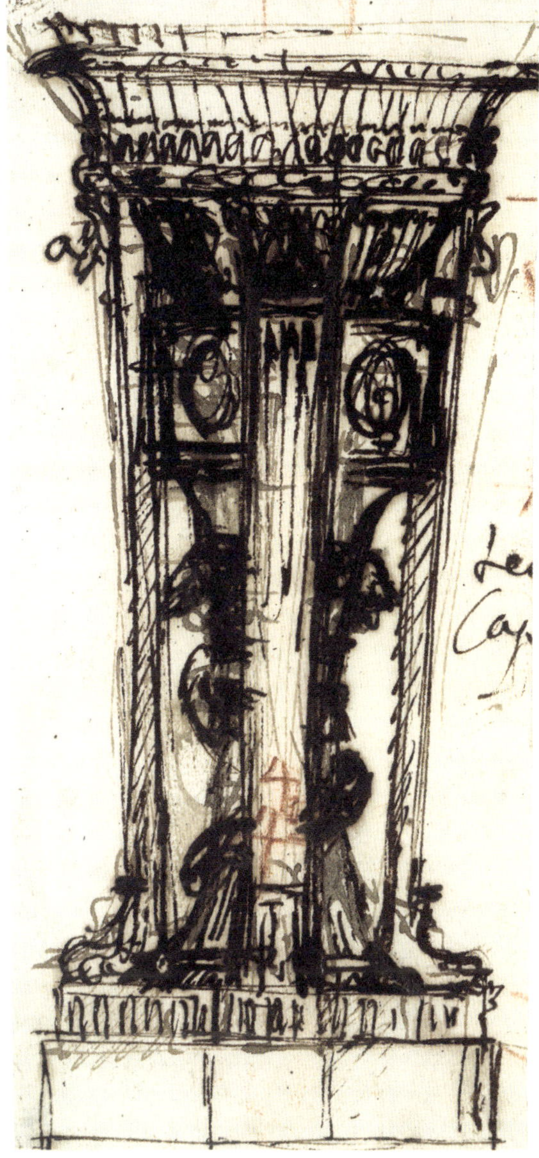

50.

View of the Strada Consulare with the Herculaneum Gate in Pompeii

c. 1772–78

Pen and brown ink (in two shades), brown
wash, on three conjoined sheets
inscribed 'Veduta del Inte/rno della porta/
della Città di Pom/pej' and numbered
373 × 864 mm (14¾ × 34⅛ in.)
1905,1110.64

Provenance: Ludwig Hermann Philippi (L. 1335)
Exhibitions: London 1968, part of no. 36;
London 1978, no. 318
Literature: Giesecke 1911, p. 99; Hind 1914,
p. 187; Hind 1922, p. 20; Thomas 1952–55,
pp. 20, 26–27, no. 8, fig. 14; Thomas 1954,
no. 62; Scott 1975, p. 331, fig. 294; Bettagno
1978, under no. 82

This drawing is one of about fifteen made
during Piranesi's visits to Pompeii in the
1770s (see also cat. 51). Another drawing
of the Strada Consulare, but seen from
the opposite direction, is in the George
Ortiz Collection.[61] The British Museum
drawing was one of eight from the
Pompeii series later used by Piranesi's
son Francesco as the basis for prints in
his three-volume *Les Antiquités de la Grande
Grèce* (Paris, 1804–7), in this case plate
XXIV in volume I.

There has been some debate about the
nature of Piranesi's involvement in some
of the Pompeii drawings (see cat. 51), but
there is no doubt that the present drawing
is by his own hand. The buildings, figures
and hatching are all executed with the
same thick reed pen and dark-brown ink,
and the draughtsmanship has the vigour
and density that are entirely consistent
with Piranesi's work at this late period.

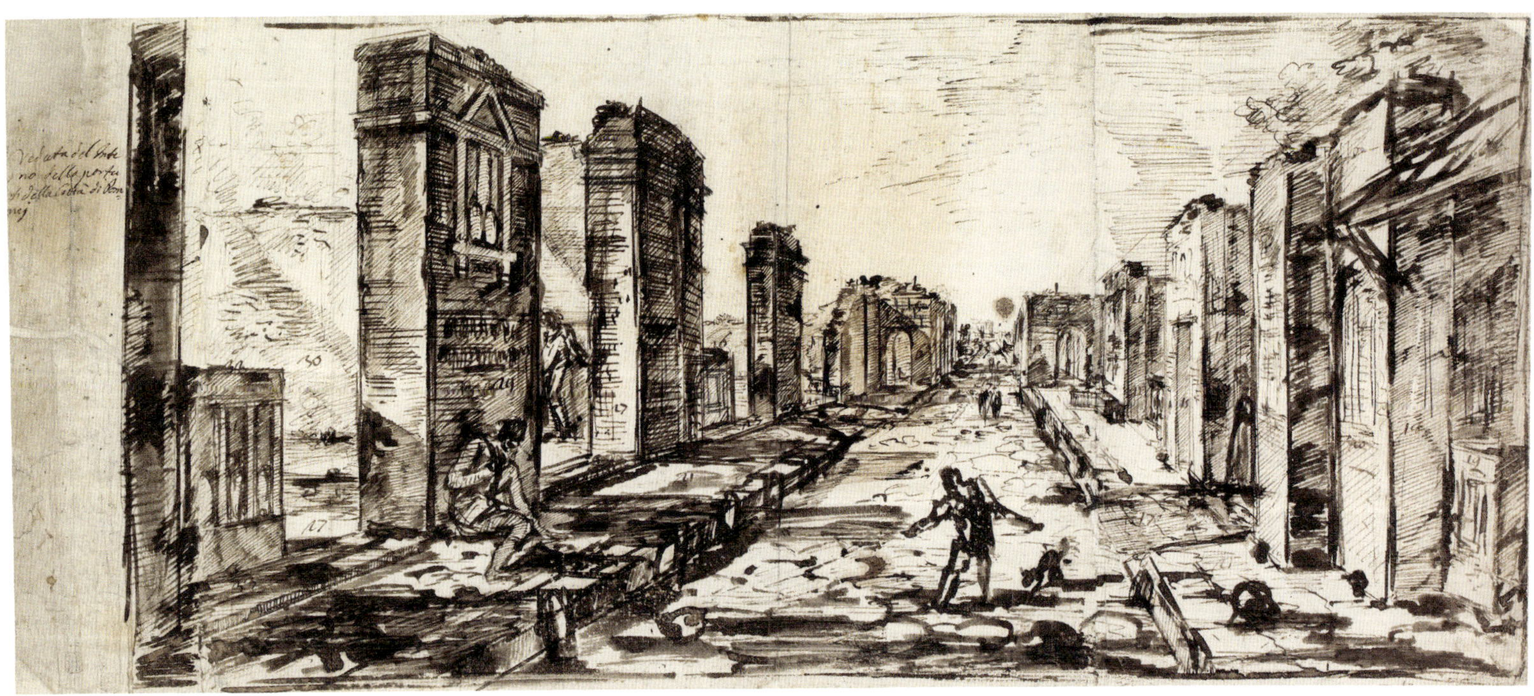

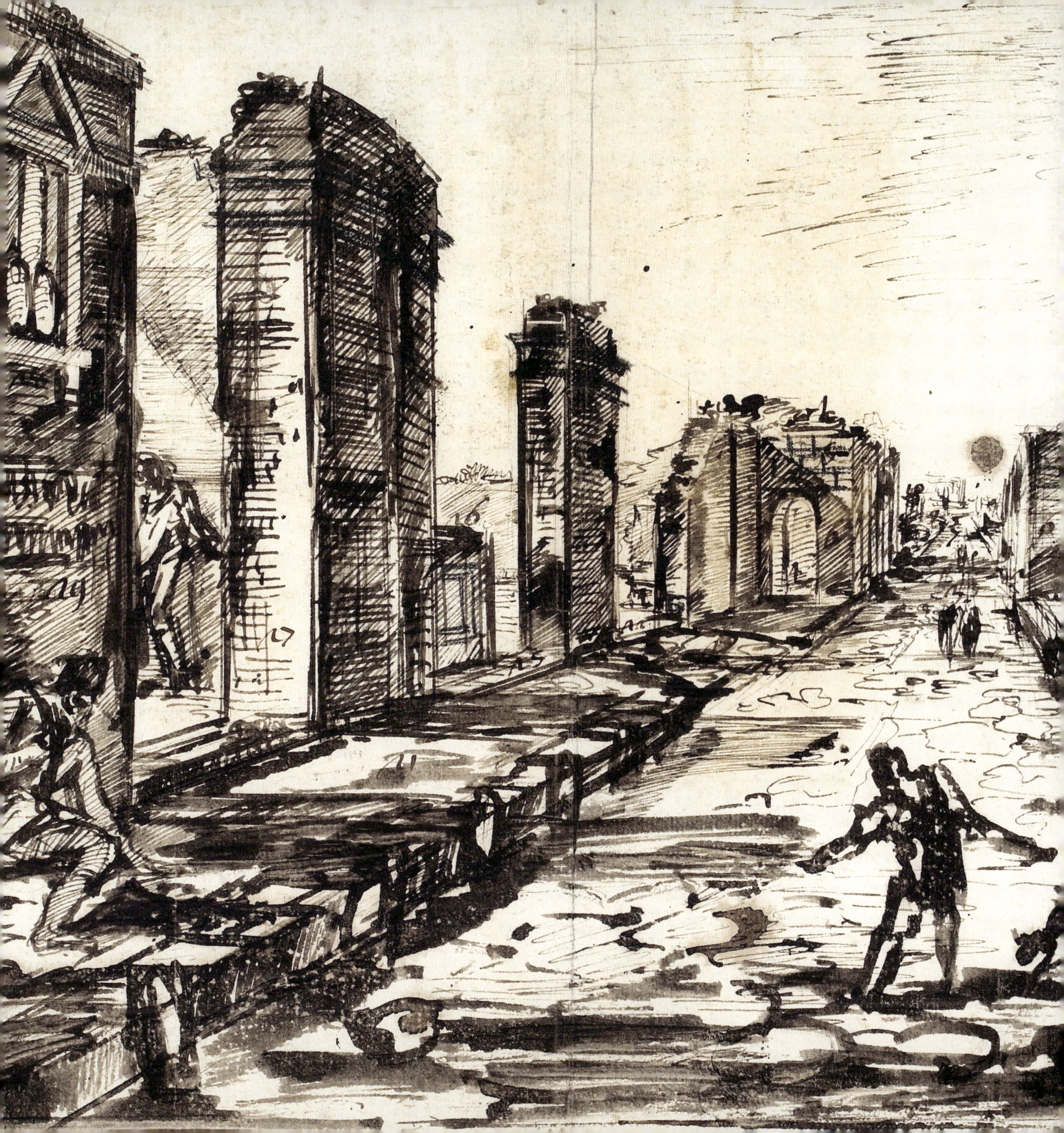

51.

**The Temple of Isis in Pompeii, seen
from the rear**

c. 1772–78

Pen and brown ink, over black chalk,
additions in reed pen and darker brown ink
495 × 750 mm (19½ × 29⅝ in.)
1905,1110.63
Provenance: Ludwig Hermann Philippi (L. 1335)
Exhibitions: London 1968, part of no. 36;
London 1978, no. 319
Literature: Hind 1914, p. 188; Hind 1922, p. 20;
Thomas 1952–55, pp. 23–24, 28, no. 18, fig. 14;
Scott 1975, p. 331, fig. 296; Bettagno 1978,
under no. 80; Wiles 1996–97, under no. 36

This is one of seven views of the
Temple of Isis from Piranesi's studies of
Pompeii.[62] Debate over the attribution
has hinged on the differing levels of
quality within the drawing. It seems
reasonable to assign the methodical base
design, including the ruled black-chalk
underdrawing and the careful delineation
of the building, to an assistant (either
Piranesi's son Francesco or another).
Piranesi's own hand, however, is clear
in the additions made with a thicker
reed pen and in darker brown ink. These
include the ornamental cornice along
the top of the building; the niche, the
columns and the vigorous hatching in
the sky. The authorship of the figures
is uncertain, as they are stockier, more
classical and on a larger scale than those
that usually appear in Piranesi's drawings.
They may well be by Francesco. The
drawing does not relate to any finished
print by either Piranesi or Francesco.

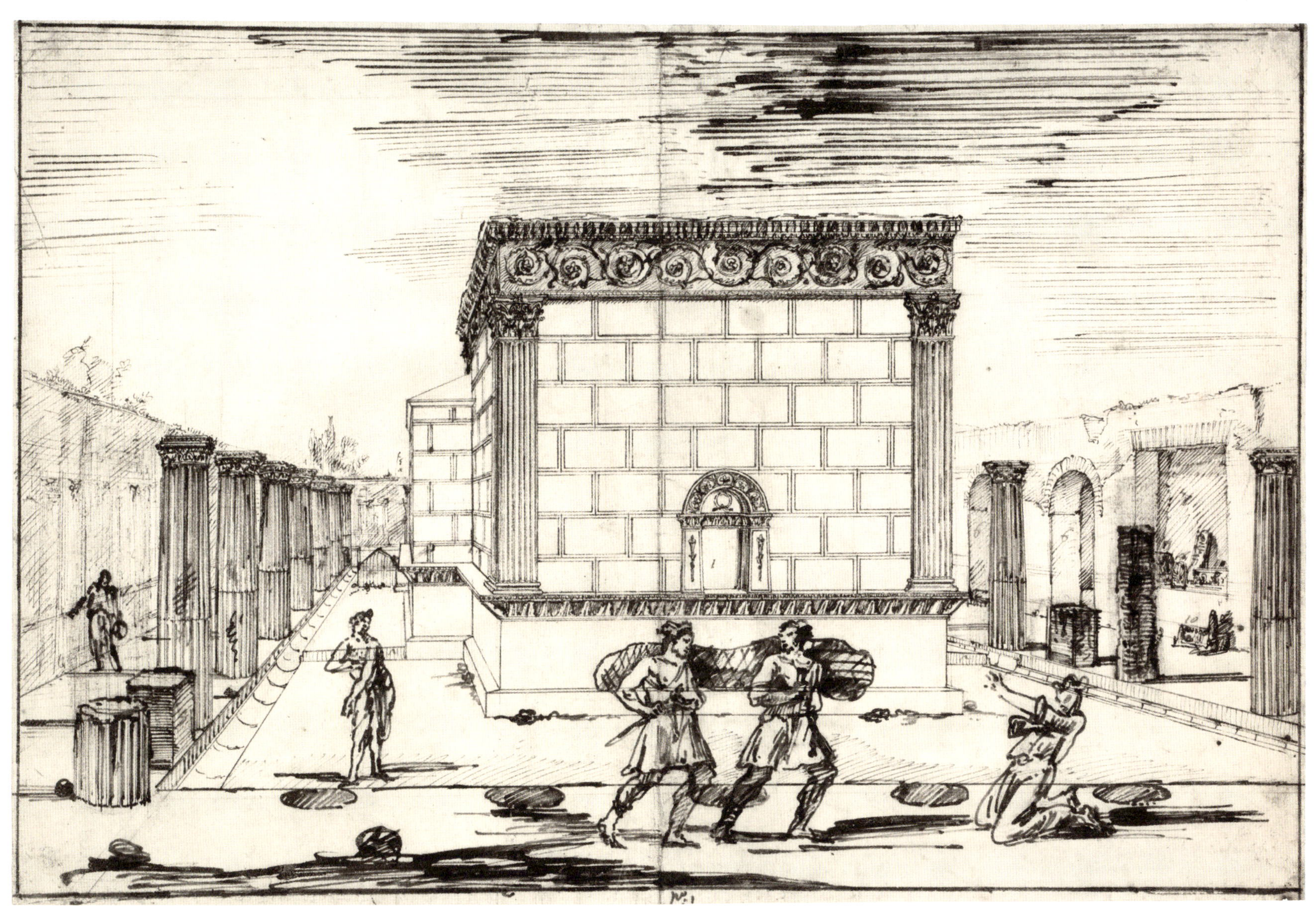

N.º 1

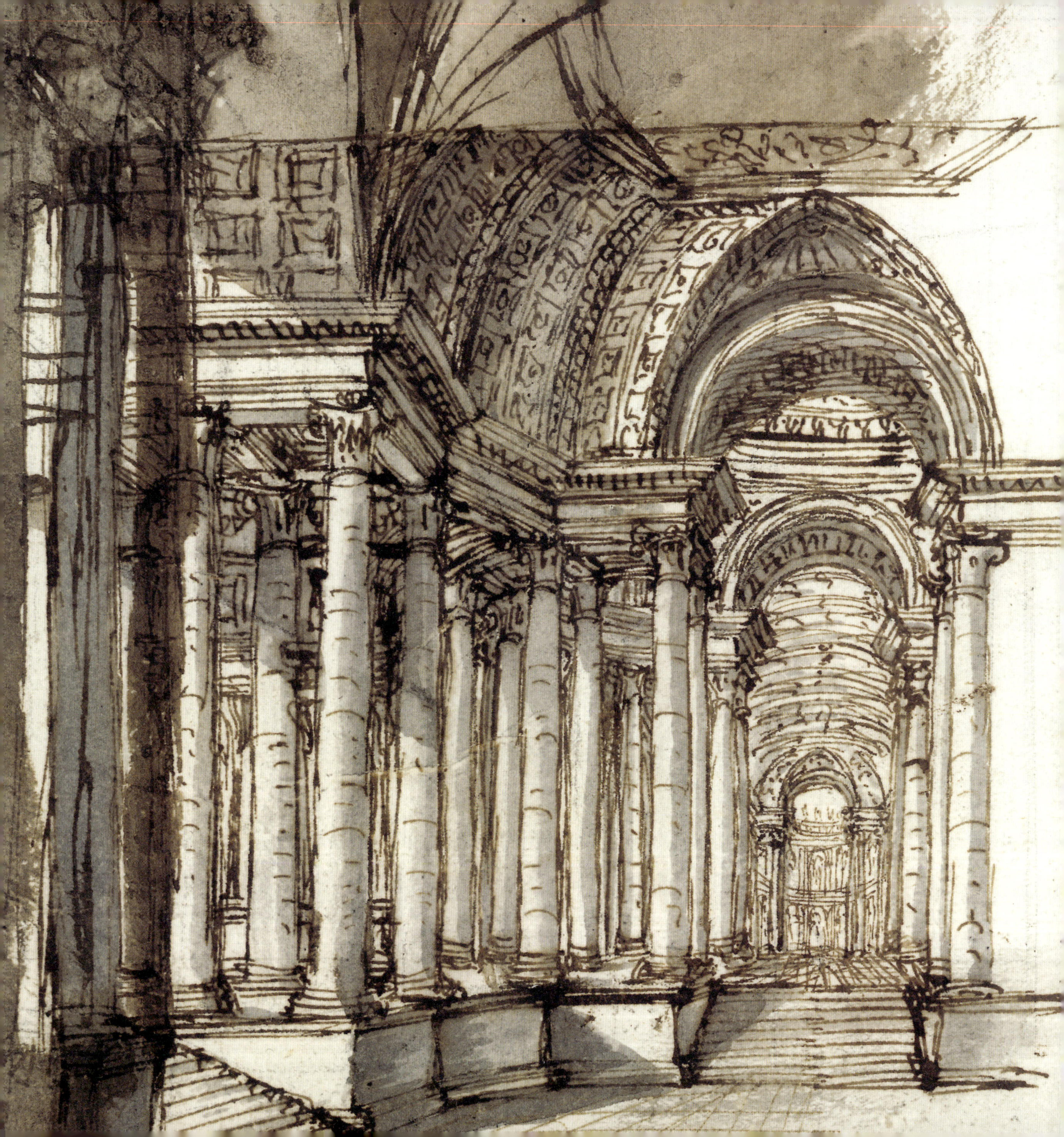

Chronology
Notes
Bibliography

Chronology

1720   **4 October** Piranesi is born at Mogliano, Veneto, on the mainland near Venice, to Angelo Piranesi, a master mason, and Laura Lucchesi

8 November Christened in the church of S. Moisè, Venice

1730–40   Undergoes training as an architect first with his uncle Matteo Lucchesi and then Giovanni Antonio Scalfarotto

May have studied etching with the print publisher Carlo Zucchi

Probably studies scenography and perspective with the Bibiena family

1735   Probably accompanies Scalfarotto on a trip to study and advise on the restoration of the Triumphal Arch of Augustus in Rimini

1740   **September** Leaves Venice for Rome as a draughtsman in the entourage of the Venetian ambassador Francesco Venier, and takes up residence at the Palazzo Venezia in Rome

1740–42   Studies etching with Giuseppe Vasi, although their relationship swiftly breaks down

Probably studies scenography and interior design with the Valeriani family

1740–45   Contributes views to the *Varie Vedute*, a series of small-scale landscapes of Rome by numerous artists intended to be bound into guidebooks

1742   Begins work on the *Prima Parte di Architetture, e Prospettive*

1742 or 1743   Visits Naples, Herculaneum and Portici, where finds from the excavations are displayed

1743   **July** Publishes the *Prima Parte di Architetture, e Prospettive*

Works with the map-maker Giovanni Battista Nolli on his large-scale engraved map, *Nuova Pianta di Roma*, for which Piranesi contributes vignettes of Rome

1744   **May** Returns to Venice for the summer due to lack of funds, stopping in Florence en route

While in Florence, engraves a view of the Medici Villa L'Ambrogiana, based on a drawing by Giuseppe Zocchi, who then publishes it in his *Vedute delle Ville e d'altri luoghi della Toscana* (1744)

September Returns to Rome for the winter

Possible further period of work with Giovanni Battista Nolli

1745   **May** Returns to Venice for a longer period

1745–47   Possibly studied or worked as an assistant in the studio of Giovanni Battista Tiepolo in Venice

1747   **September** Returns to Rome, where he sets up a Roman shop for the Venetian publisher Joseph Wagner and settles in the via del Corso

Begins printing the *Grotteschi* series

Autumn Begins work on the *Vedute di Roma*, a series of large-format engraved views on which Piranesi continues to work intermittently, publishing as he goes, until his death

1748   Publishes the *Antichità Romane de' Tempi della Repubblica*

1749   Publishes the last of the four prints in the *Grotteschi* series

Prints the first of the prints in the *Carceri* series

1750   Prints the last of the prints in the *Carceri* series

Publishes a volume of collected works including prints from all his series so far, titled *Opere varie di architettura, prospettive, grotteschi, antichità*

Publishes a collection of prints of Roman tombs, *Le camere sepocrali degli antichi Romani le quali esistono dentro e fuori di Roma*

| **1751** | Publishes *Le Magnificenze di Roma* |

| **1752** | Marries Angelica Pasquini |

Publishes the *Raccolta di varie vedute di Roma*

| **1753** | Publishes the *Trofei di Ottaviano Augusto* |

| **1755–61** | Revisits and reworks the first edition of the *Carceri* series |

| **1756** | Publishes the *Antichità Romane* in four volumes |

| **1757** | **24 February** Elected as an Honorary Fellow of the Royal Society of Antiquaries in London |

Publishes the *Lettere di giustificazione scritte à Milord Charlemont*

| **1758/59** | Birth of Piranesi's first child, Francesco |

| **1761** | Elected to the Accademia di S. Luca in Rome |

Publishes the *Della magnificenza ed architettura de' Romani*

Publishes the heavily reworked second edition of the *Carceri*

| **1762** | Publishes three archaeological works: the *Campus Martius antiquae Urbis*, the *Lapides Capitolini* and the *Descrizione e Disegno dell'Emissario del Lago Albano* |

| **1763–64** | Visits Chiusi and Corneto to study Etruscan tombs and antiquities |

| **1764** | Publishes the *Antichità di Albano e di Castel Gandolfo* |

Publishes a series of prints after drawings by Giovanni Francesco Barbieri, il Guercino, *Raccolta di alcuni disegni del Guercino*, for which Piranesi contributes a frontispiece

| **1764-65** | Restores the church of S. Maria Aventina, Rome (also known as S. Maria del Priorato) and designs a new façade |

| **1765** | Publishes the *Osservazioni di Gio. Battista Piranesi sopra la Lettre de Monsieur Mariette aux Auteurs de la Gazette Littéraire de l'Europe.* |

This publication includes two further small treatises, the *Parere sul'Architettura* and the *Della introduzione e del progresso delle Belle Arti in Europa nei tempi antichi*

Begins to show much more extensive interest in Egyptian and Etruscan motifs

Republishes the *Antichità Romane de' Tempi della Repubblica* under a new title, *Alcune vedute di Archi Trionfali*, to avoid confusion with the four-volume *Antichità Romane*

| **1765–66** | Visits Tarquinia to study Etruscan tombs and designs |

| **1767** | **16 January** Appointed Cavaliere degli Sproni d'Oro (Knight of the Golden Spur) by Pope Clement XIII |

Submits a series of designs for the reconstruction of the choir of S. Giovanni in Laterano, although he is not selected for the work

Submits designs for the Quirinal Palace to Cardinal Rezzonico

Visits Hadrian's Villa at Tivoli

| **1769** | Publishes the *Diverse maniere d'adornare i cammini*. The introduction of the series is the treatise *Ragionamento Apologetico in difesa dell'Architettura Egizia e Toscana* |

Reissues the *Parere su l'Architettura* with six new additional plates

| **1770s** | Visits Pompeii and Herculaneum on several occasions |

| **1773–75** | Publishes large-scale engravings of Trajan's Column and the Column of Antoninus Pius in the *Trofeo o sia Magnifica Colonna Coclide di marmo* |

| **1777** | Visits Paestum and oversees the production of drawings of the Doric temples |

| **1778** | Publishes the *Vasi, candelabri, cippi, sarcofagi* |

9 November Piranesi dies; buried in S. Maria Aventina, Rome

Notes

1   Scott 1975, pp. 7–8.

2   Ibid., p. 7; Nevola 2009, p. 4.

3   Nevola 2009, p. 5. Scalfarotto's brother-in-law Gerolamo Temanza was godfather to Piranesi's brother Giacomo Mattia.

4   Erouart and Mosser 1978, p. 223.

5   Puppi 1983, pp. 244–46; Nevola 2009, p. 10.

6   Nevola 2009, p. 6.

7   Scott 1975, p. 302, note 6. Lucchesi's arguments were made in the form of an attack on Scipione Maffei, *Riflessioni sulla pretesa scoperta del sopraornato Toscano espostaci dall'autore dell'opera: Degli anfiteatri* (1730).

8   Erouart and Mosser 1978, p. 223; Scott 1975, p. 10.

9   Robison 1986a, pp. 12–13.

10 Bevilacqua 2006, p. 29.

11 Kantor-Kazovsky 2006, pp. 30–36.

12 Ibid., pp. 47–50.

13 Hyde Minor 2015, pp. 61–65.

14 Vincenzo Brenna in a letter cited in Bevilacqua 2016, p. 223: 'guasi lasciato da incidere, e si è buttato a traficare di marmi antichi' (my translation).

15 Erouart and Mosser 1978, p. 246: 'ne voyez-vous pas que si mon dessin était fini ma planchet ne deviendrait plus qu'une copie; lorsqu'au contraire je crée l'effet sur le cuivre, j'en fait un original' (my translation).

16 Research is ongoing at the time of publication and the full implications of the material in the Karlsruhe are yet to be published. Kabierske 2015 offers an introduction to the material.

17 For the Paestum drawings, see J. Wilton-Ely, *Piranesi, Paestum and Soane*, Munich, 2013.

18 F. Stampfle, 'An unknown group of drawings by Giovanni Battista Piranesi', *The Art Bulletin*, 30, no. 2 (June 1948), p. 129.

19 Sotheby's, London, 20 March 1908, lot 172 (sold to the dealer Bernard Quaritch and afterwards purchased from him by the British Museum). The Sotheby's sale, and the letter to the Trustees requesting £80 for the purchase from Quaritch, refers to forty-six drawings, but the British Museum's register lists only forty-four. There is no record of what happened to the missing two drawings. Perhaps they were not by Piranesi and were removed from the album before the purchase from Quaritch.

20 'Joseph Gott', in Mapping the Practice and Profession of Sculpture in Britain and Ireland 1851–1951, University of Glasgow History of Art and HATII, online database 2011 (http://sculpture.gla.ac.uk/view/person.php?id=msib3_1202815313, accessed 4 June 2019).

21 Leeds, Brotherton Library, Gott Papers, MS.194/5/6(i).

22 Ibid., MS.194/0/18.

23 Ibid., MS.194/6/147 and 194/6/148.

24 Ibid., MS.194/6/46.

25 Ibid., MS 194/6/48.

26 Ibid., MS 194/6/51.

27 Ibid., MS 194/6/56.

28 Nevola 2009, p. 91, fig. 73.

29 As Andrew Robison first noted (Robison 1986a, pp. 18–20).

30 Denison et al. 1993, no. 27.

31 Robison 1986a, pp. 18–20.

32 As suggested by Robison 1986a, p. 14. Bibiena's print was also published as plate 48 in his *Direzioni a' Giovani Studenti nel Disegno dell'Architettura Civile* of 1731–32; illustrated in Robison 1986a, fig. 5.

33 Robison 1986a, p. 14.

34 Inv. 1966.11:2.

35 As first observed by Robison 1986a, pp. 19–20.

36 As Croft-Murray suggested in the 1968 British Museum exhibition.

37 As first noted by Sørensen 2001.

38 Biblioteca Estense, Campori, 1523, fol. 41 recto; see M. Bevilacqua, *Piranesi: Taccuini di Modena*, Rome, 2008, pl. 41v.

39 By Robison 1986a, p. 66.

40 Nevola 2009.

41 Ibid., p. 165.

42 Focillon 1918, 12.20; Hind 1922, p. 80, no. 24; Robison 1986a, p. 116, no. 20, state 2 of 5; Wilton-Ely 1994a, vol. 1, p. 41, no. 21.

43 Ashmolean Museum, Oxford, inv. WA 1948.111.

44 Kupferstichkabinett, Berlin, inv. KdZ 8458.

45 Robison 1986a, p. 40.

46 Ibid.

47 The related engraving is reproduced in Scott 1975, fig. 50.

48 Wilton-Ely 1994a, vol. 2, no. 577.

49 Ibid., vol 1, no. 189.

50 A. Robison, 'Dating Piranesi's early "Vedute di Roma"', in *Piranesi tra Venezia e l'Europa*, ed. A. Bettagno, Florence, 1983, pp. 32–33.

51 Formerly in the collection of J.E. Safra (Sotheby's, New York, 29 January 2015, lot 91).

52 As observed by both Seckler (1962, p. 346) and Gavuzzo-Stewart (1999, pp. 86–87).

53 One formerly on the art market (Christie's, London, 12 December

1985, lot 318) and one in a private collection in Montreal (*From the Hands of the Masters: A Private Collection*, exh. cat., Montreal, Museum of Fine Arts, 2013, no. 62). Andrew Robison is said to have suggested the date.

54 Sir John Soane Museum, illustrated in J. Wilton-Ely, 'Piranesian symbols on the Aventine', *Apollo*, 103 (1976), fig. 11.

55 For the frontispiece, see Wilton-Ely 1994, no. 1015. For the plates etched by Piranesi, see Wilton-Ely 1994, nos. 1016 and 1018.

56 1966.11:19–20; John Marciari, personal communication.

57 57 Jacob 1975, nos. 869–70.

58 Ibid., no. 867.

59 Wilton-Ely 1994a, vol. 2, no. 650.

60 Kabierske 2015.

61 See Venice 1978, no. 82.

62 Four others are in the Kunstbibliothek, Berlin (Jacob 1975, nos. 863–66), and two in the Morgan Library, New York (Stampfle 1978, nos. A-7 and 11).

Bibliography

Exhibitions

Bonn 2012–13: 'Treasures of the World's Cultures', Art and Exhibition Hall of the Federal Republic of Germany, Bonn, 2012–13

Cologne, Zurich and Vienna 1996–97: 'Capriccio', Wallraf-Richartz Museum, Cologne, December 1996–February 1997; Kunsthaus, Zurich, March–June 1997; Kunsthistorisches Museum, Vienna, July–September 1997

Hull and London 1995: 'Drawing the Line', Ferens Gallery, Hull, May–June 1995; Whitechapel Gallery, London, July–September 1995

London 1965: 'Masterpieces of the Print Room', British Museum, London, 1965

London 1968: 'Giovanni Battista Piranesi', British Museum, London, 1968 (exh. cat. ed. E. Croft-Murray)

London 1972: 'The Art of Drawing', British Museum, London, 1972

London 1978: 'Piranesi', Hayward Gallery, South Bank, London, 1978 (exh. cat. ed. J. Wilton-Ely)

London 1984: 'Master Drawings and Watercolours in the British Museum', British Museum, London, 1984

London 1990: 'Treasures of P&D', British Museum, London, 1990

London 1994: 'The Glory of Venice', Royal Academy, London, 1994

London and elsewhere 2002–4: 'Piranesi's Carceri', touring exhibition: British Museum, London; Northumbria University Gallery; York City Art Gallery; Milton Keynes Art Gallery; Victoria Art Gallery, Bath, 2002–4

London 2003: 'Museum of the Mind', British Museum, London, 2003

New York and Haarlem 2007–8: 'Piranesi as Designer', Cooper-Hewitt Museum, New York, September 2007–January 2008; Teylers Museum, Haarlem, February–May 2008

Paris 1971: 'Venise au dix-huitieme siècle: peintures, dessins et gravures des collections françaises', Musée de l'Orangerie, Paris, 1971

Poole and elsewhere 2016–18: 'Lines of Thought: Drawing from Michelangelo to Now', Poole Museum, September–November 2016; Brynmor Jones Library Art Gallery, University of Hull, January–February 2017; Ulster Museum, Belfast, March–May 2017; New Mexico Museum of Art, Santa Fe, May–September 2017; RISD Museum, Rhode Island School of Design, Providence, October 2017–January 2018

Rome 1998: 'Piranesi e l'Aventino', Grand Priory of Rome, 1998

Rome, Dijon and Paris 1976: 'Piranesi and the French', Villa Medici, Rome, May–June 1976; Musée des Beaux-Arts, Dijon, July–September 1976; Hotel de Sully, Paris, October–November 1976

Sheffield 1988: 'Piranesi's Prisons', Graves Art Gallery, Sheffield, 1988

Southampton and Manchester 1995: 'Drawing the Line', Southampton Gallery, January–March 1995; Manchester Art Gallery, March–April 1995

Venice 1978: 'Piranesi', Fondazione Giorgio Cini, Venice, 1978

Washington 1978: 'Piranesi: The Early Architectural Fantasies', National Gallery of Art, Washington, D.C., 1978

Literature

Bacou, R., 1974, *Piranèse, gravures et dessins*, Paris

Bettagno, A., 1978, *Disegni di Giambattista Piranesi*, exh. cat., Fondazione Cini, Venice

Bevilacqua, M., 2006, 'The young Piranesi: the itineraries of his formation', in *The Serpent and the Stylus: Essays on G.B. Piranesi*, Michigan, pp. 13–54

Bevilacqua, M., 2016, 'Piranesi's ironies: the Egyptian and Etruscan dreams of Margherita Gentili Boccapaduli', in *Giovanni Battista Piranesi, predecessor, contemporanei e successor: Studi in onore di John Wilton-Ely*, Rome

Borenius, T., 1926, 'Renderings of architecture', *The Architect's Journal*, LXIII, no. 1634

Corfiato, H.O., 1951, *Piranesi Compositions*, London

Denison, C.D., Rosenfeld, M.N., and Wiles, S., 1993, *Exploring Rome: Piranesi and His Contemporaries*, exh. cat., Pierpont Morgan Library, New York

Erouart, G., and Mosser, M., 1978, 'A propos de la "Notice historique sur la vie et les ouvrages de J.-B. Piranesi": origine et fortune d'une biographie', in *Piranèse et les français: Colloque tenu à la Villa Médicis, 12–14 Mai 1976*, ed. G. Brunel, Rome, pp. 213–56

Focillon, H., 1918, *Giovanni-Battista Piranesi*, Paris

Gavuzzo-Stewart, S., 1999, *Nelle Carceri di G.B. Piranesi*, Leeds

Giesecke, A., 1911, *Giovanni Battista Piranesi*, Leipzig

Hind, A.M., 1911–12, *Vasari Society*, 1st series, VII

Hind, A.M., 1914, 'Giovanni Battista Piranesi: some further notes and a list of his works', *Burlington Magazine*, XXIV (January 1914), pp. 187–89, 192, 193, 196–200, 203

Hind, A.M., 1922, *Giovanni Battista Piranesi: A Critical Study*, London

Hyde Minor, H., 2015, *Piranesi's Lost Words*, University Park, PA

Jacob, S., 1975, *Italienische Zeichnungen der Kunstbibliothek Berlin*, Berlin

Kabierske, G., 2015, 'A cache of newly identified drawings by Piranesi and his studio at the Staatliche Kunsthalle Karlsruhe', *Master Drawings*, 53, pp. 147–78

Kantor-Kazovsky, L., 2006, *Piranesi as Interpreter of Roman Architecture and the Origins of His Intellectual World*, Florence

Lawrence, S. (ed.), 2007, *Piranesi as Designer*, exh. cat., Cooper-Hewitt Museum, New York

Leporini, H., 1925, *Die Stilentwicklung der Handzeichnungen*, Vienna

Murray, P., 1971, *Piranesi and the Grandeur of Ancient Rome*, London

Nevola, F., 2009, *Giovanni Battista Piranesi: The Grotteschi – The Early Years, 1720–1750*, Rome

Penny, N., 1978, *Piranesi*, London

Puppi, L., 1983, 'Appunti sulla educazione veneziana di Giambattista Piranesi', in *Piranesi tra Venezia e l'Europa*, Florence, pp. 217–64

Robison, A., 1977, 'Preliminary drawings for Piranesi's early architectural fantasies', *Master Drawings*, 15, no. 4, pp. 387–401

Robison, A., 1986a, *Piranesi: The Early Architectural Fantasies – A Catalogue Raisonné of the Etchings*, Washington, D.C.

Robison, A., 1986b, *Piranesi: The Early Architectural Fantasies – A Guide to the Exhibition*, Washington, D.C.

Robison, A., 1996, 'A façade with bizarre ornaments', in *Master Drawings from the Woodner Collections*, ed. M. Morgan Grasselli, exh. cat., National Gallery of Art, Washington, D.C., pp. 302–5, no. 84

Samuel, A., 1910, *Piranesi*, London

Scott, J., 1975, *Piranesi*, New York and London

Seckler, P.M., 1962, 'Notes on old and modern drawings: Giovanni Battista Piranesi's "Carceri" etchings and related drawings', *The Art Quarterly*, XXV, no. 4, pp. 330–63

Sørensen, B., 2001, 'Two overlooked drawings by Piranesi for S. Giovanni in Laterano in Rome', *The Burlington Magazine*, CXLIII (July 2001), pp. 430–33

Stampfle, F., 1978, *Giovanni Battista Piranesi: Drawings in the Pierpont Morgan Library*, New York

Thomas, H., 1952–55, 'Piranesi and Pompeii', *Kunstmuseets Årsskrift* (Journal of the Statens Museum for Kunst, Copenhagen), pp. 13–28

Thomas, H., 1954, *The Drawings of Giovanni Battista Piranesi*, London

Thomas, H., 1957, 'De Tekeningen van Piranesi in het Museum Boymans', *Bulletin Museum Boymans*, 8, pp. 10–20

Vasari Society, 1912–13, *The Vasari Society for the Reproduction of Drawings by Old Masters*, VIII

Vogt-Göknil, U., 1958, *G.B. Piranesi's 'Carceri'*, Zurich

Wiles, S., 1996–7, in *From Mantegna to Picasso: Drawings from the Thaw Collection at the Pierpont Morgan Library, New York*, exh. cat., Royal Academy, London, pp. 72 and 73

Wilton-Ely, J., 1976, 'Piranesian symbols on the Aventine', *Apollo*, CIII (March 1976), pp. 214–27

Wilton-Ely, J., 1978, *The Mind and Art of Giovanni Battista Piranesi*, London

Wilton-Ely, J., 1994a, *Giovanni Battista Piranesi: The Complete Etchings*, 2 vols, San Francisco

Wilton-Ely, J., 1994b, *Piranesi* [Italian edition of *The Mind and Art of Giovanni Battista Piranesi*], Milan

Picture credits

The publisher would like to thank the copyright holders for granting permission to reproduce the images illustrated. Every attempt has been made to trace accurate ownership of copyrighted images in this book. Any errors or omissions will be corrected in subsequent editions provided notification is sent to the publisher.

All works illustrated in this book are from the collection of the British Museum and © The Trustees of the British Museum unless otherwise stated. Information about the provenance of exhibited works can be found with the main catalogue entries (pp. 29–133).

Further information about the Museum and its collection can be found at britishmuseum.org.

Fig. 2. The Metropolitan Museum of Art, New York. 37.45.3(1). Harris Brisbane Dick Fund, 1937

Fig. 3. Woodner Collection. Courtesy National Gallery of Art, Washington, D.C. 1991.182.17

Fig. 4. Victoria and Albert Museum, London. E.382-1927

Fig. 7. The Morgan Library and Museum. 1966.11:10. Bequest of Junius S. Morgan and the gift of Henry S. Morgan

Fig. 8. The Morgan Library and Museum. 1966.11:14. Bequest of Junius S. Morgan and the gift of Henry S. Morgan

Fig. 10. The Morgan Library and Museum. 1971.4. Purchased as the gift of Miss Alice Tully

Fig. 11. Rijksmuseum, Amsterdam. RP-P-ON-39.428

Fig. 12. NPG x16474 © National Portrait Gallery, London

Fig. 14. The Metropolitan Museum of Art, New York. 37.45.3(18). Harris Brisbane Dick Fund, 1937

Fig. 15. The Morgan Library and Museum. 1959.14. Purchased as the gift of the Fellows

Fig. 16. The Metropolitan Museum of Art, New York. 37.45.3(19). Harris Brisbane Dick Fund, 1937

Fig. 18. The Metropolitan Museum of Art, New York. 37.45.3 (38). Harris Brisbane Dick Fund, 1937

Fig. 19. Hamburger Kunsthalle. 1915-649. © bpk / Hamburger Kunsthalle / Christoph Irrgang

Fig. 20. The Metropolitan Museum of Art, New York. 37.45.3(13). Harris Brisbane Dick Fund, 1937

Fig. 21. Hamburger Kunsthalle. 1915-640. © bpk / Hamburger Kunsthalle / Christoph Irrgang

Fig. 22. The Metropolitan Museum of Art, New York. 37.45.3(15). Harris Brisbane Dick Fund, 1937

Fig. 23. The Metropolitan Museum of Art, New York. 37.45.3(41). Harris Brisbane Dick Fund, 1937

Fig. 24. The Metropolitan Museum of Art, New York. 37.45.3(7). Harris Brisbane Dick Fund, 1937

Fig. 25. The Morgan Library and Museum. 1974.27. Gift of János Scholz

Fig. 26. National Galleries of Scotland. D 1858. Lady Murray of Henderland Gift, 1860, as a memorial of her husband, Lord Murray of Henderland

Fig. 27. The Arthur Ross Collection, Yale University Art Gallery. 2012.159.11.102

Fig. 28. The Morgan Library and Museum. 1966.11:52. Bequest of Junius S. Morgan and the gift of Henry S. Morgan

Fig. 29. The Morgan Library and Museum. 1966.11:19. Bequest of Junius S. Morgan and the gift of Henry S. Morgan

Fig. 30. The Ashmolean Museum of Art and Archaeology. ANMichaelis.241. © Ashmolean Museum, University of Oxford

Acknowledgments

First thanks must go to Hugo Chapman for originally suggesting the project and for supporting me through the challenge of researching and writing a book in such a short time. My project editor at the British Museum, Kathleen Bloomfield, has done more than anyone else to shape my text into the final book and I am enormously grateful for her patience, her guidance and her eye for a good image. Claudia Bloch has provided further invaluable support and suggestions. At Thames & Hudson, Susannah Lawson has overseen the project and Susanna Ingram took on the challenge of fine-tuning the images to capture Piranesi's draughtsmanship in all its nuance. I am grateful to both of them for their enthusiasm for the subject. While preparing the text, I was fortunate enough to have illuminating conversations in both London and New York with John Marciari of the Morgan Library, who also kindly agreed to read a draft of my text. Needless to say, any remaining errors are mine alone.

I must also acknowledge my colleagues here at the British Museum who have worked so hard to prepare the exhibition that accompanied the publication of this book. Jenny Bescoby and Rebecca Snow worked tirelessly on the conservation of the drawings, revealing new insights into Piranesi's career, while Christina Angelo and David Giles oversaw the mounting. Hannah James has approached the challenges of installation with her usual calm and reassuring competence. Peter Macdermid and Helen Adrados have produced a beautiful overall design and graphic panels respectively. And I am especially indebted to Thorsten Opper, with whom I spent a fascinating few days studying the Karlsruhe Piranesi albums, and who guided me through the British Museum vaults to learn more about Piranesi's career as a dealer of Roman antiquities. The exhibition could not, however, have come to fruition without the generous sponsorship of the Tavolozza Foundation, under the direction of Katrin Bellinger, to whom I offer my deepest thanks for her ongoing support of the Prints & Drawings Department. In Karlsruhe I also enjoyed the chance to discuss Piranesi's works with a group of generous and experienced scholars, chief among them Christoph Frank and Andrew Robison, whose work on Piranesi has done so much to shape our understanding of his graphic oeuvre.

Most of all, I am grateful to my friends and family, especially Nick, who have encouraged and supported me throughout the last year, even at moments when I risked becoming lost in *carceri* of my own making.